The Saturday Book 3

The Contents

This book, published in October, 1943, was made and printed at the Mayflower Press (of Plymouth), at St. Albans, by William Brendon & Son, Ltd., and is produced in complete conformity with the authorised economy standards. The photogravure plates on pages 153, 154, 157, 158, 159, 160, 163, 164, are the work of the Grout Engraving Co., Ltd. MSS., correspondence, etc., should be sent to the Editor, 47, Princes Gate, London, S.W.7.

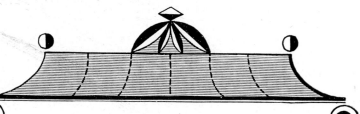

THE
SATURDAY
BOOK
3

edited by
Leonard Russell

with decorations by
Laurence Scarfe

HUTCHINSON

Editor's Note

THE SATURDAY BOOK Office,
47 Princes Gate, Kensington, S.W.7.

When the first SATURDAY BOOK appeared in the autumn of 1941 the more vigilant reviewers looked at it glumly. Something wrong, they said. The most vigilant of them all was a Manchester writer who, exhibiting original notions of literary criticism, began by weighing-in the book on his kitchen scales. This was a start which Sainte-Beuve never thought of, and it led to a powerfully delivered verdict : too heavy, out of condition, should never have appeared in the ring. Editors have their feelings, and this one nearly took to the woods. In time he recovered himself sufficiently to train a new candidate, and when it appeared before the boxing critics in the autumn of 1942 its reception was greatly improved. Now with this third volume he presents what he believes to be an even better Game Chicken, trained to the last ounce and ready to go twenty rounds with anyone. And others will follow it.

For the rest, the SATURDAY BOOK is a miscellany, and its contents are necessarily miscellaneous. But the editor will venture to observe that a certain unifying mood appears and reappears in number three : a factual mood expressed in factual writing. In the world of the cinema the book would perhaps be called a documentary. It was, in fact, as a documentary of past and present that it took shape in the editor's mind. All the contributions were specially written (or in one instance translated) for the volume, and thus make in these pages their first appearance. Many of the photographs also appear for the first time.

YESTERDAY

The Saturday Book Album

The first photograph in this Album was taken about a hundred years ago : the three young ladies seen below stand, as it were, on the threshold of the modern age. Thereafter the Album gives a tiny news-reel of English life as the camera has seen it throughout practically a century. To show the sprawl of that century across the page of history is impossible here. But perhaps some of the photographs in this collection may be regarded as footnotes to the story.

Octavius Hill

Sailors of the Forties

Soldiers of the Forties

✒ The publication of *The Times* commenced at a quarter to 7 o'clock yesterday morning, and finished at 20 minutes to 11.

LONDON, THURSDAY, DECEMBER 4, 1845.

The decision of the Cabinet is no longer a secret. Parliament, it is confidently reported, is to be summoned for the first week in January; and the Royal Speech will, it is added, recommend an immediate consideration of the Corn Laws, preparatory to their total repeal. Sir ROBERT PEEL in one house, and the Duke of WELLINGTON in the other, will, we are told, be prepared to give immediate effect to the recommendation thus conveyed.

An announcement of such immeasurable importance, and to the larger portion of the community so unspeakably gratifying, almost precludes the possibility of comment. No pen can keep pace with the reflections which must spontaneously crowd upon every thoughtful and sensitive mind. They who have long desired this change, and have long traced its manifold bearings on the welfare and happiness of the world, will in one moment see the realization of that fair prospect, and will hardly endure to be informed of what they already behold. The approaching event, therefore, which we this day communicate to our readers, must be left to speak for itself.

It is understood that until Parliament meets nothing is to be done. For the Legislature will be

From **The Times,** *1845*

Louis-Philippe

The 1840s.
An England very different from the England of the Georges is evolving. The Repeal of the Corn Laws represents a victory for the new

The Iron Horse, 1842

industrialists over the landed aristocracy. Railways are spreading over the land. Chartism at home, revolutions abroad, and Louis-Philippe loses the French throne. Lear publishes his *Book of Nonsense* in 1846. Dickens is idolised.

Charles Dickens, 1849

Queen Victoria and Prince Albert

The 1850s

Propriety reigns at Court, and Victoria and Albert, ideally married, set a pattern for Victorian domestic behaviour. The Queen has ceased to exclude Albert from political matters. Now he is her adviser, tutor, master.

'**M**an is a fighting and quarrelling animal,' said Palmerston, and as Foreign Secretary he became the darling of the country by asserting England's watchful eye and strong arm. Nor was he noticeably subdued in his constitutional struggle with the Queen.

Palmerston

This was the type of seaman that Palmerston sent to blockade the Piræus.

May 1, 1851. The Great Exhibition opens in Hyde Park, to give, as Albert said, a picture of the point of industrial development reached by man. The Exhibition is also called a Festival of Peace : fierce international rivalries will abate under its influence. They didn't. Soon there were many wars, and Britain herself, after forty years of peace, was fighting Russia in the mysteriously-generated Crimean War.

Sebastopol, 1855

Tennyson

Darwin

succeeded Wordsworth as Poet Laureate in 1850.

published his epoch-making *Origin of Species* in 1859.

F. Beato

The Indian Mutiny

Before the Indian Mutiny broke out in 1857 the affairs of India troubled few in this country. The more benumbing therefore the news that Hindus and Moslems, native princes and native soldiers had combined in an attempt to destroy the British. India was transferred to the Crown in 1858.

A Country House Group, 1860

Nevil Stor Maskelyne

Ellen Terry

The 1860s

The rugged industrialism of mid-nineteenth century England found no time to spare for the arts. But Ruskin raised his voice on their behalf, and two other artistic forces in Rossetti and William Morris rebelled against the prevailing ugliness, the one being the inspirer of the Pre-Raphaelite Brotherhood, the other a craftsman of genius. The influence of both can be traced far beyond their own time. Mrs Julia Margaret Cameron, whose photograph of Ellen Terry as a girl appears above, was a disciple of the Pre-Raphaelites with the camera.

Ruskin and Rossetti

Matthew Brady

LATEST INTELLIGENCE.

A portion of the following appeared in our Second ¦tion of yesterday :—]

(REUTER'S TELEGRAMS.)

AMERICA.

¦ER COLUMBIA, *via* GALWAY AND ST. JOHN'S.)
NEW YORK, MAY 4.

¦he blockade of the Southern ports is to be en-¦ced immediately.

¦ifty vessels, with steam transports and 20,000 ¦n, are ready.

¦he North Carolina Legislature has been con-¦ned.

¦he State is virtually out of Union, and is ¦ipping for war.

¦Maryland and Western Virginia are true to the ¦ion.

¦entucky will maintain a neutral position.

¦o attack has yet been made on Fort Pickens.

¦n insurrection has broken out at Yucatan. ¦teen British officers were killed. (?)

¦ regiment (?) has left Ruatan for the scene of ¦ion.

¦he Columbia left Boston on the 30th April, and ¦ John's on the 6th inst. She brings the mail¦

May 15, 1861. Alarming news for readers of *The Times* : civil war in the United States. Originally middle-class English feeling was with Lincoln. It veered under various influences, including the Lancashire cotton famine.

The first volume of Marx's *Kapital*, whose effect on the world's labour movement has been dynamic, appeared in 1867. Most philosophers, Marx believed, merely try to understand the world; his task was to change it. He did not foresee that backward Russia would be the first great nation to test his theories.

Karl Marx

African exploration was a subject of extraordinary fascination to the Victorians. The most appreciated episode of all began in 1869, when H. M. Stanley, that marvel of endurance, received the terse instruction from Gordon Bennett, of the *New York Herald*—'Find Livingstone.'

H. M. Stanley

Gladstone

The 1870s

Interest in home politics now reached an intensity never equalled since. Gladstone versus Disraeli secured attention exceeding even that which later generations gave to sport.

The Telephone Arrives

When Prussia overwhelmed France in the war of 1870, and Napoleon III and the Second Empire were snuffed out, a new phase began in Europe. The long political predominance of France was ended. Germany had supplanted her. The triumph— if that is the word—was Bismarck's, who in creating this Prussianised Germany set her feet upon the path which was to lead her into two world wars.

Napoleon III and Eugénie

The First Woman Typis

Unlike the internal combustion engine, the typewriter has been an unmixed blessing. The inevitable inventor with an idea appeared as long ago as 1714, but the first practical machine dates from 1874—the Remington.

W. G. Grace

If W. G. Grace has a social significance, it is that he made watching cricket an amusement of the masses. A grateful country gave him a first national testimonial of £1,500 in 1879, and another of about £10,000 in 1896. He played first-class cricket for 36 years, and lived on until 1915.

Cardinal Newman

It is not easy to exaggerate the importance of the Pulpit in Victorian England. The sermons of a Spurgeon or a Newman were matters of debate among the working or educated classes. Newman, converted to Rome in the forties, was made a Cardinal in 1879.

The children in the photograph had, very probably, never been to school in their lives. England lagged behind every other great nation in education for the poor, and before Forster's Education Act of 1870 two-thirds of the children of the country were without any instruction at all. By making education national the Act made us a literate people.

This three-wheeled car—or motor carriage as it was called—is an 1885 model, made by Karl Benz. Its speed was ten miles an hour. Another German, Gottlieb Daimler, put motoring on the map by inventing, round about the same time, a petroleum engine.

The 1880s

The succulent lady on the opposite page is there to remind us that the status of women was considerably improved by the Married Women's Property Act of 1882. The apostolic-looking gentleman on the right was the inventor of the incandescent electric lamp, working independently of Edison and anticipating him. Below, action photographs by Muybridge foreshadow motion pictures.

Sir Joseph Wilson Swan

At Bow-street, on Saturday, Oscar Wilde, described as a gentleman, of Tite-street, Chelsea, was placed in the dock, before Sir John Bridge, charged with offences under the 11th section of the Criminal Law Amendment Act. Mr. C. F. Gill, instructed by Mr. Angus Lewis, of the Treasury, prosecuted. At the commencement of the hearing the prisoner was defended by Mr. C. O. Humphreys, the solicitor who conducted the proceedings at the police-court when the Marquis of Queensberry was prosecuted by Wilde for libel. At a later stage the prisoner was represented by Mr. Travers Humphreys. Mr. Gill said that the precise nature of the charges he should ask the magistrate to commit Wilde upon would depend on the evidence disclosed on the depositions after the matter had been thoroughly inquired into. The case he proposed to proceed with in the first instance related to Wilde's conduct with regard to a young man named Charles Parker. Wilde would also be charged with conspiring with Alfred Taylor. Mr. Gill then explained the circumstances under which Parker was brought into contact with Wilde. Parker was a valet out of place. He had a brother named William Parker, who was a groom. At the end of February or the beginning of March the brothers went to the St. James's Restaurant. They were there approached by Taylor. He supplied them with drink, and got them to write down their names and addresses. He then gave his own address, and said that Oscar Wilde was a man who would give them money. After one or two interviews between Taylor and the lads, the prisoner Wilde being in communication with him by telegraph, they were invited to go to Kettner's Restaurant. They went, accompanied by Taylor. When they arrived they were shown into a private room, where dinner was laid for four. Soon afterwards the prisoner arrived, and the boys were entertained to a sumptuous repast provided by him. After dinner Wilde took Charles Parker to the Savoy Hotel, where he had a suite of rooms. He plied the lad with drink, and subsequently gave him £2. They met again on several other occasions. Wilde gave the youth money, a gold ring, and a silver cigarette-case. There were, counsel added, a number of cases against the prisoner. Wilde had already had an opportunity of explaining these matters, and, if he chose, he could get into the witness-box and give any explanation he liked. It was an unpleasant case, but it was one of enormous importance. It was of enormous importance to show that people who committed these offences were bound to be brought to justice. Charles Parker was the first witness. Whilst he was giving evidence Alfred Taylor, alluded to by Mr. Gill in his opening statement, was placed in the dock and charged with conspiring with Oscar Wilde. Parker, in the course of his further evidence, said that on several occasions he visited Wilde at the Savoy Hotel and had champagne and chicken. Wilde gave him money to buy clothes with and made him other presents. The last time he saw Wilde the latter, who was in a cab in Trafalgar-square, told him he was looking as pretty as ever. William Parker, brother of the previous witness, gave corroborative evidence. Mrs. Ellen Grant, Little College-street, Westminster, proved that Taylor occupied rooms there, for which he paid £3 a month. Daylight was always excluded from the rooms. She understood that Taylor was a bachelor. She had heard him speak of "Oscar," but she had never seen Wilde. There were a number of visitors. Alfred Wood, formerly a clerk, spoke of his acquaintance with Wilde, and said he went to America to get rid of "these people"—that was, the people who went to Taylor's tea parties. Sidney Arthur Mavor and some other witnesses were then examined, and the case was adjourned till Thursday. Mr. Travers Humphreys applied for bail for Wilde on the ground that he knew the warrant was being applied for on Friday afternoon, but made no attempt to leave London. He had no intention of leaving the country, and he was the only person who could properly instruct solicitor and counsel. Sir John Bridge said it was not a case for bail, and the prisoners were removed in custody.

At Marylebone, Emma Beattie, aged 44, described as a cook, with no fixed abode, was charged before Mr. Plowden with wilfully and maliciously breaking a coloured-glass window, valued at £4, the property of Christopher Eales, architect, 9, Welbeck-street, Cavendish-square. Mr. Baker, solicitor, appeared to prosecute, and stated that the prisoner entered the prosecutor's service as cook in November last and left

Oscar Wilde

The 1890s

The massive edifice of Victorianism began to break down in the nineties. Its great ones were gone, or soon to go, Demos was beginning to stir, dissolvent æsthetic doctrines were in the air. It was to Pater that the æsthetes of the nineties turned, and the idea which spread among them was that Art was all, and good and evil nothing more or less than material for the artist. The arrest in 1895 of Wilde, the populariser of the Art for Art's sake doctrine, gave England a sort of Dreyfus case. It also led to the exclusion of Aubrey Beardsley (a design by whom is on this page) from the *Yellow Book*, and practically eclipsed the decadent movement. Wilde's legacy to the twentieth century was his gay and amoral attitude to life. Finally, there is Hardy, who published *Tess* and *Jude* in the nineties: a giant in a world from which giants were vanishing.

Thomas Hardy

AVBREY

Can-Can Girls

The raffish, or Pink 'Un, side of the times—the legendary 'naughty nineties.'

Paul Martin

August Bank Holiday

Hampstead Heath is still a place to go on August Bank Holiday, but they dance like this no longer. In the nineties the day was an eagerly-awaited carnival.

Organised British Socialism was born in the nineties. Keir Hardie was elected Labour M.P. for West Ham in 1892, and arrived at Westminster accompanied by a brass band. In the following year the I.L.P. was formed under his chairmanship. The life of the people was changing, and they were even, like the eminent, coming before the camera on informal occasions. Paul Martin took both photographs on this page and the five which follow them.

Kruger

The Original Commandos

Winston Churchill (second row, second on left) **Morning Post** *War Correspondent*

The Boer War—another of those wars that were to be over by Christmas—cost us two and a half years' fighting, 20,000 lives, £200,000,000. It is easy, putting aside the heroism, to dislike practically everything about it—the obstinacy of Kruger and the jingoism of Joseph Chamberlain, the mafficking hysteria, the muddles' the Khaki Election. Winston Churchill, present as a war correspondent, provided one of its more agreeable episodes in his escape from the Boers.

£25

(Twenty-five Pounds stg.) REWARD is offered by the Sub-Commission of the fifth division, on behalf of the Special Constable of the said division, to anyone who brings the escaped prisoner of war

CHURCHILL,

dead or alive to this office.

For the Sub-Commission of the fifth division,
(Signed) LODK. de HAAS, Sec.

1901

The old century died, and with it the old sovereign. Edward VII, who came to the throne in his sixtieth year, was crowned in 1902.

No. 270.

Special Army Order.

SOUTH AFRICAN FIELD FORCE.

ARMY HEADQUARTERS,
PRETORIA.
24th January, 1901.

DEATH OF HER MAJESTY QUEEN VICTORIA—

The following telegram has been received from the Adjutant-General, War Office, dated London, 23rd January, 1901:—

"Commander-in-Chief deeply regrets to inform you of the death of Her Majesty Victoria, Queen of the United Kingdom of Great Britain and Ireland and of the Colonies and Dependencies thereof, Empress of India, who departed this life at 6-30 p.m., 22nd January, at Osborne House, Isle of Wight."

The following from Lord Kitchener has been sent in reply:—

"The news of the Queen's death has been received with the greatest grief by the Army in South Africa. In their name I beg to express our sincere condolences with the Royal Family on the great loss sustained by them and the Nation."

By Order.

W. F. KELLY, Major-General,
Adjutant-General.

1902—1914

The relations of the Kaiser with his uncle, Edward VII, seem to parallel the situation that was arising between the two countries. 'He is a Satan,' the Kaiser had said —'an old peacock,' with 'a false and intriguing nature.' Britain began to fear German hegemony in Europe. Germany in return spoke, as usual, of encirclement.

King Edward, the Duke of Connaught, and Kaiser William II (1907)

The First Aeroplane Flight

The air age is coming and the horse age, with its hansom cabs, dying. On December 17, 1903, Wilbur and Orville Wright flew the first aeroplane. The ladies on the opposite page are at a balloon meeting at Ranelagh, 1906.

The Keystone Cops

Off to a Fire in the City, 1911

Crippen in the Dock

Comic films, the horse-drawn fire engine, Crippen—all may be given a tiny place in the Edwardian mosaic. The Crippen case has not proved as perishable as most sensations of the kind, possibly because the mild murderer, like a figure in folklore, continues to claim our sympathy. Finally, there is that curious minor Edwardian character, the wig-maker, Willy Clarkson, tending a sea-sick friend at a photographer's studio—a bizarre postcard in an era of postcards.

Willy Clarkson

Freud

H. G. Wells

Suffragette at Buckingham Palace, 1914

Mr and Mrs Lloyd George, 1911

New men are appearing, among them Freud, who published *Traum-Deutung* as long ago as 1900, and Wells, who with his scientific romances behind him went on to social and political criticism and a dazzling career as a novelist. That other phenomenon, Lloyd George, is here to remind us of the high blood-pressure days of the People's Budget of 1909–10, when 'Mr Balfour's poodle'—the House of Lords—revolted. While the struggle between Lords and Commons was still on, Edward VII died.

WORLD WAR No. ONE
1914–1918

Germany was the enemy—that much everyone knew long before the war broke out. Yet as late as the end of July, 1914, when the enemy was ready and had even found a *casus belli*, the Irish crisis was still mesmerising the country. The war that followed so rapidly was volume one, had we but known it.

Recruiting at Walham Green

Mud and Blood

E. O. Hoppé

The war ended, and the Unknown Soldier was buried in Westminster Abbey, and the men from the trenches returned, rather bewildered, to the loud-voiced civilian world of which they had long been suspicious.

The 1920s

The great housing shortage began in the twenties, and property values rose steeply. Few new houses were built until the latter half of the decade, and then came a building boom. But the slum problem remained, and children continued to grow up in surroundings of inexcusable squalor.

Bill Brandt

Out of the miners' strike of 1926, and of the confusion and discontents arising from severe unemployment and high cost of living, came the general strike of 1926, which was called off unconditionally after nine days. Trade unionism was severely chastened, and a year later a new Trade Disputes Act made the general strike illegal. These were tragic years for the miners. One of their penalties was lengthy loss of public sympathy in their claim for better conditions. But now the necessity for a new deal is widely understood.

The General Strike, 1926

Big-city life had its extravagances in the twenties, but no reprobation need fall on the man on the pogo-stick or the woman on the motor-scooter. Or, for that matter, on Mayfair's Bright Young People, whose treasure hunts and other activities managed to annoy quite a lot of people when reported in the newspapers. The hedonism of the twenties was certainly not confined to one class, the party-going class, of the lines—

Lenglen at Wimbledon

Mrs Smarty
Gave a Party
No one came.

Her brother
Gave another
Just the same.

Tennis was played generally, and watched by fair numbers. Radio was making great strides here and in America, whence comes the photograph of the man having his heart-beats broadcast to illustrate a Poe story.

On the Air

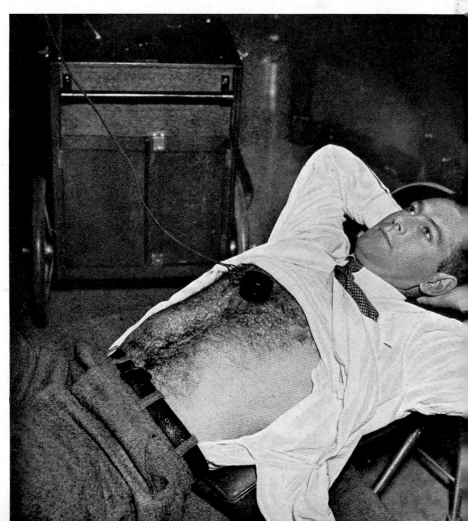

T. E. Lawrence

Chaplin

Film stars—and T. E. Lawrence —were the fabulous heroes of the period. Chaplin did more than anyone to start the cinema-going habit in this country, and became the pet of the intellectuals. Garbo is still the supreme woman star. Of Rudolph Alfonzo Raffaele Pierre Filibert Guglielmi di Valentina d'Antonguolla, or Rudolph Valentino, there is space to say nothing at all.

Greta Garbo, 1923 *Arnold Genthe*

Rudolph Valentino

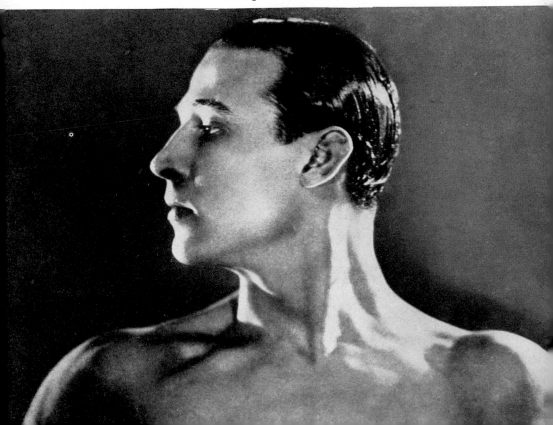

Einstein

E. O. Hoppé

Epstein

George Platt Lynes

Gertrude Stein

Einstein was very big news, and was treated with something approaching reverence. Epstein was news, but was treated with irreverence. Gertrude Stein was always good for a debunking paragraph or two. How sick, through no fault of theirs, one became of the trio! No wonder somebody wrote—

I don't like the family Stein!
There is Gert, there is Ep, there is Ein.
Gert's writings are all punk,
Ep's statues are junk,
And nobody understands Ein.

Augustus John

Eliot, Huxley, Coward—on their various levels they express the disenchantment of the twenties, unlike John, who always seems to be enjoying himself. At the same time they foreshadow, again on their own levels, the desire for moral certitudes which was to characterise the frightened thirties.

Noel Coward   **Aldous Huxley**   **T. S. Eliot**

The 1930s

The fear of the thirties—the greater because not yet experienced—was the fear of bombs. This picture, a portent, was taken in Downing Street when a ball was thrown and mistaken for a bomb. The woman has completely shielded one child.

In 1933 began Hitler's Germany and Roosevelt's America. The Nazis celebrated by burning down the Reichstag and fathering the plot on the Communists. Hitler's 'Brown terror' was under way.

The Depression, 1930

Unemployed Demonstration

The depression of 1930, following the Wall Street crash, saw the emergence of Mosley's New Party. Something happened to its policy of action, and Mosley reappeared with home-bred fascism in the shape of the British Union of Fascists, whose violent and fantastic meeting at Olympia on June 7, 1934, put an end to any chances of success the party may have had.

Sport, 1934

Mosley meets Friends

A storm broke in 1935 : Abyssinia invaded, and the League a failure. There followed the reoccupation of the Rhineland, March, 1936, the war in Spain, July, 1936, and Japan's attack, in July, 1937, on China.

Japanese Barbarism : Bayonet Practice on Living Chinese

Franco's Victory Parade

Haile Selassie

Life and the building-up of the German air force went on. Back in 1934 Churchill had warned Baldwin : Germany was re-arming on land ; she was rearming also to some extent at sea ; but what concerned us most was the rearmament of Germany in the air. Again and again the theme of his speeches was Germany's undeclared war, but the words, for all the practical effect they had, fell on deaf ears.

Baldwin and Ramsay MacDonald

The Coronation

King George V died in January, 1936 ; King Edward VIII abdicated in December of the same year, after a reign of 325 days ; King George VI succeeded to the throne, and was crowned on May 12, 1937. Thus (in case you've forgotten) three Kings reigned in one year. Stanley Baldwin retired after the Coronation, bearing handsome bouquets for his handling of the Abdication crisis, and stepped immediately into something indistinguishable from oblivion. Neville Chamberlain succeeded him as Prime Minister.

Feliks Topolski

Away from it All : 1—Hot Music

2—All-In Wrestling

3—Holidays Abroad

Lancelot Vining

4—Bottle Party

Lancelot Vining

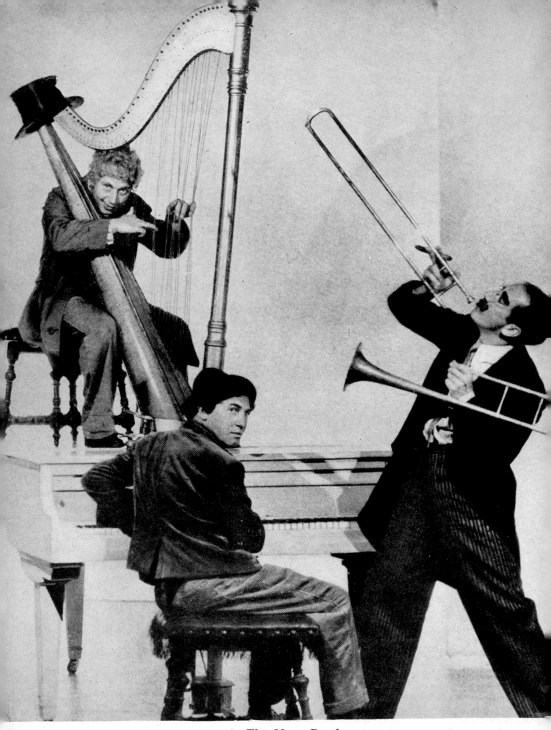

5—The Marx Brothers

From America all through the thirties came a flow of screwball humour, in films, magazines, and books. The Marx Brothers were pioneers, and no one had any difficulty in understanding their sort of surrealism.

David Low

Sir Max Beerbohm

Edith Evans

John Gielgud

Before this Album comes to a close, thanks to Low for great work in the thirties ; to Max, who doesn't entirely belong to the Beardsley period ; to Evans and to Gielgud. (*Cecil Beaton took the last three portraits.*)

'*We've Got to be Prepared*'

Lancelot Vining

September, 1938. Crisis in Czechoslovakia, queues for gasmasks in England, trenches being dug in gardens and parks, 'We've got to be prepared' posters everywhere, first-aid lessons and girls with false wounded arms—the dress rehearsal for a

YORK Tribune

LATE CITY EDITION

OCTOBER 1, 1938

THREE - CENTS
New York City and Vicinity

Britain and Germany in Compact Never to Fight Each Other Again; Nazi Troops Cross Czech Border

Hitler's Vanguard Passes Austro-Czech Frontier at 1 A.M., an Hour After Deadline He Had Fixed

General Settlement Expected in Berlin

Deal on Spanish War, an Air Pact and Limit on Arms Due, Plus 4-Power Accord Sought by Italy

By The Associated Press

BERLIN, Oct. 1 (Saturday).—The first contingent of German troops crossed the Czechoslovak frontier near Aigen, Upper Austria, early today, starting the Nazi occupation of territory granted to Chancellor Adolf Hitler by the four-power Munich accord.

The gray-clad German infantrymen marched over the border shortly after 1 a.m. (7 p.m. Eastern standard time, Friday), little more than an hour after the midnight deadline Hitler had set for his occupation.

An infantry battalion, numbering about 600 men, advanced along several roads from Aigen to take possession of posts immediately behind the Czechoslovak frontier in southwestern Czechoslovakia. It was explained that this movement was regarded as merely a vanguard operation, reconnoitering the terrain and preparing for the main army of occupation to march in later today, taking over the first of four districts granted to Hitler by the Munich pact.

The main body of troops, 30,000 men, assembled along the border of

Herald Tribune radio photo—Acme
Prime Minister Chamberlain at Heston Airdrome yesterday

Czechs, Bowing to Munich Pact, Get an Ultimatum From Poland

Warsaw Demands Evacuation of Teschen Today; 'We Want to Fight,' Prague Crowds Reply to Plan; 50,000 Non-Nazis Flee Sudetenland

Chamberlain Reveals New Pact of Friendship to Crowds Wildly Cheering Him on Return Home

Tells Them He Won 'Peace With Honor'

'I Believe It Is Peace for Our Time,' He Asserts; Later Parley Expected to Give Reich Colonies

By Joseph Driscoll
From the Herald Tribune Bureau
Copyright, 1938, New York Tribune Inc.

LONDON, Sept. 30.—Prime Minister Neville Chamberlain, returning tonight to receive a grateful welcome from hundreds of thousands of peace-loving Britons, brought from Munich not only the four-power agreement which authorizes Nazi Germany to take over Czechoslovakia's Sudetenland by gradual stages, but an Anglo-German pact of friendship, by which the two nations resolve never to go to war against each other and to settle all disputes by consultation and negotiation.

When his American Lockheed airliner brought him back to English soil at Heston Airport this afternoon Chamberlain received his first hearty welcome, which was followed by stirring street scenes the like of which had not been equaled in London since Armistice Day, 1918. The Prime Minister responded by reading, for the benefit of the newsreels and television apparatus, the text of the peace pact to which he and Hitler had affixed their signatures.

From the **New York Herald Tribune**, *October 1, 1938*

year later. On the 15th Chamberlain flew to Berchtesgaden to see Hitler. There was another meeting at Godesberg. Then on the 29th they met for the Munich Conference to satisfy Hitler's last territorial demands. Czechoslovakia was dismembered. On March 15, 1939, Germany occupied the remainder of the State.

11 a.m., September 3   *11.30 a.m., September 3*

The era of undeclared wars is over. The paralysing years epitomised in the satire

on the Left as the years of 'Waiting for the end, boys, waiting for the end,' are

over. Shocks and miseries and victory are to come.

L.R.

Acknowledgments

The editor's thanks are tendered to : J. W. Drawbell, for generously allowing
reproduction of a photograph from his own book, *All Change Here* ; Arnold Genthe,
George Platt Lynes, and Walker Evans, with whom the editor has been unable to
get into touch ; Messrs. John Lane for the Topolski drawing, from *The London
Spectacle*, 1935, and Messrs. Hamish Hamilton and F. L. Allen for a plate from
Since Yesterday ; Edison Swan Electric ; and E. O. Hoppé.

Kotelnikovo

By Alexander Werth

In the dark the ambulance stopped, and a lanky corporal conducted me and Edgar Snow to the house where we were billeted.

'Mind your head,' said the corporal, as we entered a tiny hut, with a dim light showing through the second door. We had to bend down to get in. The house consisted of two tiny rooms, lit by a small kerosene lamp. The first was the kitchen, the other our bedroom. Between the two was a large Russian stove, and it was very warm. We were greeted with a great display of cordiality by a middle-aged, very exuberant woman, plump, with fat arms, and with two golden front teeth which glittered in the light of the kerosene lamp. 'Pozhalte, pozhalte,' she chattered away, 'how nice to see some real friends, allies, after all we've gone through. Americans? British? You speak wonderfully good Russian, probably lived in our Soviet Union for quite a while, eh? And this is babushka,' she went on, pointing to a tiny shrivelled creature who sat silently in the corner of the kitchen, near the blacked-out window. We paid our respects to babushka. The corporal departed, telling Elena Nikolaevna to take good care of us, and saying he would call again in an hour to conduct us to our eating place. Elena Nikolaevna took the kerosene lamp and took us into the other tiny room, leaving babushka in the dark. 'Babushka will be all right,' she said; 'she is used to peeling potatoes in the dark.' Here was a table, and a large bookcase, and two beds, one a big homely affair with a lot of blankets and pillows, the other flimsier. 'You, the little one,' she said to Edgar Snow, 'had better sleep on this one. What a life we've had in Kotelnikovo these last five months,' she exclaimed, without even being asked any question. 'First we had some Rumanians here, and then the

65

E

Germans—a tank crew of five men. Very rough people ; but then, I suppose, it's because they regarded us as enemies ; I don't know what they would have been like in peace-time.'

A plane was zooming overhead, very low by the sound of it. 'That's a German plane,' said Elena Nikolaevna, 'I know it from the sound.'

'A German plane wouldn't fly so low,' I suggested, and at that moment we heard a stick of bombs go off with a whine, and somewhere, a long distance away, there was the sound of two not very loud explosions.

'Makes me a bit nervous when they fly about at night,' said Elena Nikolaevna. 'It's these transport planes that take food to the Germans encircled at Stalingrad. They keep flying all the time at night ; don't see why they should drop bombs at Kotelnikovo.'

Elena Nikolaevna was an elementary school teacher. When the Germans were approaching Kotelnikovo in August, 1942, the secretary of the Raikom said that Kotelnikovo would not be evacuated, but that if it were they would be warned in good time. So the teachers were left behind when it came to the point. One or two even went to the German commandant to inquire when the school would open again, but they were informed 'not yet.' So the teachers went on living, without any jobs. The local population was summoned to a general meeting to elect the starosta, or mayor, of the town ; at first one man was elected and then another, but both were invalidated, Elena Nikolaevna wasn't sure why ; and then a third one was elected, a railwayman called Paleyev, aged about 38. He was known to be quite a good man, but later he must have sold himself to the Germans. There were also a number of railwaymen who formed the bulk of the local police ; these policemen, Elena Nikolaevna said, used to chase about the local population, especially young girls, who would be forced to carry bricks and dig and build fortifications.

'One of the first things the Germans did,' she said, 'was to open the church. At first there was a Rumanian priest, and later they unearthed a Russian priest from somewhere, a very old man. The church used to be crowded with Rumanian officers and soldiers, and the population also used to go, or rather put in an appearance, because there was a fine of a thousand roubles if you didn't go to church. Gai and I went there once or twice— just looked in.'

'Who's Gai ?'

'Oh, you'll see Gai,' said Elena Nikolaevna ; 'Gai is my son, a clever boy ; you'll like him. And the choir,' she continued, 'was composed of very old women of the town. I don't know how the service was conducted ; the only two times we went the Rumanian priest was still in charge, and I couldn't make head or tail of it, and I don't even know what they were praying for.'

'Well, but how did you live ?'

'You can hardly call it living,' said Elena Nikolaevna. 'We were very short of food. We only received 250 grams of flour per person per day—nothing else.'

'How can you live on that ?'

'I used to do a little extra work for the Rumanian officer when he lived here ; his orderly once gave me an enormous pile of washing ; I spent four days washing his stuff, and then the Rumanian orderly gave me half a loaf. It was really a shame, and I couldn't complain. But then, I suppose, the Rumanian orderly hadn't anything else to give me. The Rumanians were a measly bunch, and simple in their behaviour. Some of their soldiers, far from giving us anything, asked us for bread ; I would give them a slice ; it was better that way, or they might have taken it anyway. The Germans are very proud people, very different from the Rumanians. Occasionally they'd give me something— a tin of fish or a cigarette—yes, just like one of those English cigarettes you've got.'

'Will you have one ?'

'Thanks,' said Elena Nikolaevna, putting the Players' between her gold teeth. 'You may think it shocking to see a lady smoke, but it's just an old vice with me.' She laughed in girlish fashion. 'Yes, all the time they were here, they gave me two tins of fish. It wasn't much, was it ? I used to wash and scrub for them all day, and they'd send me out for water to the well. It was a slave's life. And Gai and babushka and I had to live in the little kitchen, all huddled together, while the five of them lived here, in this room—two on the beds and three on the floor. They had a lot of drink, and a lot of food, these Germans had, and they seemed very confident at first they would stay here indefinitely. But a day or two before they left, one of them got up in the morning and shouted as usual : "Matka"—they used to call everybody Matka, damn cheek !—"Matka, Wasser zu waschen." But

I don't know why, that morning I had a hunch the Russians
were coming back, and I just couldn't force myself to take out
the pail. So I said "To hell with you !" and one of them started
smashing up the stove with the butt of his pistol, and another
fired his pistol into the ceiling, and they gave babushka a heart
attack—she nearly passed out. . . . Here's the hole in the
ceiling, you can still see it. But I wouldn't budge, and in the end
one of them went out for the water himself.'

There were two occasions on which the people of Kotelnikovo
thought that the Russians were coming back—in November and
then again at the end of December. But by the middle of
December one of the tank men said to Elena Nikolaevna, 'Russ
nicht zurück'—'we've chased them back eighty or ninety kilo-
metres.' 'It was quite true,' she said ; 'the firing had become
very distant again. But on December 28 one of the tank men
said to me : "Russ kommt zurück." You see, one wants to live,
especially when you've got a young boy to look after, so I expressed
no joy. And four of them went away that day, without a word,
but the fifth one said : "Auf wiedersehen, Matka." They were
very gloomy. They weren't so bad, these five Germans, but they
thought we were just slaves—only there to work for them. In
other houses they behaved much worse. They wouldn't leave
the women alone ; and the Rumanians were terrible. There
was a lot of rape in the town, though I admit I hardly ever saw
anybody during the occupation. We just stayed indoors. Only
once I went out to my vegetable plot outside the town, and the
Germans had stolen all the vegetables, and stamped everything
out. I didn't hear of anybody being shot at Kotelnikovo ; but
thirty or maybe fifty people were taken away by the Germans.
Or maybe they followed them voluntarily, people like the priest
and the policemen. They were going to mobilise all the young
people for work in Germany, and they sent out leaflets, but I
don't think they had time to do anything much.'

Later, I was to hear more about the rather peculiar behaviour
of the Germans at Kotelnikovo. This was Cossack country, and
it seems they refrained from large-scale savagery in the hope that
the Cossacks would eventually accept them. They encouraged
some people who showed willingness to co-operate.

'Yes,' said Elena Nikolaevna, 'some queer things happened,

I can tell you. But it was very depressing after all the freedom we enjoyed under our dear Soviet régime.' And then she spoke of her last night under German rule. 'That last night,' she said, 'there was much firing going on in the neighbourhood. The three of us and twenty other people escaped to the basement of a big stone building not far away. Outside was a German battery. It fired to split your eardrums. Then, later, somebody said : "Just look out." It was terrifying. It seemed as though the whole town were in flames. Actually, a large part of the town was in flames—most of the public buildings. And when we went out to look it was so strange : there were neither Germans nor Russians in the town. Earlier that night I had seen many of the Germans going away somewhere, with their gun-carriages and a lot of tanks. I did not see any Rumanians, though ; they may have surrendered to our people by then. But I didn't know they were all going away. That night the town was empty. Our people didn't come in till the next morning. It was funny, the Germans and Rumanians didn't get on at all ; they didn't live in the same houses ; they didn't even live in the same streets. . . .'

And this was the room in which the German tank crew had lived, these were the beds in which two of them had slept. The house was intact—partly, no doubt, because it was hardly worth looting. Here were many family photographs and snap-shots on the wall, stuck untidily into large frames, an old calendar with a picture of Lermontov contemplating the Caucasus, lace curtains, a balalaika in the corner, a bookshelf with school texts on physics and chemistry and Russian literature, and, on the table, a copy of the *Wittgensteiner Zeitung* of December 4, with an editorial : '50. Geburtstag Francos : der Erretter Spaniens,' and—how sickening !—an index of the Paris Métro. Pages of it. Almost every street meant something to me, some unimportant but still precious memory of Paris. . . .

The corporal called for us and we went and had supper. Through the dark he showed us home again, and we went to bed. In the morning I found Edgar lying on the floor. 'It's these bedbugs,' he said ; 'I've got a complex about bedbugs. Couldn't stand them even in China.'

Elena Nikolaevna came in, looking very distressed. 'I noticed when I got up at six this morning that your friend was sleeping on the floor. Did he have bugs ? I looked very closely

through the bed, I swear there wasn't a bug to be seen anywhere
—only two little ones, and I killed them. Do you mean to say
there were really bugs in your bed ?'

Snow said something had definitely bit him during the night.
'But please don't worry,' he added.

'Worry !' cried Elena Nikolaevna, 'I'll worry all day. It's
terrible. But,' she said, almost with tears in her eyes, 'what can
you expect if you've had Germans sleeping in your house for *five*
months !'

The next night I took the small bed, and the bugs did not
bother me. Elena Nikolaevna may have killed the last bugs, or
perhaps I was more thick-skinned than Edgar.

That morning we met Gai, Elena Nikolaevna's only child. He
was fifteen, fairly tall but almost unbelievably thin. Gai was the
Cossack name his mother had given him, but no youngster was
less sturdy than he. He had an extremely bright, intelligent,
slightly monkey-like face, thin, skinny little hands, wrists and
arms not much thicker than a walking-stick.

'Is that what the Germans have reduced you to ?' I said.

'No, I was always rather thin,' said Gai, 'but of course it was
upsetting to live under the Germans. We didn't have enough
food, and all that sort of thing has an effect on your nerves, you
know,' he added with all the earnestness of a grown-up. 'But
when I went with mother to Stalingrad last year to consult a well-
known doctor there, he said there was nothing wrong with me
really—lungs and heart perfectly all right, just slightly anæmic.'
He spoke beautiful Russian, in a clear, silvery voice. 'I'm sorry
I wasn't here last night,' he said, 'but when the Germans were
here we never went out at night and very seldom during the day—
one just didn't feel like it. Now I go out at nights to see my pals—
the fellows I used to go to school with. There are some still left
at Kotelnikovo.'

'Yes, it's a blessing,' said Elena Nikolaevna. 'Gai will now
be able to go back to school. He's a bit skinny, but,' she added
proudly, 'he's the cleverest boy in his form—full marks in every
subject. He has read everything—all the classics, but his chief
interest is science, and he wants to go into the Navy.' We did
not pursue the subject, as we had to go out, but we saw a lot
more of Gai that night and during the following days.

That morning we had our first proper glimpse of Kotel-nikovo—and of our house. It was very like the other houses around—a small cottage with whitewashed outer walls and a touch of blue paint round the windows, and a gabled iron roof. Between the cottages were spaces of some ten or fifteen yards—these were vegetable plots, I suppose, though now they were all covered with snow, and there were no fences left to mark the separate gardens : they had been used as firewood during the occupation. Our house was one of many in one of the main streets of Kotelnikovo—Lenin Street.

Some military lorries and horse-drawn sleighs drove along Lenin Street. At one corner I noticed a German sign-post by which Lenin Street had been given the non-committal name of Chaussee-Strasse. Our improvised canteen was in a street parallel with ours, and we walked across the snow, winding our way among the cottages, trees and privies. On our way we ran into Handler, another newspaper correspondent, who said we must go and have a look at his house. He was living in a larger and more prosperous-looking cottage. In the garden outside some-thing unusual was happening. Here were four Cossack women—one very old and three younger—and a child, and they were standing among a large pile of belongings—bedding, blankets, barrels of salted tomatoes and cucumbers, a map of Europe, a Singer's sewing-machine, and large quantities of old-fashioned crockery and kitchen utensils. A fifth woman, with her head protruding from a large hole in the ground, was passing them more blankets, dishes and eiderdowns. It was a deep, almost bottle-shaped hole, cemented on the sides, and here they had kept their most valued belongings during the occupation.

Here in the garden, beside the people, also stood a cow, and several chickens were scuttling about. 'How did you manage to keep these ?' I asked. One of the younger women—she was one of the old dame's three daughters—said that the Germans liked to have milk, and so the cow was kept for their benefit. As for the chickens, she pointed to a small wooden door at the foot of the house.

'We managed to keep twenty chickens there right through the occupation. At first we were frightened they would cackle, but they never do in the dark. Whenever the Germans were away—and they didn't usually stay here throughout the day, we'd take corn to the chickens ; and here they are,' she added, with a touch of triumph.

'These people aren't lacking anything,' said Handler ; 'you should have seen the breakfast they gave me—cabbage pie and tea and sugar and milk and sour cream and preserved fruit— terrific. The husband has a job on the railway, so he is able to keep a cow and a big vegetable plot, and another of the daughters is a big shot on one of the kolkhozes, and what they don't grow here they get from the kolkhoz in exchange for some of their own produce. They did very well before the occupation, and having lost very little, through sheer foresight and presence of mind, they'll be back to prosperity before long. In fact, they're pretty prosperous already.'

The Cossack girls were big buxom wenches. I asked how many more sisters or brothers they had. Their one brother, they said, was in the Red Army, and one little sister, the youngest one, had been an anti-aircraft gunner at Stalingrad, and she had been killed. And suddenly all three, and the old mamma, began to cry.

'Weren't they awful brutes, the Germans ?' I asked old mamma.

'No, I wouldn't say so,' she said ; 'some were very nasty people, but those we had here—if you were polite to them, they'd be quite polite to you.'

I imagine the Germans must have treated these 'kulaks' fairly well, with the cow as the real basis of their *modus vivendi*. Mamma and her three daughters had clearly been pursuing a policy of waiting. After all, there wasn't much else they could do, and maybe they benefited to some extent from the relative politeness with which, for reasons of their own, the Germans considered it advisable to treat the more prosperous part of the population in this part of the world. First, they had the idea that the Cossacks might be used for political ends, and secondly, the front was so near that it was better not to antagonise the people and drive them into open opposition and desperate sabotage. But the interesting thing is that the Germans had really no consistent policy about the Cossacks. In some cases they used the velvet glove, in others the gallows, the firing squad and the deportee train. And when they thought they would be chased out for ever, they became particularly horrible—witness Krasnodar, the capital of the Kuban Cossacks. At Kotelnikovo, during most of the time, they imagined the country already belonged to them, and until the final introduction of the New Order it would be simpler to keep the place more or less as it was. To let the old Cossack woman keep her cow was in the interests of the German army, as it happened. . . .

Elena Nikolaevna and Gai were waiting for us. I had given her the butter I had brought from Moscow, and although she and the boy had probably tasted no butter for months she had insisted on baking little pastries for us, and, as the kettle was boiling, Edgar produced the remains of his coffee and we all had a little feast together. Babushka, with her funny little wrinkled face and equally wrinkled hands, stayed in her corner, but obviously enjoying her coffee and cookies.

'It's wonderful,' babushka said, 'having you here, instead of these Germans. I just used to cry and cry all day and all night, ready to die, and leaving my dear ones to all this misery.'

'Babushka is really very brave,' said Elena Nikolaevna ; 'perhaps it's because she's a bit deaf. Last summer she'd go right across the yard, to get water, with firing and bombing going on all over the place. And she'd just toddle along with her pail, taking no notice of anything. I'd shout to her, "Come back, babushka," but she'd just say, "It's all right, dear, I shan't be long." '

Babushka, who perhaps didn't know what was being said, continued her own train of thought. 'Ah, yes, I thought I'd die, but now that our own people are back I think I could live to a hundred,' she said, as her little face screwed up in a toothless smile. 'English, American ?' she went on, talking almost to herself. 'I used to know English and American gentlemen. My husband used to be an *izvostchik*, had a fine phaeton on springs ; he used to drive English and American gentlemen across the Don—they were engineers. Long time ago that was, still under the Tsar.'

'I'd like to see America some time,' said Gai. 'I know the names of all the big towns—New York and Chicago, Washington and New Orleans and San Francisco.' Elena Nikolaevna proudly flashed her golden teeth.

'Gai knows a lot ; he's first in all subjects ; he's very good at geography, too.'

Gai was enjoying himself. He was showing off in his fifteen-year-old way. 'What papers do you write for ?' he said.

'Do you know any of our papers ?' I asked.

'Yes,' he said, rattling off another list of names. '*Times, Daily Worker, Daily Telegraph, Morning Post* . . .'

'Any American ones ?'

'No, I don't think I know any American papers.' Gai was a fine kid. He talked and talked in his clear silver voice—about everything—about himself, and his future career, and about the Germans, and about the films he had seen. 'I like American films,' he said. 'Here in Kotelnikovo *Song of Love* and *The Great Waltz* were a great success. Before the war we had a very good time, you know. I was a pioneer myself, and would be in the Comsomol by now, but for the German occupation. All our younger people were preparing to be engineers, or doctors, or surgeons, or scientists. But if the Germans had stayed here there would have been no education for us. The girls would have been expected to wash floors, and the lads to look after the cattle. They didn't regard us as human beings at all.' Gai said he was anxious to enter the naval academy. 'There is room for a lot of specialists in the Navy—for electro-technicians, and physicists, and all sorts of skilled people. We had some Black Sea marines at Kotelnikovo last summer. They fought here. They said that although I was a bit sickly the sea would put me right. There's one fellow they told me about ; used to be as thin as me, and now, after two years' training, he's manning a gun on a cruiser, and is perfectly all right. I've never seen the sea,' said Gai, 'but I've read a lot about it.'

Elena Nikolaevna said proudly, 'Oh, Gai is a great reader."

'Gai, tell us, what was it like under the Germans ?'

'Well,' he said, shrugging his frail shoulders, 'they didn't consider us as people at all.'

'Did they kick you about ?'

'No, they simply took no notice of me. Sometimes they'd ask : "What form are you in ? Where's your father ?" I'd say he was in the Red Army. They'd look cross but say nothing.'

'Did they ever say what sort of government they were proposing to establish here ?'

'Yes ; they would say : "Everybody will work for himself ; no more kolkhozes and no more communism. We aren't going to stay here ; we have only come here to liberate you from the Jews and the Bolsheviks." They put up a picture of Hitler on the walls ; it was called "Hitler the Liberator." ' Gai made a wry face. 'He hardly looked human. A completely beastly face. Terrifying. Like a native of the Malay Islands. They opened the church ; first they had a Rumanian priest, later a Russian. I once went when the Rumanian was still there. Crowds of Rumanian soldiers. At one point they'd all go bang down on their knees. Then they would carry around a dish, covered with a napkin, and the Rumanians would put money on it —roubles, or marks or lei. Didn't make much difference, all money was pretty useless. The mark was worth ten roubles, but the marks that circulated here were some special kind of occupation marks, without any watermark. The Germans had a passion for destroying things,' said Gai ; 'it was quite absurd some of the things they did. They tore up all the vegetables in our allotment outside the town, and stamped everything to blazes, so that you couldn't grow anything there next year. They burned down the library. They wouldn't even leave my little library alone,' said Gai, pointing at the bookcase. 'They tore up the Russian magazines, and tore out of all the books the Lenin and Stalin pictures. So silly—don't you think ? It was these tank men. Queer chaps. You should have seen them at Christmas. They went all sloppy. They got a lot of parcels from Germany with coloured cards, with robins and things. They sat here, and lit the candles of a tiny paper Christmas-tree they'd got from home, and they unwrapped enormous cakes, and opened tins and bottles of rum, and they got drunk and sang sentimental songs about something or other.'

'Where were you at the time ?'

'Just where we always were,' said Gai, 'in the kitchen, where the three of us would sleep.'

'Didn't they offer you any cake ?'

'No, of course not. It wouldn't even occur to them.'

'Weren't you hungry ?'

'Of course,' said Gai, 'but I would have hated to take part in any of their festivities.' He produced a lighter from his pocket. 'They left it here by mistake ; after they'd gone I found it under one of the beds. We haven't any matches, and it's a useful gadget, but I don't like having anything from these people. . . .'

'Yes,' said Gai, 'I got thin, even thinner than I was. The bombs got on my nerves, I suppose. And when one no longer feels a human being—for they kept rubbing it in that we weren't *people* any longer—it has a bad effect, too, on one's health. But the doctor says I'm quite sound. They had no respect for anybody ; they'd dress and undress in front of women ; we were just a lot of slaves. . . . And, of course, there was no food ; 250 grams of bread a day was all we'd get ; they also opened a shop where one could buy some rye flour—9 kg. a week for the three of us, for 10 roubles 60. But there was no market ; nothing came from the kolkhozes ; we didn't see any fats at all,' said Gai, with a scientific air. 'And what a nice little town our Kotelnikovo was,' he said, 'not like Moscow, of course—I want to go to Moscow to see the Metro and the escalators—but nice in its own small way. The Univermag—the department store—was quite a big one, though even before the fritzes came it no longer had anything to sell except a few rubbishy odds and ends—thousands of collar studs, for instance ; and then there were five other big shops, and about twenty booths, and a summer restaurant where they sold very good ice cream and vatrushki (cream cheese pie). And I've already told you about the cinemas. One of my favourite films— I saw it several times—was Charlie Chaplin's *City Lights*. . . .' He babbled on and on, till it was time for us to go. Elena Nikolaevna listened admiringly to her boy.

'Yes,' she said, 'he took it much to heart, all this humiliation we suffered from the Germans and Rumanians. They are proud people, the Germans. Only sometimes they would joke, and say : "Matka, we think you're a Jewess." "Sure I'm a Jewess," I'd say, and they'd all laugh. The Rumanians were more down at heel. We used to call them "the Gipsies." '

That night and during the subsequent days I also learned much more about Elena Nikolaevna, and got to like her better than at first. First of all she told me the story of her two gold teeth. There was nothing wrong with her teeth, but when she and her husband and little Gai and the inevitable babushka—'we've taken her around everywhere,' she said—lived for some years in Kazakhstan, it was the fashion among Russians and Kazakh women there to have two, or even all, the front teeth crowned in gold. Elena Nikolaevna was not by tradition a Bolshevik. One day, as we came back to the cottage, she was singing a sentimental Essenin song. 'Perhaps this is forbidden now,' she said, with a shrug, 'but it's just a passion with me.' She had studied singing at Novocherkassk Musical Academy. She had gone there, as a young girl, soon after the civil war. She belonged to a Cossack family in one of the big *stanitzas* on the Don. 'My father,' she said, 'was what you might call a small *seredniak* (a 'below average' farmer). He hadn't much of a business head, and during the civil war we lost everything. We were literally reduced to starvation, and father, who, poor man, had lost his head, and didn't know how things would work out, sold the farm to a Kulak for ten sacks of flour. We moved to Novocherkassk, where we lived in a small flat. But before we had settled down properly my father and my brother died in the typhus epidemic of 1921. I was still at school then, finishing my seven-class course. When my father and brother died there was nothing much to hope for. I entered the Comsomol, and went to the musical academy where they began to teach me singing. I was quite good at it, but I had to look after mother, and my stipend was very, very small ; so when my future husband met me and asked me to marry him, I agreed. He had a job as a railwayman—which meant a regular job.' To this last survivor of a Cossack family ruined by the turmoil of the civil war, her marriage to a railwayman seemed rather a *mésalliance*. 'He's a good man, my husband,' Elena Nikolaevna would say, 'though he hasn't much of an education. Yes,' she would add, 'he's in the right Bolshevik tradition. He's been a railwayman all his life, and so was his father. His father, who had been a railway conductor for forty years, received an inscribed gold watch from Kaganovitch himself.'

Later, after her marriage, and after settling down at Kotelnikovo in her husband's home, she took a correspondence course in elementary teaching. It was during the days when thousands of schools were opened throughout the Soviet Union, and Elena Nikolaevna was as good as anybody for this simple job. This coquette of thirty-eight or so no doubt dreamed of all she might have been but for the civil war ; she would talk of her youth when she 'looked pretty good and kulturno, with her hair waved and a pretty summer frock' ; and one of the Rumanians had told her that if a Rumanian was fond of a girl called Elena, he called her by the affectionate diminutive of 'Enutsa.' She giggled in a girlish way, but added : 'I told the little swine I wasn't Enutsa to him, thank you.'

Elena Nikolaevna was happy she had lived safely through the ordeal of the German occupation, and that babushka and Gai were safe, too. Gai and babushka were really her life now ; and she was grateful to the Soviet régime. 'Thanks to our Soviet régime,' she once said, 'we pay only five roubles rent a month for this little house of ours, and,' she added, 'you can say what you like'—not that either Edgar or I had said anything—'but it's a good régime. Even babushka, to whom it was all very new and strange at first, has become very fond of it.' As for the husband, they had last heard of him in June, 1942. He was on the Voronezh front then. Now that the postal service was about to be restored at Kotelnikovo they might hear from him soon. . . .

Many weeks later I received a short letter from Gai. It came by ordinary post.

> Good morning, dear Mister Werth.
> I have a great piece of news for you. Our school has opened, and to-day is the first day. The post is working well, and we regularly receive newspapers, and even magazines. Please send me your magazine, and also some books, if you can.
> The fritzes have stopped flying over us.
> Please write to me in detail, and tell me how you are living. How is Mister Snow feeling ?
> All is well here. We have had several film shows, and already one concert. Greetings to Mister Snow.
> Write letters.
> > Yours,
> > > Gai.

The letter was written in a good, mature hand.

So life was going back to normal at Kotelnikovo ; and there was no longer any need for the fritzes to fly to Stalingrad to supply von Paulus's troops. They were all dead or in prison camps. But Gai's father, the railwayman—where was he ?

Are You Happy in Your Work

By J. Maclaren-Ross

Work for me starts normally at nine. The rattle of my type-writer coincides with the arrival downstairs of the Second-in-Command, whose clerk I am. At the moment he's on leave, so we'll leave him. Then shortly afterwards a shout of SHUN shakes the house and that is Company Evidence. C.O's Evidence follows later and then you get ESCORT AND ACCUSED SHUN. While this is going on downstairs I enter despatches. There are many items to be entered, including the annoying return required urgently by the adjutant three days ago and duly despatched to him ; returned by BHQ in error that evening ; the next day again sent off by me marked ADJUTANT ; returned the same afternoon with *HQ Company* on it and ADJUTANT rubbed out ; redirected and returned promptly with new markings on it and moreover with one corner missing : it's beginning to come to bits. The only solution is to seal it up to ensure the adjutant gets it, otherwise he'll be raising hell. I pick up a sticky label : by the middle of the morning my mouth is sour with gum arabic and my tongue stuck to my teeth.

The CSM enters with an Offence Report in his hand. A spot more crime to add on, he says. Who's it to-day ? Bloody Bates and Hubbard. What, again ? Yeah. They'll be for the clink this time that's one comfort. We'll soon be rid of em. What shall I put down. The usual ? A.W.O.L. ? That's the ticket. Thank you.

The CSM always says Thank You, he also says Please, which is what makes him different from other Company Sergeant Majors. His name is Denton, although recently when a phone message came through to him from Major Glover, the signaller on phone duty transcribed it as 'TO MAYOR KENTON FROM MAYOR GLOVER,' whereupon the CSM said to him, If a Mayor gets more pay than I do then I am willing to be one, but my name I have had for 37 years and I'll be damned if I change it now.

CSM Denton is a regular soldier and has seen service in most parts of the world : he can talk entertainingly about them all. His attitude towards most things is one of cheerful je m'en foutisme, and is frequently expressed by him in its literal English equivalent.

Tall and straight and thin, with a rigid back, a lean mobile face, a high neighing laugh, he has only one aversion : OCTU candidates. And this is natural, since you cannot expect him to willingly salute, on their return to the unit as officers, lance corporals of 19 who when sent to OCTU were probably not in receipt of proficiency pay, having less than six months service in. In any case CSM Denton always says that he does not salute anything below the rank of Captain.

Returning to his office the CSM almost collides with Sgt Legge, the pay NCO and Company Clerk, rushing down the corridor with a casualty state in his hand. Sgt Legge grins Sorry over his shoulder and roars out in the same breath RUNNER. This is the signal for everybody in the building to roar out RUNNER simultaneously. Corporal Dexter, the Orderly Sergeant, emerges from his bunk and leans over the banisters. RUNNER ! RUNNER !! RUNNER ! ! ! The shout echoes down the stairwell ; it is taken up from every office, like the barking of dogs in a countryside at night.

Sgt Legge is by now in my office ; big and burly, with curly hair and a large grin, he drops the casualty state on my desk. Nicknamed Smiler for obvious reasons, he speaks always explosively. Where are the expurgated runners ? I don't know. Well send one of the expurgators down to me will you when they roll up.

Legge goes out, he is stopped on the landing by a corporal for a confidential talk about the tarts they met at the dance last night. What she said what I said and did you and did I, it was a proper laugh.

Sgt Legge is the Company Romeo. Once he became monogamous : it was a telephone girl. Then there was a bust up and he ceased to live up to his nickname. For days he went about looking black ; blokes coming to him for casual payments got their heads bitten off. He drank all his pay and was broke by Monday. I said to console him There are more fish in the sea. He said he ruddy well knew it but in his present state of mind he didn't feel like fishing. I could understand that, having been offered the same advice in similar circumstances myself. But it is good advice all the same and later Sgt Legge took it and the other fish is blonde and wears the uniform of a WAAF.

I enter a despatch SUBJECT Discipline. It's one of the C.O's special stinkers and should wake everyone up. I read it with satisfaction. Cpl Dexter puts a sick report on my desk. Look at this here.

The M.O. has written across it, This man was recommended for 14 days Sick Leave in hospital but states he has been given detention instead.

Some ruddy mess-up I reckon, Cpl Dexter says buttoning his blouse, I don't know nothing about it.

Then the runners come trooping in, they've been in the tea-shop. Two of them are immediately nailed down and sent out on messages. The remaining two, Wells and Williams, sit at opposite ends of the desk.

Wells comes from West Ham and plays the accordion in the unit dance-band. With his cap cocked on one side, nervous rolling eyes, a deep guttural voice, he is actually timid despite a rather raffish exterior. He is easily elated and depressed ; he is nineteen years old. He starts now to write a letter in pencil but not as formerly on my best notepaper, as I have locked this up in a cupboard. Wells's letters are either Dear Mum and Dad or else to his girl. His girl is generally known as Bleeding Rosie. She has puritan instincts and is constantly repudiating the plans put forward by Wells for their wedding night. When he is on leave she wears frocks buttoned to the neck and leaves nothing to chance. Get something, Wellsy ? they ask him on his return. Yerce, he tells them gloomily ; a slap in the chops.

Wells's wedding is always being postponed. His mum interfered when the banns were put up and there was a row which ended in Wells being kicked out of home. Everyone gave contradictory advice and Wells nearly went out of his mind. Eventually it was smoothed over, the wedding fixed for his next seven days, and correspondence with Mum and Dad, interrupted during the breach, continued as usual. But Rosie advises Wells in her latest to bring home with him a tin opener or better still two, in case one breaks.

Williams, on the other side of the table, leans forward with a burnt-out fag-butt in his mouth and in an accent at first unintelligible to me but which I have got gradually used to, asks if he can have one of my lights. Like most Welshmen he buys few

F

matches and then only on Fridays. I tell him he can have the rest of the lights to-morrow. He sits back with his legs stuck straight out, puffing at his fag and smiling foolishly. As usual his jacket and collar are undone.

Williams is lanky and owing to adolescence and the condition of his skin might easily be mistaken for a case of scabies. One day he was and spent a blissful five days in hospital, where he got off with a nurse. When he first arrived as a runner I thought he was either foreign or else congenitally unable to understand what was said to him. Both turned out to be right, as in his native village he spoke only Welsh, but his knowledge of English slowly improves, although it's still confined mainly to swearing.

The other two runners are Pritchett and Dobb. Pritchett is the banker of the quartet : he lends money out to the other three at interest. He collects threepenny bits and is continually counting his money over in the kitchen. He keeps a reserve fund of half-a-crown concealed under his cap-badge in case of need. His other money is kept in two separate pockets : one for silver, wrapped carefully in a handkerchief so that no coin jingles ; the other for coppers, which he brings out and displays as his entire means if approached for a loan by anyone other than his regular clientele. He is a practised dodger and an actor of no mean ability. If sent up the town on a message he spends the afternoon in the cinema ; consequently I employ him only for local jobs from two o'clock onwards.

During the winter he volunteered for the job of looking after fires ; thereafter officers used to comment on him commiserat-ingly as he staggered manfully in with a coal bucket full to the brim. One of the officers, feeling particularly sorry to see him so laden, offered to help. He lifted the bucket ; it was astonishingly light and proved on investigation to be stuffed with paper, a few knobs of coal artistically arranged on top. After this he was in disgrace and Dobb took over the fires from him. The job suited Dobb because it permitted him to be revoltingly dirty at all times without being checked for it.

Dobb is another cockney but of a repellent kind. Almost a dwarf, he is always shadow-boxing about the office and telling about the time he knocked out a fascist with a righthander in Whitechapel. It transpired that the righthander was delivered by Dobb while three of his mates held the fascist down, one of them sitting on his head. I have tried hard to dislodge Dobb but without success. Once he was transferred but he came back ; no one could handle him. Now, without the excuse of fires, he still contrives to be almost completely black ; one day when he had a bath he left his boots behind in it.

Wells scrawls a signature in pencil and beneath it embarks on a series of crosses. I count forty-six. Wells searches among my papers for an envelope, sticks it down, writes SWALK on the flap. RUNNER is called out in the voice of the CQMS. Williams, flinging away his fag, lopes off along the corridor ; Wells starts on a long yarn about his cousin who has inherited a hundred pounds and how can he go about tapping her.

Now there is a sudden speeding-up of work, people run in and out with papers to be sent off, the Education Officer drops two letters in front of me, the P.T. Sergeant wants a sports programme typed, a lieutenant asks me how to spell loofah.

Wells has picked up a magazine of mine and opening it is faced at once with a painting by Dali. What the deleted's this ? he says. It's a picture. Yerce but what's it meant to be.

A scraping of rifle butts on the landing advertises the presence of men waiting outside the CSM's for their leave passes. It must be ten o'clock. Thank God for that. At half-past I can slip out for a break. A sudden shout goes out. One of the passes, supposedly for seven days, is found to be made out for fourteen. A row begins, the guardroom is mentioned. The CSM gets the best of it, the man doesn't get his pass, Wells gives up Dali as a bad job. Can he post his letter ? Yes but don't forget to come back. Garn whatcher take me for.

I examine the postage book. Somewhere there's been a ballsup. I count my remaining money and stamps. I'm a shilling short. I go over the account day by day, it goes back weeks. The totals add up wrong, I'm in a whirl. Suddenly a slip of paper hitherto unnoticed catches my eye, *Respirators will be worn by all ranks to-day from* 1030 *till* 1115 *hours.* That makes me pause. Respirators ? Three-quarters of an hour ? Not bloody likely. I grab my cap and the two letters dumped by the Education Officer and make for the stairs. There is no official break time for office personnel : mine is known as going to the post. I do in fact go there but afterwards. First I go to Mercer's Café.

It's down on the front by the Pier and is civilian, that is to say although patronised mainly by the troops there are tablecloths and the atmosphere is not that of a canteen. A stag's head, antlers on the wall, a banner : PLEASE BRING YOUR OWN BAGS AND PAPER. There is a downstairs room for the officers where everything costs more. Once we had a subaltern of socialistic views who objected to the implied class distinction and also to the twopence extra on tea ; for two mornings he sat upstairs with the other ranks but we damn soon showed him what was what and after that he too went below with his brother officers.

Gradually the café fills up : the CSM, the Messing staff, the two educational sergeants (at other times invisible), the orderly sergeant, a few corporals, the training sergeant-major in shirt-sleeves with his crown strapped to his wrist like a watch, and of course Smiler, roaring with laughter and with a face like the rising sun. He is surrounded by WAAFs and one WREN, a girl with eyes starting out of her head. There is backchat with the waitresses : the big frizzy one, the smaller one in the green smock who looks always as though she had awakened from a night of love, the buxom sophisticated one that Wells has his eye on. Coppers rattle in the china bowl, cream doughnuts are consumed by the score. There's an argument over who pays. The waitress says Come on, Smiler says I'll toss you. Who's got any sporting blood. Toss you hell, they say, pay up it's your turn. But in the end they toss for it ; Cpl Dexter says Let's see them all go up same time. He loses, it costs a tanner.

The wireless plays Music While You Work ; in the middle of this Wells suddenly appears. Rossy, they all got respirators on. So what ? Well I ain't got mine, are we safe in here. Safe as houses.

Wells, after eyeing my black coffee with apprehension, as though it were a potion about to turn me into Mr. Hyde, orders a tea. He signals to the sophisticated one : a screwed-up note changes hands. Dating her up, Wells explains, 8 o'clock to-night. What about Rosie ? Well she won't know will she.

The hands of the clock point to eleven, it's time to go. I leave Wells, who's officially supposed to be taking a message to the Transport Officer, and make my way through back streets to the post office. The entrance to the grocery shop which houses it is guarded by an enormous black ferocious-looking but docile-natured dog of indeterminate breed, chewing a bone that must have come from the Dental Centre. At any rate it is mainly teeth. The letters drop in the box ; as it's Thursday I withdraw five bob from the savings bank.

Coming out a man bicycles past me with his respirator on, I am shaken by the sight. I crawl in through barbed wire the back way. I cower in the downstairs lavatory hearing the muffled voices of men calling out through their gasmasks. Surely time must be up now ? At last ! The voices begin to shout normally ; I emerge, walk past a regimental policeman wiping his face-piece with anti-dim, and slide up the stairs to my office. There the table is almost completely covered with papers brought in during my absence for despatch : it looks as though there's been an avalanche.

I sit down and straighten it out : to X Company, to BHQ, Sealed PERSONAL to Adjutant, local stuff ; a kit inventory to the QM, a dental card, a medical history sheet to the M.I. Room. A completely silent man, category C, slips into the room like a shadow and removes the salvage sack from its hook on the cupboard where I keep my manuscripts. Several figures in denim suits present themselves paybook in hand and are redirected to Smiler in the pay office. Then there are men asking to see the CQMS, they want a new cap-badge, a cake of blanco, one has lost the whole of his kit. He's in his office, in the stores, up the town, in bed asleep, how should I know, get the hell out.

Dobb puts his nose round the corner, wiping it with his sleeve. He gets the local despatches given him. I just bin out, it ain't my flicking turn. Go on, get going. Wells got the flicking bike. You don't need the bike to go round the corner. Dobb goes off moaning. It ain't his turn, it ain't fair, he gets all the flicking work, he's thorough browned-off. All the men in denims return in a body, they can't find the Colour Bloke nowhere. Well come back at two. We're on parade at two. Well come back after parade.

I struggle again with the postage account, end by putting one of the shillings from my savings into the wallet where I keep the postage money. From upstairs comes a stampede of men clattering knives forks and spoons. Dinner time. I fall in on parade outside ; we march down to the cookhouse.

The duty officer for the day is also the Messing Officer. We are given open order march and our hands and eating utensils are inspected. Several men are sent off to wash. Suddenly after all this a gigantic M.T. corporal appears, in denims soaked with oil and stained with grease ; he salutes the Messing Officer with a hand as black as a negro's. The Messing Officer gives up ; we get Front Rank right turn quick march. We file into the cookhouse ; it's in the basement of a large empty hotel supposed to be haunted. The ghost used to appear in winter dressed as a waiter. Several people saw it ; there was at the same time an epidemic of pinching. Then one man shot another by accident and a third got sent to detention and the ghost ceased to walk. We drew our own conclusions but we're not sure.

The dinner is principally stew. I get a bone for my ration and lots of men begin to bark. There are also shouts of Fido and Good Dog. The Messing Officer asks any complaints. It's a rhetorical question. No answer is given or expected. After that we get duff. It's good but I am put off my portion by the sudden appearance of Dobb in front of me. Here I ain't had no flicking grub. Why not ? They won't give me none not without a chitty. See the orderly sergeant. Dobb retires muttering, I finish my duff.

Back to the office. There I find the rest of the runners about to operate on Williams's more outstanding blackheads. Those on the back of his neck are now receiving attention. Williams is screaming blue murder ; Pritchett, grinning in the background, has whipped a pin from his lapel and is gouging with it at something that turns out to be a mole. This pastime is curtailed at my entrance ; the runners go off after cups of tea.

I do the sports programme for the P.T. Sergeant : it includes a series of exercises for unarmed combat : how to disarm a sentry, Japanese stranglehold, etc. The siren goes ; Jerry flies low over the roofs ; ack-ack gunfire flaps like washing in a wind. Sound of aeroplane engine receding ; the all-clear coincides with the arrival of to-day's Despatch Rider, a man about seven-foot tall, his height added to by his crash-helmet, who once figured prominently in a court-martial case. I ask him What's the time. Twenty past two. The time is eternally twenty past two according to the despatch riders. They are always eager to get off and twenty past two is the time scheduled for their departure. They are not so eager to come back, especially those with homes in the neighbourhood of BHQ. Of course there are always excuses—a new motor-bike, hold-ups at Companies, engine trouble, a breakdown miles from anywhere. At one time all these reasons for delay recurred regularly, sometimes all at once, and Don-Rs started to roll in after dark. I then instituted a time-sheet to be sent in to the adjutant once a month, on which the names or Don-Rs returning late were entered in red ink. Engine trouble immediately ceased, Companies dished out despatches on the dot, and Don-Rs, muttering Rotten regimental basket under their breaths, were in the office by half-past four.

But now the time is twenty past two according to the Don-R ; two o'clock according to everyone else. He has twenty minutes' wait, he does it in the teashop downstairs. I finish off the P.T. programme, concluding with a blood-curdling exercise of combined arm-lock and kidney-punch.

Again the despatch rider climbs the stairs and stands with his top boots and his yellow gloves, and despatch case invitingly open. The RSM appears at the last moment with a colossal package of Training Pamphlets to be tied on to the back of the bike. At last he's off, then everybody remembers something urgent they should have sent. Too late, save it, 'll do to-morrow.

What's that noise on the landing outside? Sounds like rifle butts again. The noise resolves itself into a shout from downstairs of EMPLOYED MEN GET ON PARADE. Pritchett rushes in with his rifle and says Rossy have you forgotten. Hell, I had. It's Thursday, when half the employed personnel do their rifle revision ; the other half who do it on Monday go to the baths. Get my equipment quick. He brings it down, I buckle on belt and bayonet, sling my rifle, and we thunder down the stairs. The parade has marched off, we can't see anyone at all. There's a squad in the distance but it turns out to be the NCOs Cadre drilling under the RSM. He waves us sternly towards an even further group of men, at first invisible because they are lying flat on the ground behind bushes. As we approach they turn into familiar figures : Bentick, the one-eyed storeman, Hansford from the Officers' Mess, L/C Smith of the QM's, Kirkland and Draper. They have small targets stuck in the ground in front of them and are in charge of a corporal new to the company.

He gives them UNLOAD, they work their bolts and stagger to their feet, Kirkland losing his balance completely and falling to the ground. Pritchett and I line up with the rest. The corporal scratches his head. What they give you usually on these parades. The rifle, Corp. Yes I know but which lesson. We was on the lying load last time. Okay we'll carry on with that. All of you got dummies.

Pritchett and I haven't ; we get five apiece. Squad, lying— LOAD. Down we get, fumbling with our pouches. Keep your eyes on the target, look down only when inserting the rounds in the breech-charger guide. There's a further delay while I get my glasses out and adjust them. We fire five dummies, reload with a further five (imaginary). You, third man, what's your name, Draper : what's the first rule of aiming. Keep the sights upright, Corporal. Why don't you do it then. Right, rest.

We lie on our sides ; the corporal squats on his hams beside us. How long's this thing go on for ? Three quarter hour Corp. Ah to hell. The ground is hot, there's a smell of sun-warmed grass and rifle-oil. Bentick sings out suddenly, Watch your step, Corp, here comes an officer. Righto, blokes, look as though you're doing something. The officer draws near, it's Lieutenant Stroud. The corporal says in a loud voice as he comes level : Give us the six aids to good shooting. We rattle through them, the corporal salutes, Lt. Stroud passes on, switching at the long grass with his stick. We relax immediately, the time is looked at. Ten minutes to go. 34 Platoon marches past with their towels on the road, bound for the baths. There are distant shouts from squads drilling out of sight somewhere. ONE two-three ONE. ONE two-three ONE. ORDER—hup ! Old Smudger Smith, the post corporal, cycles past with a sack slung over his shoulder.

What's the time now. Quarter to, Corp. Right, unload. Clip up your dummies. As I rise my equipment falls off me. But who cares, the parade's over. Squad Dis-miss ! Pritchett limps along beside me telling about the gangster film he saw last week. I hand over my equipment for him to take upstairs ; Smudger Smith, locking his door, says Nothing for you Rossy. There seems to be no one else about ; I enter the CSM's office for our afternoon chat. He's sitting at his desk, fags are mutually offered. The conversation opens on traditional lines. Well sir how are you. Proper browned-off. So am I. Roll on the end of the war.

We count the number of absentees, read out the choicest entries in the crime-file. Cpl Dexter's latest romance, the time when the CSM was fed through his ankles. He pulls down his socks to show me the scars where the tubes were inserted. And believe it or not you felt as though you'd had a blinking good meal afterwards.

A knock on the door. Come in, yes what d'you want. It's Pte Ames. Can he have his afterduty pass please sir. All right, half a tick. But when it comes to the point the pass cannot be found. We look in all the boxes, in the pay office, under the tablecloth. No pass anywhere. Are you sure you put it in. Pte Ames is positive. He has begun to sweat and to nervously unclasp his hands. He joins in the search. We look in the corners, under the table, the CSM turns out his pockets. A screwed-up ball of paper in the washbasin : ah, what's this ! Ames's pass is found. The list of cricket fixtures that the CSM's been looking for all morning also comes to light in this way. Ames snatches his pass, counterfoil and all, and dashes down the stairs before anyone can stop him, pursued by a shout of laughter from the CSM.

We look out of the window. About time that blasted despatch rider rolled in. A tramp of feet on the stairs. Ah, that's him maybe. But no, it's the rest of the staff back from wherever they've been. Are the despatches in. No not yet. Wells comes back from the baths with his face all covered with blood and crimson lipstick. He'd slopped a tart about in the doorway, had a fight with a sailor. The sailor, obscurely connected with the tart in some fashion, had socked Wells without warning on the snout. The story is told several times, Wells mops at his nose with the bath towel. Flicking nuisance, may spoil my chance with that waitress to-night. Dobb creeps up the staircase clean for once : he's been supervised by a lance-corporal in his bath.

Then a motor bike shudders to a standstill outside. We all rush to the window ; it is, it isn't, it is. The despatch rider drops packages and receipt books on my desk. He proudly says, Dead on time ; the red ink bottle is not uncorked. Everyone descends on me before I can sort anything out ; I say For Pete's sake. Signatures are scrawled, the motor bike roars off up the street. The despatches are ready for distribution. WELLS WILLIAMS PRITCHETT DOBB. They appear but minus Dobb. Whose turn is it to take the stuff out. Ain't mine. Nor mine. I took em yesterday, it's flicking Dobb. Where is Dobb. Echo answers where, Dobb doesn't answer his name. Cpl Dexter is called in, he keeps watch and pounces on Dobb creeping out the back way.

What, me again? Cor stone a crow I done em Tuesday. Wells says Bleeding liar ; gets his cap knocked off by a right-hander. Dobb dances about with his fists up, Cpl Dexter says That'll do. At last Dobb bicycles off, bent low over the handle-bars. I stuff the 2nd-in-Command's stuff in a special envelope and throw it in a cupboard to await his arrival from leave. Padlock off, padlock on. Key in pocket. I prepare to knock off. But no, there's a sudden outcry. It's the Captain. The urgent return to the adjutant has reappeared once more, inscribed in green pencil THIS RETURN IS INCORRECTLY RENDERED. READ A.C.I.'s. A.C.I.'s are thumbed through, at last the required pro-forma is found, I rattle it off on the Imperial. The men in denims are queuing up outside the CQMS. But he's gone, so they're foiled again. Come back to-morrow.

Now I really do knock off. Down the road past the swimming pool and the sign STATIC WATER. Up the town.

The town is approached only by hills. The most convenient is one appropriately named Convalescent Hill. Trees lean drunkenly sideways with the effect of surrealist landscape. I climb through a barricade, bump my head once, recover my balance and make for a café. Bacon chips peas two cheese sandwiches and a black coffee. The order is as invariable as the day's routine. The café is all right to eat in but not for any other purpose. I emerge into the highstreet again, there are few people about and nothing to do. At the Plaza Mickey Rooney ; at the Picturedrome Madame X. The shops close at six. There is a public library and two canteens : the Y.M. and the Methodist. I choose the latter ; too many matelots in the Y.M. Under the stone lintel a neon-lit WELCOME. Orange juice and sandwiches at the counter : a white-haired woman in a picture hat presides. The Minister circulates among the ping-pong players. I enter the reading room : stained glass windows, leather chairs, a bookcase containing an odd assortment of children's and religious books : 'COPPER NOB SECOND MATE,' 'SIMPLE TALKS ON THE HOLY SPIRIT.'

I settle down to write, someone plays the same tune over and over again on a cracked piano in the games room. Men step over your feet with plates of cakes and cups of tea slopping into the saucer. One trips and drops the lot. Shattered china and a steaming brown puddle on the floor. An incredibly old man with a purple nose peddles newspapers : anyone like the latest ? A lance-corporal asks me for a light ; some men start singing to the piano ; a girl of about sixteen, daughter of one of the servers, sits down in the next armchair and talks. I kissed her once under the mistletoe at Christmas and she's never got over it. It's impossible to work here, I decide to go back and type out what I've written.

Down the hill ; along the sea-front ; the women's services in pairs, arm in arm, trailed by soldiers and aircraftmen on the hunt. The chase comes to a giggling conclusion among the laurel bushes and benches of the gardens overlooking the sea. I go the opposite way : in the Jazz, the huge hotel of black and blue bakelite (best appointed ballroom on the coast) there's a dance on : Smiler waltzing with his WAAF, the officers saying Have another in the upstairs lounge. The signals office is surrounded by small civilian girls who've not long left school but have already the airs and graces of the Garbo. The picquet man clicks his heels at the door of HQ. There is funny business of a mock salute and requests for rude books to read. The jankermen are reporting to Cpl Dexter in full pack. What about your water-bottle ? Forgot to fill it Corp. If you was in the flicking desert you wouldn't forget. Double back and report again with it full.

I sit at the window in the fading light ; downstairs the black-out boards are being manœuvred into position. I've half an hour to do some typing before lights out. To-morrow the 2nd-in-Command comes back, I shan't have time. Bed and before you know it, reveille ; breakfast ; and then the major's bell, silent for the past seven days, starting to ring. Despatches and postage ; typing and Mercer's Café ; Wells and Rosie ; Dobb being dirty ; Williams being Welsh. The same day after day ; the only change recorded on the calendar. My leave's not due for another two months.

Intruder Ops

By Flt. Lt. K. M. Kuttelwascher, D.F.C. and bar

[EDITOR'S NOTE: *Flight Lieutenant Kuttelwascher, famous as a night fighter, served in the Czech Air Force and the French Colonial Air Force before he joined the R.A.F. during the Battle of Britain. As these extracts from his diary show, he introduced Intruding on a big scale with all his Flight and with Squadron Leader J. A. F. MacLachlan. For day fighting, anti-shipping operations, and night fighting Kuttelwascher holds the record for destruction of enemy aircraft.*]

February 12, 1942

To-day we had one of the most hurried orders for readiness ever. I was awakened by the sound of a W.A.A.F.'s voice over the loudspeaker calling, 'All stations in readiness.' Rough luck, since I had only gone to bed three hours before, at 7 a.m. But out of bed I tumbled and managed to be in dispersal in record time. (How I did it I cannot remember, but it has taken me a long time to find my pyjamas to-night, and only after a long search do I realise that I've had them on all day under my flying kit.) In a few minutes all the pilots were in dispersal, and each one asking the same question—What's up? We soon knew the answer : the orders have come through for one flight of our squadron to stand by for anti-shipping ops.

Within twenty minutes my flight was airborne, and, escorted by Spitfires, we were soon hedgehopping our way towards the coast. After flying for fifteen minutes we reached the sea, and setting our course at 110° continued for another ten minutes at 0 feet. We suddenly saw some destroyers steaming N.E.-wards, and the near one fired some recognition rockets. At that moment one of my flight called out, 'O.K., Kuttel—they are ours.' I was trying, in very bad weather conditions, to identify them, when suddenly, beyond these destroyers, I caught sight of some battleships. Above them some fierce fighting was going on between our fighters and some MEs. To our right was the French coast ; from there we were already being fired on by A.A. guns, and I realised that the ships were not ours at all, but German ones. Here was my predicament. Should I attack the destroyers or join the fight over the battleships ? Our mission was anti-shipping, so I decided to attack the destroyers immediately. Quickly turning

FLT. LT. K. M. KUTTELWASCHER

to the left, and switching on my cannons, I led my flight towards the destroyers, flying in open formation. By now the destroyers had opened fire on us, and I could see clearly that the particular destroyer which I was attacking had six guns blazing away at us. My good old Hurricane rocked rather a lot as some shells burst around me, but there is no turning back in a fight, and I just kept going straight ahead until I had the whole ship beautifully in my gun-sight. I was about 800 yards away when I first fired, but unfortunately it was a little bit short and hit the water near the destroyer. Pulling the plane up a little and firing with all my cannon, I let the destroyer have it, and saw my shells piercing the bridge. Through the corner of my eye I saw one of my boys crashing into the sea before I hopped the nose of the destroyer and went dodging from side to side to avoid the shells, which were pursuing us relentlessly. On my right Ginger clung to my tail faithfully, and it was not until I tried to call him that I realised my wireless had gone. I wanted to tell him to open formation as we afforded the gunners too good a target by flying together, but Ginger stuck to me like glue. All my ammunition was gone so the only thing to do now was to make tracks for home, with Ginger following.

We had to be careful in beating a retreat, as there were plenty of enemy fighters around. We kept a sharp look-out in all directions. I must say I was perturbed to see two MEs flying in the same direction as us about 500 yards to our left. This was certainly a tight corner, but we were very lucky, and the MEs turned to the left, apparently without having seen us. I can imagine now what an easy prey we would have been with no ammo, no wireless, and very little petrol. The prospect of an icy bath in the North Sea in February did not appeal to me at all, and what a relief it was to see the two MEs turning left and making their way back towards the French coast. Without any further incident Ginger and I reached the English coast, and before very long arrived at our base. I was very anxious to know whether all my flight were safe, as I had lost sight of them since we first went into attack. After reporting to the Intelligence Officer I waited for a couple of hours, hoping that maybe they would turn up. Two of my boys came back soon after Ginger and me, but we heard later that one of the two who didn't return was a prisoner of war and the other missing. By this time I realised that I was very hungry, and had a good meal. Now, after writing all this, I feel dog tired, and am going to continue the sleep which was interrupted this morning.

February 19

It's been a lovely sunny day, followed by a bright moonlit night, and at dusk I received the order to stand by for night ops over the S.E. coast. I had a feeling that to-night there would be something doing, so I chose all the best night-fighters to make up my flight. Shortly after dusk we were called to patrol an area on the S.E. coast, and I was first to take off. The moon was so bright that every house was plainly visible, all the roads looked long and well-defined, and the rivers looked like satin ribbons in the moon's reflection. Orientation was as easy as in broad daylight, and everything looked extremely languid and peaceful, that is, everything except the place for which I was heading. Soon I beheld some glowing fires and saw strings of A.A. shells shooting up in pursuit of German dive bombers. After the peaceful scene I had encountered a few moments ago, I felt suddenly infuriated at this scene of wilful devastation, and went at top speed towards the unfortunate target, determined to make some of those pirates pay for their crime. I was there in a matter of seconds, and started patrolling at 7,000 feet. In order to look around with unrestricted vision, I opened my hood, and suddenly there it was—caught in a searchlight beam. I dived immediately, but realised in a second or two that 'it' was only a balloon ! Feeling very disappointed, I returned to my former height and continued patrolling. I knew there were some Jerries about, because I had seen a few bombs burst on the town below. However, my luck was out, as I had the order to return to base about ten minutes later, without having seen a single raider. Now I'm back in dispersal with nothing worthwhile to report, and we are spending the last hours of our duty sitting around a lovely fire. When dawn comes we shall give over to the day boys.

March 26

We went on duty at dusk as usual last night, and somehow all the boys, including myself, were feeling somewhat bored with life. After playing cards, reading, and doing a score of other things to while away the time, we were relieved to have the order that some of us were to be released for the night. I was one of the lucky ones, so leaving Harry Connolly in charge, I soon made my way to bed. In about two hours, however, my batman awoke me, saying that Connolly wished to speak to me on the phone. I soon learned what he wanted. One of the bombers returning from night ops needed an escort over the Channel, as dawn was approaching and the plane would make an easy target for enemy fighters. I decided that I would take Connolly along with me, and, getting down to dispersal in five minutes or so, we were soon off on our mission. The air was crisp and fresh as we set off, and made one feel so wideawake and energetic. This was, however, no time to be rhapsodising on the glories of the morning, so we just kept our eyes opened, in case we should meet some enemy planes. All we saw was the bomber we had come to escort home, and I believe the crew were relieved to see us. The escorting over, the bomber landed on our drome. I was very surprised to find that the crew was made up of my fellow countrymen. Knowing this, I was very gratified to have been given the opportunity of escorting them back to England, and of course the discovery called for a celebration.

April 1

To-day I've been busy since early afternoon making preparations for a longer trip than usual. My Hurricane has been transformed into a long-range fighter, and to-night it was successfully put to the test. When I asked my commanding officer a few days ago whether I could make a trip to the Paris area, he seemed to be very tickled. His instant retort was, 'So you want to go to Montmartre to see some of the girls there, eh?' We had a long talk about it, and after I had explained all my plans to him he finally gave way, helping me tremendously in getting it sanctioned by the Superior Commands. As a result, this afternoon has been spent in testing my plane, studying maps (although my orientation over France would be easier as a result of my flying activities there before the capitulation), and checking up weather reports. My mechanics had put in a splendid job of work on the plane, realising the importance of the work that lay ahead of me and how any success achieved would reflect their excellent craftsmanship. By dusk everything was ready, and after an hour of waiting in dispersal and a nice cup of English tea I set off. All the boys wished me luck and told me that they would wait in dispersal until I returned.

It seemed to me that I had never before in my life taken off so smoothly. I felt so free and exhilarated, with the half-moon shining above me, and the Channel already in sight. I lowered the revs, for economy's sake, and with a smoothly purring engine I left the English coast behind me. I passed over a hundred miles of calm sea before reaching the French coast, where I pinpointed my position and set my course afresh. A couple of searchlights were playing below, but I avoided them and carried on without any opposition. It seemed to me that I should by now be nearing my target, but I could see no landmarks because of a slight haze beneath me. Peering down in the hope of finding my bearings, I saw a few lights, and on closer examination I found that I had come across an aerodrome. They must have known I was hovering around, because they immediately switched off the lights. Almost simultaneously another lot of lights were switched on, which reminded me of Christmas trees of my childhood days. Red, green, blue and yellow lights were all over the place, and I said to myself, 'Crikey, Moses, you can't fox me with this, boys. That's definitely a dummy.' Turning to the left, I located once more the real aerodrome with its flare-path dimmed, and there I saw a plane taxi-ing with its navigation lights on. He was just taking off, and I swooped down to get behind him. I passed through his slipstream and got rather a bomp, but, slowing my speed a little, I was able to get within firing range. With my gun sight and firing button already switched on, and the plane looming up right in front of me, I gave it a long burst, and saw it catch fire in a matter of seconds. I was obliged to pull out quickly to the right to avoid colliding with it, and I watched it hit the ground and burst into flames. I made a half-circle to the left and saw, just in time, another plane taking off. Again I dived, opened fire from slightly above and behind him, but at that moment I was caught by four searchlights and fired on with streams of shells from the ground defences. I had to be content with only damaging this second plane, as the firing still continued from the ground. It was not very accurate firing, but it was time for me to make my way home. I flew north, scanning the sky as I went, and after a while I looked down, seeing to my surprise the Champs-Elysées and the Arc de Triomphe, and, lastly, I caught sight of the Seine. In a split second I was caught in a searchlight beam but managed to manœuvre my way out of it very quickly. Using the Seine as a landmark, I made my way to the French coast, which I crossed without further incident. Again I was flying over that 100-mile stretch of calm sea, and after having permission to land, I found myself surrounded by a dozen eager faces, all with the same question to ask : 'How did it go ?' They all listened avidly as I made my report to the Intelligence Officer, and when I finished I had to promise to take all of them with me next time. With a JU88 destroyed and another damaged, I made short work of breakfast of bacon and eggs, and so to bed.

April 27

After a fortnight or so of unfruitful attempts at securing a kill, this night has been successful. For some time now, Mac and I have been putting in a good many hours on our new job of intruding. We both took off about the same time to-night, and made our way to France ; he going to Western France and I to the North. It was rather chilly as I took off soon after midnight, and I felt suddenly lonely as I crossed over the sea all on my own. However, I did not feel that way for long, because when I was a few miles from the French coast I caught a glimpse of a signalling beam which aroused my interest. By this time I had crossed the coast at a low altitude to avoid detection, and saw a few lights turning in the distance. It took me longer than I expected to reach the locality, as visibility was good, making distances rather deceiving. I made sure of my position and instantly knew that there was an aerodrome here. Besides, I could just see the emergency flarepath which was illuminated below me. Something must be happening here, I thought, and I was right, because after hovering around for five minutes or so I caught sight of a plane silhouetted against the moonlit sky. I did my best to close in as soon as possible, but I lost him. Deciding quickly that he must be coming down, I waited for him on the side from which he would have to land. I hadn't long to wait ; in a moment or so I again saw him. I was in a good position to close in for the attack, being just behind him and slightly below. I gave him a long burst to make sure that I'd get him first time, as I was too low to attack him repeatedly. He turned steeply to the left and then crashed among the hangars, where he immediately burst into flames. In about three seconds I was a bit startled to see a stream of tracer bullets passing about ten feet above me. The only answer was that an enemy night fighter was on my tail, so I quickly pushed my stick forward, and he went roaring over my head at a terrific speed. Instantly hurrying my plane up, the position was reversed, and I was now on his tail, firing madly at him. He started to climb, but with his extra speed I could not catch him, and finally I lost sight of him as he climbed to the left on the dark side of the sky. By now I was rather short of ammo, and without reaching my original target I decided to return to base. On the way home I fell to thinking how near I had been to becoming an 'also ran.' If the night fighter had made the most of his opportunities he could, I realised, easily have got me. As it was, I reached base with news for the boys of an additional obstacle in our new game of intruding—the presence of night fighters.

April 30

My destination to-night was W. France. My main object was to wreak vengeance on these blasted Jerries for having, in the early evening, blitzed one of the most beautiful of English towns, which was purely a non-military objective. I took off well before midnight in bright moonlight, and flew on a direct course from base to the target. I came right over the target, and was obliged to fly south to confuse the ground defences, as they had already detected my presence there.

On the almost completely blacked-out drome I spotted a plane with its navigation lights on. As he was taking off I dived after him and manœuvred so that he was between me and the moon. He immediately switched off his navigation lights, but he was too late, as he was already well placed in my gun sight.

I fired three short bursts. There was no result from the first two, but after the third the aircraft turned steeply downwards and exploded on the ground. My plane rocked violently as if in a terrific gale. The enemy plane must have been loaded with bombs to have exploded like this, and it gave me great satisfaction to know that he, at least, would never again deliver any of his loads on English soil. I waited there for about five minutes, and seeing no more activity I decided to fly northwards to another drome near the coast. There I saw a plane with its tail navigation light on, but unfortunately lost him when he switched off his light. I then flew around for another ten minutes and saw a second plane, fully lit up, and about to take off. Its lights were switched off before becoming airborne, but I followed the direction in which he went. After a few minutes I saw him against the moon, just above me, and managed to come dead astern. Giving him two bursts from short range, I saw his starboard engine was shot to pieces. By now we had crossed the coast, and after two short bursts the plane plunged straight into the sea, sinking immediately.

May 3

Mac and I to-night decided to swap our hunting-grounds, so he took the north and I took western France. Not a very successful shuffle from my point of view, as Mac got two Jerries, and I got only a train and an E boat. I got to my target without incident, but after flying around for over an hour I had still not seen a single plane. I therefore decided to make tracks for home, and tried to find some other target on the way. Before reaching the French coast I came across a goods train puffing slowly up the valley. I went in to attack three times, hitting some of the trucks but chiefly attacking the engine. After the third time the train stopped, and seeing billows of smoke pouring from the engine I knew I had definitely destroyed it, so continued my way home. I had already crossed the coast when I saw a stream of tracers coming toward me from below. Luckily they all passed over my head. 'That's asking for it,' I told myself, so I turned back quickly to do some investigating. Seeing an E boat going slowly westward just below me, I returned to the French coast to make my attack from behind. The E boat fired furiously at me during the first attack, but in the second there was no fire at all. Its engines had already stopped, and as I finished my shells I saw the ship listing very badly to port. Feeling a little more satisfied, I turned for home, and got into dispersal before Mac. He came

in a little later with a face like the rising sun, wildly waving his
artificial arm, which was very badly bent and had to be discarded.
On seeing me he rushed over with the question, 'What luck,
Kuttel?' on his lips. I rather disconsolately told him I had not
seen anything with wings so had had to confine myself to the
train and E boat. Whereupon he gave us all the news about his
shooting down two Jerries, but at the expense of his artificial arm.
I noticed that during breakfast he ate about three times as much
as he usually did, and decided that to-day he must be a happier
man than I.

May 4

In the last twenty-four hours I have been out twice on intruding
ops. From my early morning trip I came home without having
had any luck at all and with engine trouble. This job had not
in any way been to my liking—having to cross over a hundred
miles of sea with a faulty engine makes one think rather a lot and
anticipate quite a few unpleasant happenings. The second trip
I made just before midnight and, oh boy, what a grand do it was!
Knowing that a large force of enemy planes were attacking
England, it was decided that the intruders should go out in
strength. We did so, and were fully rewarded for our night's
work. I took off when the attack on one of our towns was
finishing. I made my way post-haste to a French aerodrome
which, I felt sure, they must be using for this attack. Some boys
had already got there ahead of me, so I hurried to join them
at the last minute. What a spectacle confronted me on arriving
at the aerodrome! Again I thought it resembled a Christmas
tree, except that this one was suspended in mid-air. About
twenty Jerries were awaiting their turn to land and, being in a
hurry, they flashed on and off all the lights they had. Pounding
into the *mêlée* with the ferocity of a tiger, I was in just the right
mood for a kill, but pulled myself together. knowing that unless
I was calm and calculating I should be able to do nothing at all.
I remembered also that my mother had always told me, 'Grab all
and you gain nothing.' The one problem now was how many
of those b——s I could finish with my ammunition. I decided
I had better get within close range and give my victim short
bursts in order to make my cannon shells go further. Jerry

knew that we were hovering around in strength and so they kept switching their navigation lights on and off to fox us. We, however, went boldly after our prey, knowing that there was no danger from the ground defences while their own planes were flying around. As I was waiting for an opportunity to get at the Jerries I saw one pass right over my head. In a split second I had pulled my stick back slightly and had fired two short bursts at him. Flames shot instantly out of one engine, and down he went in a steep dive to hit the ground. Again pulling my plane quickly to the right, I did the same to a second one which had been simply begging for it with his navigation lights full on. He, too, caught fire and hit the ground with a shower of sparks flying all around him. All this shooting had taken place in one minute, and now I had the opportunity of looking around me a little, as there was nothing in my vicinity at the moment. I saw one of our boys also doing his best and sending a Hun hurtling earthwards in flames. I once more fixed on a Hun to shoot down, but it took me three minutes to get within close range as the devil kept on switching his navigation light on and off as he waited his turn to land. At last I got into position for the attack, but this time it took me a little bit more ammo to finish him off. He turned into a steep left-hand dive, with me on his tail firing ceaselessly. I was obliged, however, to pull up my plane and climb once more to a safer height, as I was too near the ground. I ran out of ammunition at the same time, so there was no more firing at him. I was going to claim him as a 'probable,' because I saw my shells hit him and it would have been almost impossible to come out from such a steep dive at this low altitude. But when we got back it transpired that Willie, one of the boys, had seen this action and the plane crashing in flames. So I had definitely shot the third down after all. Instead of going to bed when our duty was over, we stayed up in the mess for hours, talking of the nice work and drinking to the success of future ops.

The Tube-Dwellers

By Mass-Observation

'**B**ut why the devil do they *still* come here ?'

The speaker was a middle-aged business man, making his way irritably through the straggling group of shelterers on a North London tube station one evening. The shelter marshal smiled resignedly, and said : 'Oh, I don't know. They get used to it, you know.' And with this seemingly inadequate reply the questioner had to be content.

The problem is one that has puzzled many people. How is it that, nearly two years after the last serious raid, there are still several thousand Londoners who continue to come to the tubes night after night ; that there are children nearly three years old who have never spent a night in their own homes ?

To solve the problem we must go back to that winter of 1940-41, and consider what were the feelings and motives that first took people to the tubes. For it was not merely a desire for safety, as might at first be imagined. During that winter this country saw the first stages of the formation of a new community ; perhaps one of the strangest communities in recorded history. In vast caverns tens and hundreds of feet underground civilised people of all sorts and classes were gathered —not just now and then, as an emergency measure, but for months on end. For the first time in many hundreds of years civilised families conducted the whole of their leisure and domestic lives in full view of each other. To anyone of a sociological turn of mind the situation was full of possibilities—for the first time sociologists could watch the living process of highly civilised individuals adjusting themselves to a pre-civilised, communal form of society.

For this is in fact what it amounted to. Most of these people were not merely sheltering in the tubes ; they were living there. The completeness with which their new home filled the time and thoughts of the tube dwellers is well shown by the following description by a Mass-Observation investigator on the spot, during the height of the blitz winter.

The scene is a West London tube station, the time 2.30 p.m. The weather is damp and windy. Outside the station there is a queue of about a hundred people, mostly middle-aged and elderly working-class women. About 20 per cent are children. A few men, mostly shabbily dressed and with a rather down-and-out appearance, are among them. A short distance from the queue, lined up against the wall, is a row of perambulators and push-carts, some empty, some piled with bedding. Several have a sack or a piece of tarpaulin laid over the bedding—it has been raining earlier in the day. A typical bundle of bedding consisted of a worn grey rug, rather torn ; inside that a green and pink eiderdown, faded, and apparently much of the inside gone ; inside that, pillows without cases. The whole bundle is done up with a piece of thick string. In the same perambulator are a pair of strap shoes and a man's overcoat.

The crowd seems placid and fairly cheerful. The investigator was struck, however, by an apparent lack of any interest in appearances. Many of the women have their hair in curlers still ; and the bundles of bedding show no attempt to hide tears and stains, or to put the best-looking article on top, or anything of that sort. Children are in the main subdued but not unhappy. They mostly stand quietly, holding or sitting on their bundles. Two little boys are playing with one of the empty prams. They are picking up handfuls of leaves, putting them into the pram and then shovelling them out through the hole in the bottom.

Conversation in the crowd is very largely about air raids :
'What was that ?' says a woman suddenly.
'Car, that was.'
'Funny, the things you think you hear, isn't it ? Everything gives you a start. Can't hear a leaf falling without giving a jump, can you ?'

Talk about local damage. An old man recounts a story he has heard about people dug out of a wrecked pub. 'And when they'd got them all out they went back for the things. They got out an old chest with hundreds of pounds' worth of gold and silver stuff in it—plate and that. It belonged to a Jew man, see, and when they'd got it out—twenty of them had been at it—when they got it out he gave them three shillings between the lot of them.'

'A Jew, that was.'
'Terrible, isn't it ?'

At about half-past three there is a sudden awakening of the crowd and a moving forward.
'They're opening !'

'They're opening !' says the woman next to me, and begins trying to push forward. Several people begin to run, and are shouted at angrily by the others. About a dozen people in the front burst into the tube in a sort of headlong rush ; after that the police get control and make the others enter in a more orderly fashion. There is a lot of grumbling.

'Some of them they've only just come ; pushing forward like that ! We've been here since six o'clock this morning. Pushing in front like that !'

'They ought to have it how they did ; go in two and two. They ought to stop the rushing and scrambling. It's not fair.'

'What time did *you* get here, you sod ?' yells a woman with a huge roll of bedding and a young baby to a pale, puffy-faced man who is hurrying past her. Later, the investigator's report continues:

I am near the back of the queue, and when I reach the platform I find all the places on platforms and lower passages already booked up. Booking is usually done by laying a blanket folded into a long strip along the wall. I talk to a little girl of eight, who is minding some places by the entrance to the platform. She says she has been queuing since six o'clock in the morning.

'I haven't had my dinner yet,' she says.

'Do you *have* to start queuing so early ?' I asked.

'Oh, yes ; you don't get a place if you don't come early.'

'Do you sleep all right down here ?'

'Oh, yes ; it's all right on the platform ; it's warm. Don't go by the stairs. It's cold by the stairs.'

Farther down the platform a quarrel is going on. A little boy of about nine is standing, tearful but defiant ; four or five women are talking indignantly on his behalf. Apparently he started queuing at half-past six in the morning ; had got down first, and booked places for his whole family ; and then a porter had come and pushed his things away and given the place to an elderly woman and her daughter.

'It's wicked, do a thing like that. Freddie started waiting before it was light this morning. He was up there with the guns going and all, before any of us.'

'He has that place every night. They've no right to do a thing like that.'

'You wait till that young man comes back (the porter). I'll tell him. . . .'

The interlopers are standing by, rather embarrassed.

'Well, I didn't know. . . . He just give me that place,' says the girl.

'No, it's not your fault.'

'Oh, no, it's not her fault. It's his fault. He oughtn't to do a thing like that.'

'It's wicked. We stand out there in the perishing cold all day. It's not like we did it for ourselves ; it's for our husbands.'

Porter reappears. The women all begin talking to him at once. He shouts them all down. 'That place wasn't taken ; if I gave that place to anyone, then that's their place. I'm not going to hear any more about it.'

He stamps away and disappears through a door, slamming it behind him.

'Never mind, dearie,' says a woman to the little boy. 'They shan't get your place to-morrow. I'll keep it for you if I have to take my skirt off to put down.'

I go farther along, and get into conversation with a group of women. I ask them what makes them start queuing so early (six o'clock is the time they allege they start). Do they think it is really worth it ?

'You don't get a good place without you get there early.'

'That's right, you don't get in.'

'Funny how some people think they can get in coming at half-past three or four in the afternoon. Think they ought to get just as good places as us what's been here all day.'

As the above description shows, in the beginning tube life tended to be chaotic and undisciplined. Shelterers in the tubes and other deep shelters got a reputation for rowdyism and squabbling that was not undeserved. Again and again investigators report fights and quarrels in the shelters :

'. . . People lay everywhere. Gangways were kept by wardens, who shouted, "Keep the gangway clear, please," and "No standing about—break it up there." People were constantly walking up and down, treading over outstretched legs.

'Families quarrelled among themselves. The two fights I witnessed were both family quarrels. First was a girl, shouting and screaming at her mother. In the end, they were separated by force, and led away from each other, struggling and screaming.

'The other case was of a man and his wife. The wife wanted him to sit down, the husband wanted to walk about. She became very excited, and a crowd of "rubberers" formed round them. She bit his ear and tore out his hair. He smacked her face and threw her to the ground. The wardens split them up in the end. Said a spectator : "There's enough fighting going on outside, without having it inside as well." '

Many people used to give this as a reason for not going to the tubes and deep shelters : 'I wouldn't go there—they're a rough lot. Always fighting.' And : 'There's always a row going on down there, fighting and squabbling. One man got knocked on to the line, I was told.'

Most people assumed that the disorderly behaviour in the shelters, often calling for police intervention, meant that the people in the shelters were on the whole a rough, low type. But the real explanation seems to lie not so much in the character of the individuals as in the complete novelty of the social set-up. With the disappearance of all ordinary ways of life it was only to be expected that some of the ordinary canons of behaviour should also have been set aside. People who in their ordinary, familiar surroundings were models of respectability might easily lose some of their inhibitions when in totally new surroundings, for which no accepted standards of behaviour had yet been evolved. This point was emphasised by investigators at the time :

'Officials are few and far between, and include some women. *Individually*, there was quite a friendly attitude to them. People would go up to them and tell them long grievances which were listened to patiently and sympathetically. One did get the impression, however, that with the crowd as a whole the officials were feeling slightly out of their depth—shown by superfluous shoutings and pushings if anything went slightly wrong—e.g. a group of about thirty people starting off down the wrong stairs. Investigator felt that this may have been due to the atmosphere of social instability about the whole place ; the feeling that here were several hundred people in a situation which carries with it at present very little ingrained tradition of behaviour, such as exists in a street or at a public meeting. In a street or at a meeting people may do things wrong ; but one knows from long experience what behaviour is likely to occur. The crowd as a whole does at least know what normal behaviour is, and will readily slide back into it after any disturbance. But in these vast shelters traditions and standards of ordinary social behaviour are not settled and established, but still in the making. This makes the crowd more unpredictable, and hence more to be feared, than is usual.'

Slowly from this chaos order was established—some of it imposed from above, but more important was the code of unwritten laws which was gradually built up in most of the shelters ; such laws as the respecting of 'places'—if a person has reserved a 'place' he can go away and leave it, knowing that it will be there when he returns, provided he has covered it with a blanket. Public opinion is the strong and only assurance that such unwritten laws shall be obeyed. 'On one occasion a woman put her blanket down in an apparently empty space. Immediately a huge man stood before her, and instructed her to "Remove your rubbish ; this is a gangway." She protested that there already was a gangway, and this was sufficient. "We are looking after our own interests," he informed her. "And we want two gangways." However, public feeling was with her, and she was allowed to remain.'

With the code of unwritten laws there appeared also natural leaders and organisers from among the shelterers—some of them officious busybodies, some with genuine talent for directing and controlling others. Each shelter became more and more a self-sufficient community, with its own leaders, traditions and laws.

It is against this background that we must think of the tube-shelterers to-day. It must be clear by now that people don't go to the tubes *merely* for extra safety. In the beginning they went mainly for that reason, but they went on going for a thousand social and psychological reasons which have little or nothing to do with air raids. There were some who went for shelter and found there not only shelter but a whole new life in a new society—a society where they could start from scratch and for the first time in their lives make a name for themselves and shine in their social group. Others came from solitary bed-sitting rooms with a gas ring, and found they could spend evenings in light and gaiety, surrounded by company. Harassed house-wives found that they could halve their housework if the family spent the main part of its leisure time—i.e. the time when it makes the most mess and wants the most food—somewhere other than in the home. The trouble of preparing sandwiches and so forth to take to the shelter was found by many of them to be small compared with the work they would otherwise have to do—make beds, prepare hot meals, wash up, and keep up with the eternal tidying and sweeping that is necessitated by a large family at home. Some found themselves possessed of unsuspected talents for organising, entertaining, or what-not, which for the first time found scope and appreciation.

Can it be wondered at, then, that these people found it hard to leave their new lives when the raids ceased ? By leaving the tubes many of them were leaving a life and an environment which suited them much better than 'ordinary' life would ever do. Take the case of 'Auntie Mabel,' from a report by a Mass-Observation investigator in the spring of 1943.

'The family atmosphere, which really did seem to include all the people in the shelter, was probably as much to do with the shelter marshal as anything else. She was a small, spry woman of about 45, who came down every night, and was very proud of the fact that she ran the shelter single-handed. "They all call me Auntie Mabel here," she said. "They all know me. It's real funny sometimes. Up top, sometimes I see them outside, when I'm down in the market say with me 'usband. 'Oh, look, there's Auntie Mabel,' they say ; 'Hi, Auntie Mabel !' I should think I'm as well known as anyone in H——. Lovely people they are down 'ere. Never a cross word all the time I been down 'ere. Know everybody, I do." '

Think what it would mean to Auntie Mabel if she had to leave this life of hers, where she is known, respected, and needed, to return once more to being a nonentity of a London side-street, known only to her next-door neighbour.

Investigators studying the tube shelters in April, 1943, have found much of this sort of pleasant, social atmosphere that the people find so hard to leave. For instance, this description of a North London tube station :

'I was taken on a conducted tour to see all the young children.

They all looked most fresh and healthy. Said the warden : "We've got some marvellous children down here. Never had no trouble with them ; no scabies, no skin troubles, nothink. Come an' have a look at our newest baby, he's only three weeks old."

'These young babies were a great source of pride and interest to the women in the shelter, and as I walked round and talked to people I was several times asked if I had "seen the new baby." Mothers were very anxious to tell exactly how long each child had been in the shelter. Young women went up to each other's bunks to ask how the children were, and the old women would sit and smile round on everybody. The family atmosphere which was apparent in this particular shelter was quite remarkable. Another child in whom the shelterers were interested was George, a plump, dark-eyed, smooth-skinned little boy of five. George specialised in imitations.

' "Do Hitler," said his mother, and George pulled a lock down over his eye, put a finger under his nose and jerkily threw up his arm. "Now Mussolini," and George threw out his chin, curling his lower over his upper lip. "Tojo," and George set his lips, narrowed his eyes, and wrinkled his forehead. A few people standing round laughed a lot, and George greatly enjoyed himself.'

Of course, these tube communities will not last for ever. Like all societies whose *raison d'être* has ceased to exist, they are doomed to disintegrate ; but like all societies they cling as long as possible. In many of the tube shelters disintegration has already set in (April, 1943). The pleasant co-operative spirit has disappeared and the few remaining shelterers sit about in scattered ones and twos, silent and glum :

'After the M. shelter, the atmosphere here seemed quite inhospitable and grim. People were sitting in isolated groups and often a man or woman would be sitting alone. The shelter marshal was quite a different personality, a woman of about 50, with strained suffused eyes and a cold suspicious manner. . . .

'The children were pale and tired, one of them crying inter-mittently. Other children, poorly dressed and rather dirty, looked more tired and less healthy than in the former stations. In common with the adults with them, they were silent and apathetic.'

If the bombers come again, as they may have come before these words appear in print, new life will have been infused into these moribund communities, and Auntie Mabel may again find herself the centre of tube life, the oldest inhabitant, with a record of three years' continuous residence underground.

Meanwhile the communal atmosphere of 1940 has created something of a new tradition in London's Underground. War-time relaxation of restraint, plus the presence of members of a multitude of nations whose behaviour is normally less constrained than that of the British, have also helped to make the tube stations a more cheerful place than they were before the war. One hears stories from the suburbs about the behaviour of returning revellers, like this : 'Women drink a fat lot more than they did before the war—even I remember that. You never saw so much of it before the war started. Not that I mind a woman having a drink at a pub. I take no objection to that, not at all. But some of these lasses don't know where to stop. Do you know what I saw only last night ? I was coming home by District from Victoria, and there was three American soldiers, young chaps all, with their arms round two ATS. All twined in circles they was, and hardly able to stand, not one among them. One of the girls was sick in the train before we got to South Ken. Sick as a dog she was. The other gal came across to her and took off her cap and tried to comfort her, but she was so drunk she could hardly keep on her feet. Now that's not right to my mind.'

Mass-Observation's investigators, patrolling the tube stations at night in spring, 1943, certainly found a great relaxation of restraint in people's behaviour. Piccadilly Circus, while scarcely typical, gives a good picture of the atmosphere which diffuses itself along the line between 10 o'clock and the last train home. Here is an investigator's description of a typical night in April, 1943 : 'I arrive just after ten p.m. and see a Canadian officer going off through Shaftesbury Avenue exit accompanied by two policemen and followed by glances from the crowd. "What happened ?" says a middle-aged working-class man to a woman. Nobody seems to know. Station is packed, near entrance to trains, and there is a babel of sound. "This place is like a slum," shouts one WREN to another as they go to automatic machine to get tickets. I go into a telephone box. A few drunk soldiers gather in a neighbouring box, and the indistinguishable noise is nearly deafening. Come out again. Young prostitute with angry expression says to naval man with her : "First time I've ever had any trouble." Another angry prostitute passes with man in civilian clothes. "Behavin' like that for no reason at all," she says crossly as she passes me.'

At this point, drowned in the din of voices, the alert sounds outside. A policeman moves on two spectacled youths, and a few minutes later does the same to a group of women. Soon the station is almost cleared : 'A man of thirty, in civilian clothes, is talking earnestly to a young woman by the ticket machines. He has his hands on her shoulders and is looking with apparent sternness into her face as if exacting some sort of vow or declaration. Presently they take tickets and go off together hand in hand. A party is trying to take tenpenny tickets and the machine refuses to work ; the three men of the party take turns in kicking it ; train official watches but makes no protest. Girl comes from train with American soldier, both seem a little drunk. "Less jus' see whass going on—jus' see whass going on." Another group of three girls and four soldiers arrive. Girls start yelling, 'Where we goin', where we goin'?" '

Only at this point does the investigator find out that the alert has sounded, on getting into conversation with a station sweeper. The investigator joins the crowd taking tickets : 'There is no alarm shown. People remark, "Hope we shan't be hung up long," "Wonder how long it will last," "They stop the trains, don't they?" quite calmly.

A train is standing in the platform, and there is much dispute as to where it is going. A woman porter comes along and announces it is a Stanmore train, and there is a great scramble to get off, most people having decided it was southbound. On the platform again the investigator gets into conversation with a woman of 35 : ' "Ooh, I wish I was in my bed. I've got to get to the Elephant. I wonder how long this is going on." There is a lot of noise, but nothing can be heard distinctly except the conversation of one's immediate neighbours. "They always put it in reverse when the warning's on," says the woman. "Put what in reverse ?" I ask. But the answer is drowned.'

At last a train arrives. There is a terrific scramble to get on board. A man of fifty in imitation Harris tweed coat and with a

demoniac expression fights and kicks and elbows his way in.   The
train moves off : 'It is now as packed as the platform, and people
have to fight and batter their way out at Charing Cross, where
several people are heard saying that the all-clear has gone.   I
stand beside two Irishwomen with a coloured man in civilian
dress, only about five feet high.   One Irishwoman says, "Ah,
lovely Pete, he was a nice person, he'd never see an Irish person
want." The coloured man says, "When you leave in the morning,
you never know if you'll see it again." Presently the other Irishwoman is heard to say, "The Irish people never believe in making
a toil of pleasure." "America is the only place you can
do as you like in," says the coloured man.   Another station.
Opposite me is a middle-class woman of 35, and beside her an
older man, a hearty business-man type.   She looks very attractive
in a frosty way.   He appears to have picked her up, but is not
sure of his ground.   He keeps smiling and winking at me all the
way home.'

   This is London's underground on a typical night on a typical
last train home, slightly more crowded, slightly more gay because
of the alert, but with a live, unrestrained, cosmopolitan atmosphere.   Along the line the thinning communities of tube-dwellers
watch this new social life, wonder, perhaps, whether in the winter
of 1943 the communal existence which evolved round them two
years ago will revive in new blitzes.   A certain exclusiveness
seems to be developing among the remaining inhabitants of some
of the tubes.   The bunks, instead of being open to the public gaze,
are often shrouded with a blanket slung from the bunk above,
cutting solitary sleepers off from the rest of the world.   If blitzes
start again will the goodwill and communal spirit, the shelter
leaders and shelter characters come into their own again, or will
the private-booked bunk and potential class-differentiation between
the older inhabitants and newer residents of tubedom lead to
exclusiveness and cliques ?   By the time these words are read the
answer may be clear to anyone taking the last train home.

SCRAPBOOK
from Devon

by Douglas Glass

Here are Brixham folk in wartime. This is 'Sarge' Brown, fisherman

There is character in the face of Mrs. Crang, Devon born and bred

This is how they dry their fish in the open at Brixham

This is the gaslit interior of a fisherman's cottage

And here, work finished, men spend an hour at the Crown and Anchor

Profiles
By Dilys Powell

Great talents have sometimes been defeated by the excess of their own qualities ; Draco's penal code, for instance, left so little to chance that, had it been strictly applied, there would have been no survivors to administer it. Goofy's daring has induced in him a disregard of physical laws whose logical consequence in a logical world could only be a broken neck. Enthusiasm, resolution, contempt for the word impossible—these are the qualities which have guided not Goofy alone, but the Disney Trio in general. A man without the debonair and jovial confidence of Mickey Mouse might have lapsed into misanthropy. Less strongly armed with consciousness of moral rectitude, Donald Duck would long since have fled from the humiliations of public life. If Goofy were afraid of hard knocks he would give up sport. The Trio have never faltered. Disappointment, ridicule, the bleak hostility of the world of matter, all have been dared. It is in keeping with their curious story that in the family group only their dog, Pluto, quite escapes the melancholy shadow of the unaccomplished.

Fifteen years ago the eldest and the most internationally famous of the Trio made his debut in New York. In September 1928 visitors to the Colony Theatre were electrified by the apparition of a small acrobatic figure with globular head, protuberant ears and gay inquisitive nose, wearing patched short pants, outsize shoes and the air of a conqueror. The public were accustomed to quiet heroes. Mutt and Jeff, Felix, Valentino himself had operated in a silence broken only by the chatter of the cinema piano. For a year now the old ways had been changing. In 1927 a mort of things happened : Lindbergh flew the Atlantic, a Revised English Prayer Book was issued, Tunney beat Dempsey at Chicago and Al Jolson's voice was heard in *The Jazz Singer*. Now in 1928, year of the Kellogg Pact and the *Royal Oak* incident, the silent film suffered yet another defeat. Mickey Mouse appeared ; and he was a musical Mickey.

The whole of the huge Disney family, in the pause between the wars, came to be connected in the public mind with music, much as the Barrymore name stood for the stage. Not all branches of the family boasted performers ; perhaps some members who did perform would have done better to refrain ; and his most devoted friends will scarcely claim for Donald Duck a sensibility to pitch. To Mickey, however, must go the credit for the introduction of synchronised sound in cartoons. In music, as in other spheres of human activity (for their humanism is the first, the inescapable characteristic of the Disney Trio), he immediately showed himself a resourceful as well as a cheerful executant. His emergence coincided with the years of high living and ballyhoo ; and when in *Steamboat Willie*, beaming, he propped open the jaws of a cow and used her teeth for musical instrument, something in the public mood responded to the confident insolence of his gesture. Mickey the musician came, played and conquered.

Conquered : those were indeed the years of conquest for Mickey Mouse. First in black and white, then, from 1935, in colour, he fought a fantastic battle with a world of prodigies and portents. In 1929 the slump came to put, as an American moralist expressed it, honky-tonk in hock. Mickey went right on winning. He did not, of course, remain purely and simply the musician. A historian points out that between his first appearance and the beginning of World War II he had played 'gaucho, deck-hand, farmer, impresario, teamster, musician, explorer, swimmer, cow-boy, fireman, convict, pioneer, taxi driver, castaway, fisherman, cyclist, Arab, football player, inventor, jockey, storekeeper, camper, sailor, Gulliver, boxer, exterminator, skater, poloist, circus performer, plumber, chemist, magician, hunter, detective, clock cleaner, Hawaiian, carpenter, driver, trapper, horseman, whaler, and tailor.' Never was the American manner of life, in which White House is approached by way of log cabin and the actor qualifies first as soda-jerker or elephant-tamer, better exemplified.

In his individual adventures, maybe, he was even at the first not always the victor. The hero of a score of tussles against overwhelming odds might be defeated by the trifling opponent ; a canary and her brood, a family of young Mickeys in destructive mood might reduce to impotence the intrepid explorer, Two-Gun Mickey, the Klondike Kid. It was as the man of action that Mickey, above all in his black and white period, won an inter-national reputation. Yet already in these moments of defeat the sharp-eyed observer might have divined the shadow of the frustrated future which awaited, not Mickey only, but to an infinitely greater degree his younger brother Donald. By an ironic coincidence, in their first public appearance together in colour, Donald, the most irascible, and fated to become the most often thwarted, of the Trio, was the instrument of Mickey's most notable reverse. Friends of the family never tire of recalling the incident. It was *Band Concert*, and the maestro was conducting the 'William Tell' Overture. Stirring, exultant, Rossini's martial notes sawed through the air. The music came abruptly to the end of a phrase ; and in the momentary silence before the composer had set off on a new tack, Donald was heard continuing in the same key with a rendering of 'Turkey in the Straw.' The dovetailing of the two compositions was as perfect as Mickey's

discomfiture was spectacular. This time Donald was the winner. But something in the obstinacy with which he filled in the pauses each time Rossini and Mickey stopped for breath might have warned the onlooker that here was a being doomed to perpetual struggle. The fanatic in modern society creates his own enemies, and Donald's persistence, his refusal to entertain the idea of defeat, were to arouse the opposition of the inanimate world. So far as he is concerned, things have, not tears, but malevolent laughter.

But before Donald joined Mickey in the life of public adventure the eldest of the brothers had won the respect of a humbler companion. Pluto has sometimes been taken for a member of the family. A certain facial resemblance links him with Goofy : the long muzzle, the pendulous ears are the same. But the careful observer will mark the differences. Goofy is rigged out in formal or sporting dress ; Goofy walks upright ; Goofy talks. Pluto, to whatever degree of family intimacy he may be admitted, remains the dumb animal. From the early days—for Pluto too was born in the black and white period—he was essentially a one-man dog. Silly, demonstrative, faithful, he followed the fortunes of his master Mickey with clumsy devotion, at once pet, servant and friend. His fidelity persisted into the age of colour. Still he caddied for Mickey, still valeted his owner ; if the boss went shooting, Pluto went too, scaring the game, struggling with noisy mimicry to learn the business of a sporting dog, falling a victim at last to the insolence of the birds who perched all over him as, transfixed, he pointed. In return Mickey has always showed a special tenderness for his pet. Those who know him best say his voice takes on warmth and (if one may apply the term to so fluting an organ) depth when he instructs or admonishes Mickey. If Pluto is a one-man dog, Mickey is a one-dog man.

Other pets have entered the domestic circle in which Mickey has increasingly spent his later years : a parrot, for instance, or, a bitter pill for the favourite, a kitten. People who doubt whether dogs have a moral sense should remember two episodes in Pluto's life : his conscience-stricken dream of a Judgment Day presided over by a Rhadamanthine cat, and the battle between his higher and his lower self as the kitten in the bucket rattled down the well. Domestic cares, however, and the anxiety of bringing up a family have lain lightly on him. His chief enemy, a bulldog with whom he has had what he calls bone-trouble, he has defeated by superior dog-tactics. For the rest, he has been a happy-go-lucky creature, enjoying adventure where he found it. In his time he has done a good deal of miscellaneous swallowing. An electric torch and a magnet have continued to exercise their

functions inside him ; nothing comes amiss. Animals, they say, assume the characteristics of the human beings they frequent, and in this Pluto might be said to take after Donald, as a swallower himself no dope. Only the other day Donald swallowed an alarm clock ; its illuminated dial ticked contentedly under his vest. But Pluto is no mimic of mankind. He knows his place, on the hearth, in the kennel, in the world ; a casual worker but an exuberant friend, more often than not in hot water, but shambling clear on his huge awkward pads, touchingly confident of applause.

Donald's association with Pluto began early, but never threatened Mickey's ascendancy over his pet. The relation between Donald and Pluto was rather that of workmates : of workman, sometimes, and indolent mate. Donald, aloft, would clean the windows while Pluto snored on the sidewalk ; Donald would signal for a pail of water, Pluto, still unconscious, would hoist a bucket of clinkers. Donald's conscience has never let him take life easy. In the first years of his career he was apt to be overshadowed by his brilliant elder brother. Mickey's dash and verve, the multiplicity of his adventures, his long and picturesque romance with Minnie, all combined to make him the darling of the public. Yet there is no denying that in the last few years the gay spark has rather withdrawn from the public eye. His appearances have been rarer and on the whole in less triumphant roles. The barriers placed in his way by sardonic circumstances have been more impenetrable. And as the hedonist has retired, the apostle of stubborn endeavour has advanced.

Donald in some curious way has won fame, not as a success, but as a failure. Outwardly his career has followed the lines of his brother's. Like Mickey, he has been a rolling stone, in his time fireman, bill-poster, blacksmith, bell-boy, trapper, agriculturist and caravanner. In some of these pursuits he has been the companion of both Goofy and Mickey, for the Disney Trio, despite their occasional personal disagreements (and their curious lack of family likeness) are a united family, enjoying work as well as recreation in common. But there the resemblance stops. Donald might venture into romance with Donna. He might, in a flourish of frivolity, take up golf, hockey, motoring, fox-hunting or autograph-hunting. With transparent optimism he might engage in occupations as rich in disappointment as gardening, chicken-farming or going to bed early. It would be no dice. Donald lacked both his elder brother's bonhomie and the resilience of his younger brother. His tyres would go flat and the fox would fool him. The prairie marmot would eat his melons at fabulous speed. The cock would picket the eggs and the folding bed would fold up on Donald. Nothing if not a tryer, he would tackle each new hobby, each new job with the brisk enthusiasm of a man unacquainted with failure. He even sang at his work. 'Early to bed, early to rise,' he crooned hoarsely, tunelessly to himself, 'With a cluck-cluck here,' 'A-hunting we will go.' But only too soon the enthusiasm would turn to fury and the contented droning would swell to a torrent of abusive squawks. Animal, vegetable, mineral, everything was against him ; even the garden pump played him tricks.

With the passage of time Donald has grown more defeated and more inclined to the morose. Occasionally emotion has been known to unman him. When Admiral Byrd sent him a young penguin, Donald, under the impression that his new pet had eaten the goldfish, punished the little creature ; convinced of error, he apologised : 'I'm sorry, Tutzie,' he cried. 'Aw, be a sport, Tutzie !', and the episode ended in expiatory tears. The public still applauds his uncontrollable rages, his endless battle with the blank hostility of inanimate matter. Of late a new interest has come into his life. A sturdy moralist, he finds in the war an outlet for his patriotism. Bitten by a new enthusiasm, today Donald wants to fly. And, together with every other American caught in the draft, he discovers a fresh enemy in his sergeant. Those who have wished for Donald a taste now and then of success were gratified when the other day, by enthusiastic use of camouflage paint, he became the Invisible Private. The Invisible Man, we know, lost his reason. This time the Sarge it was who went to the psychopathic ward.

In some ways the youngest is the most mature of the Disney Trio. A comparatively late arrival, Goofy, first known as the Goof, went through an apprenticeship of some years before Mickey and Donald would allow their kid brother to make a solo appearance in public. With them he went whaling or holiday-making in Hawaii. With them he cleaned clocks, built boats and —a responsibility sustained with genial calm in circumstances of

peculiar danger—drove the car for the trailer. Donald was his favourite brother, and the pair shared certain pursuits from which Mickey was excluded ; it was, for example, with Donald as huntsman that Goofy enjoyed his first recorded adventure on horseback. This was the prelude to the experiences in the sphere of sport which were presently to rivet public attention. In 1939 Goofy went for the first time outside the circle of the immediate family, taking as his partner in a joint fishing venture a distant cousin, Wilbur. Another two years were to go by before the youngest of the Trio could be said to stand on his own feet. In 1940 the public still was not Goofy-conscious. But in 1941 the young man appeared, modestly but with an unshakable confidence, as the pupil pilot of a glider. Suddenly the world understood that here was a portent among sportsmen, a character never to be deterred by difficulties or dangers from attempting the ultimate proficiency. The great Goofy Instructional series had begun.

From that moment no field of sport was closed to Goofy. Ski-ing, fishing, swimming, baseball—again and again enthusiasts were admitted to an intimate view of the champion's progress from tyro to expert. Ignoring the risibility of interested parties, he pursued the art of self-defence and the varied activities of the Olympic Champ. Fish went into convulsions of gaiety over his fly-casting, and when his horsemanship suffered a mischance his mount lay down and laughed till it cried. Still he was the Mark Tapley of sport ; radiant, he tackled the impossible, and after each rebuff his voice, rich, unctuous, was heard recommending yet a farther step. Failure left no mark on him, and frustration has so far left unimpaired the endeavours of this pioneer in the struggle against the law of gravitation.

In their personal circumstances and characteristics the brothers are strangely dissimilar. Mickey, the only one of the three to marry and enjoy a settled establishment, is yet the rover of the family : in spite of his sentimental side a man's man, careless in his dress and, except for an occasional excursion into costume, clinging man-like to his old and shabby clothes. Donald's closest ties, apart from his brothers, are with his three nephews, an ebullient trio and a trial at times to their irritable uncle. Donald, too, is conservative in dress, wearing for preference his sailor suit. He has, however, assumed various disguises, even feminine ones. He likes gardening, cooking and the sea. When annoyed he taps with his toes, quacking under his breath. Goofy is the dandy of the family, appearing with patent delight in hunting pink or the correct swimming or ski-ing dress. He is never annoyed. Critics have observed that he is also never successful. The progress of the Disney Three has thus been from the aggressive triumphs of the early Mickey, through the exasperated defeats of the middle period Donald, to the joyful frustration of the late Goofy. The temper of the public has changed. Chaplin was once a tough and is now a sensitive ; crude conquest is no longer in fashion. The Disney Trio too have moved from victory to an uneasy truce with fortune. But to the world they are still champs.

Thanks are tendered to Walt Disney Productions for permission to reproduce the illustrations. That of Pluto on page 125 is appearing in Robert D. Feild's The Art of Walt Disney, and thanks are also tendered to he publishers, Messrs Collins, for making it available here.

To the Unknown Critic

By Stephen Potter

These notes, by a journeyman broadcaster, are dedicated to the Unknown Critic—'unknown' because no big-C Criticism of radio has yet made its appearance. There are plenty of critics, and a fair amount of criticisms, in the radio columns of newspapers or radio journals. This local analysis of individual programmes is sometimes brilliant and always pertinent, unlike the pronouncements of the unprofessional judges who, particularly since the beginning of the war, have expressed their sense of the deficiencies of wartime broadcasting by a quantity of very pugnacious dogmatism, the main drift of which has been to point out angrily that light entertainment was not serious, nor was serious entertainment light.

No wonder those who work in broadcasting so often sigh for Criticism—for a Principle, in the vitalising, procreative, Coleridgean sense of this word. A Matthew Arnold to show its relation to life, a Granville Barker to give such terms as 'good radio' as full a significance as 'good theatre,' and one or two Herbert Reads to denominate styles and trace an evolution. Most of the more significant things in radio are still nameless. The name 'radio' itself is too modernistic, snappy and un-English. 'Broadcast' is too neo-Saxon—one might almost as well call it 'cast-craft.' There is no name at all for the kind of specialised style best adapted to effective broadcast communication—as different from any literary or rhetorical style as verse from prose. There is no name for the mingling of words with music in a special pattern— that radio ballet on which so much thought and not always unsuccessful care have been expended. There are phrases like 'radio drama,' a term so loose and misleading that it includes everything from a reading of an Ibsen play to a reconstruction, with recordings, of a day in the life of a Welsh coal miner : there is no word for the combination of sounds, music, voice and action which is radio's own carefully nurtured infant. There is no word, that is, except the technical nickname 'feature'—as undescriptive and misleading a term as was ever invented.

Here the Unknown Critic smiles. 'I am afraid I never listen,' —how many times, and in what good company, has he not repeated that phrase already. He will imply, and certainly

130

believe, that broadcasting has produced nothing worthy of his study. He will be wrong. A new medium doesn't rise, flourish for two decades, attract an audience of millions, and produce nothing worthy of the critics' study. Broadcasting has evolved its own actors, writers and directors, and has induced writers and entertainers from the other arts to adapt their talents to its strict demands.

Now if there are no tenets of a radio æsthetic, the conditions which control this art, the Unknown Critic will find, are formidable and cramping. The prospective radio writer finds himself either crushed or stimulated by severe difficulties. He will realise, first of all, that he is Down the Spout, and he will realise what this means. He will perceive that not only do his radio efforts receive no help from the eye ; he will certainly discover that all his witty light little touches or eloquent closing speech are each strangled at birth by being spoken into a thing like a meat safe and received by the listener at the other end through a deplorably open-mouthed, expressionless, polished receiving set, its only claim to interest—the marvel of its internal workings—tastefully concealed from the eye by a shiny wooden front. He soon understands, moreover, that it is through sound alone that he has to engage the interest of a listener who (i) probably regards everything that comes out of the spout as the 'wireless' or the 'BBC' and has no sense that the particular department of drama, features, talks and variety who may be presenting this programme to him are as disconnected and divergent in aim as the managements of the White City, the Haymarket Theatre, the Central Hall, Westminster, and the Malvern Arts Society. He is trying also to engage the sceptical ear of (ii) someone who has not paid for his seat, or perhaps it would be fairer to say is using a seat which has cost a proportion of a wireless licence amounting, say, to 0.2 of a farthing. There is, at any rate, no sitting down to it, no unaccustomed clean collar to stimulate alertness, no difficult long journey, no exciting crush in the gangway, no glow of footlights switched on to the base of the drop curtain. Yet this half-attentive listener must be held by the ear alone.

Not that this limitation may not be a stimulating challenge to the high-spirited radio author ; and this difficulty is, moreover, balanced by advantages. It was this curious new one-sidedness of the first cinema, the all-silent film, which helped to generate its Charlie Chaplin.   There is no Charlie Chaplin of viewless radio, but there are many considerable performers who have made an art out of this attenuated form of self-expression, and thrived on it.   Radio, too, has an extraordinary freedom within the rules.   A freedom to penetrate time and place.   An absence of dependence on scene shifters.   There is considerable freedom, too, of artistic self-expression.   The radio director is far less dependent on the box-office than his colleagues in films—freer than the theatrical producer.   The producer in uncommercial radio such as the BBC can be as experimental as he likes.

Through the ear only . . . the casualness of the listener . . . the artistic freedom . . . these are some of the facts peculiar to Radio which the Unknown Critic must never forget when he makes his analysis.

Beyond that, and before 'The Good Radio' comes to be defined even in general terms, he must find out by sheer hard listening (or, better still, by sheer hard practice)—what works. Some of the things which work and do not work in Radio I propose now out of my own experience to suggest.

I suppose for any worker in broadcasting the first rule or commandment is Be Thou Intimate. Almost every listener understands the implication here.   Your audience, whether it is one million or six, is almost unthinkably large, and the old original mistake used to be to think in terms of speeches of more than Albert Hall dimensions and dramatic entertainments on an Olympian and even White City scale.   It was forgotten that these millions were divided up into groups of two or three, and that since there was no emotional current between the groups, and therefore no possibility of a mass response, this group of two or three was in fact the real audience, and that the scale must be set accordingly.

A famous fact—yet half the bad in broadcasting can still be attributed to a forgetfulness of this rule.   The audience is so unprecedentedly small.   Not only the general approach but the actual technique must be scaled down to fit.   It is like working under a microscope, and illogical as the image may be, one comes to think of microphone work as microscope work, with microscope effects, a rough edge or an abrupt movement both leading equally to a blur.   An actor speaks an emotional line.

Listen to that line in the studio and it sounds right. Let him speak the same line in the same way on the stage and it will sound not only inaudible but ludicrously under-played. But listen to it through the receiving set, and if it sounds right in the studio it is certain to sound like over-acting. Every detail of acting and voice production must be similarly scaled down. What a brilliant impression of the Cockney maid Miss X gave at the St. Martin's. But put her under the microscope and it will be seen to be just first-class stage cockney, speaking a generalised dialect not really consistent with any of the four main types of local London accent. Under the microscope, stage American, stage foreign accent, stage Scots destroy the illusion at once. Famous actor-producer de-G has a trick, at dramatic moments, of prolonging his final consonants. Miss D, similarly, lingers on her vowels. Juvenile lead B, if he wants to sound ingenuous and fresh, makes frequent and sudden ascents to his top register. Under the microscope we see the machinery in action but lose the sense of character, even the meaning of the words. And put half-a-dozen gold medallists of the Poetry Speaking Union under the lens and the results are painful. Number One (with the beautiful voice) sounds like a cinema organ. Number Two, who has studied naturalness, simplicity, and under-emphasis, doesn't sound right either. The freshness of the girl asking Miranda if she remembers an inn becomes forced and arch. And the young man reading the love lyric makes a noise which sounds, to use the description of one of the best and most effective of broadcasters, like the mating of dinosaurs. Scale down to micro-dimensions, scale it all down—feeling, hesitations, accent, characterisation, changes of mood, changes of tempo. This is the first rule.

    In a word, the Scots accent, or whatever it is, should be innate—mimicry even by the possessor of the finest ear is in danger of sounding faked. The actor's line must never be dependent for its effect on a trick or a method. Unless a certain style is being assumed for the sake of its allotted part in a pattern, words, to sound natural, must come from the thought. They must never depend on a naturalistic technique. And in the reading of poetry (it is so difficult even after five hundred auditions and fifty tests of established speakers to try to dogmatise on a Right Way of speaking verse into the microphone)—well, I believe that even in poetry 'thinking the line' is more important and plays a greater part than any other kind of verse reading, just as, antithetically, any kind of incantation has, in this medium, to be handled with far greater restraint. The broadcasting of poetry is one of the most testing ordeals through which any reader can pass. In order to read his poem successfully he must understand the words through and through, and his knowledge of verse-reading must be a combination of conscious study and natural flair. The rhythm of the poem must fairly beat in the reader's blood, and he must be impregnated with its colour and its quality. All this knowledge, half instinctive and half acquired, must be kept within the unnaturally cramping limitations of the microphone.

Control—scaling-down. In my own kind of production, in the dramatised 'feature,' it is just as important to remember that the veracity of the crucial passages bears an inverse ratio to the force of the statement. It is the casual and the under-stated which makes its mark ; hardly ever the strong line, the hit word, or the effective exit. In war features the studied under-statement habitual in the Services, for instance, must be actually exaggerated if verisimilitude is to be maintained. One so often finds that the 'throw-away' line, as actors call it—the line which the listener is not quite certain whether he has heard or not, the line which in fact he has overheard—becomes the key word in the scene. If, for instance, one wanted in a biography of Coleridge to express the selfish coldness of his attitude to his wife, one could very well reproduce that letter he wrote to her when, in order to avoid the pangs of child-bearing peculiar to men, he had got himself out of the way to observe her confinement from the safe distance of a walking tour in the West country : 'My love, my thoughts are indeed with you at this hour, and my heart trembles to think of you perhaps already with the baby at your breast. Remember to get two *pots* of butter for T. Wade and that he likes *salt* butter.' It is this final afterthought, of course, which is the key to his whole selfish attitude ; the throw-away line which, under the microscope, gives the clearest indication of character. Even the key action can most effectively be made incidental to something more trivial which is going on at the same time.

In an imaginative script on Dostoevsky recently written by V. S. Pritchett, Dostoevsky is in an agony, confessing his gambling losses to his wife :

DOSTOEVSKY : No, I'm not one of those fools who believe in a system, it is a
question of will and calm. One has to surmount oneself, look
over the wall. One must concentrate. I went to the table
and, would you believe it, there was an Englishman beside me.
He had put some perfume on. It was absolutely overpower-
ing. I could not keep still beside him. I just swayed by
the table. All I saw was the words Impair and Passe before
me, swimming before my eyes.

The adventitious Englishman miraculously heightens the point
of the disaster. More simply, any crucial line can be most
effectively given when the speaker is apparently buried in some
task unconnected with the main issue.

This close-range, small-scale work calls for a great deal of concentration on the part of the listener, and the best help to concentration is change. 'Be various' might stand as the second
commandment. Even the serious and careful listener finds the
best presentation of the bodiless voice difficult to accept in
long stretches. Movement and change keep the attention from
wandering.

In radio production this rule has to be borne constantly in
mind. Continual changes : of tempo, of length of scene, of type
of voice, of background, of acoustic. Unity in variety. It is
particularly necessary that a radio production should have the
unity not of a piece of cheddar cheese, but of an Adam house.

The fabled 'sense of radio' which successful broadcasters are
said to achieve may be very largely the sense of how to break up,
how to make a change, how to vary. A sense, that is, of the right
use of the medium.

'Use the medium' might be our third commandment. There
are certain devices natural to Radio. The soliloquy, for instance.
We accept the convention in Shakespeare or eighteenth century
comedy without difficulty. But in a modern realistic play, a
soliloquy, with its invaluable clue to what the speaker thinks of
his own problems and his own personality—such a soliloquy,
elocuted to the back of the gallery, seems absurd. But thoughts
passing through the head can very effectively be suggested by
the low whispered voice into the microphone, even in a realistic
modern treatment.

The possibilities of quick transitions in time and place should not be forgotten. The flashback is more natural to broadcasting than it is even to the cinema. On the other hand, do not misuse the uses. Do not overdo the flashback. And remember that each change of scene must be clearly led up to.

Here is a note which the Critic or writer may find useful. Say your dramatic script deals with the past, say with the Armada. Do not plunge straight into a scene like this : 'King Philip seated at his desk. Enter his secretary. Sixteenth century Catholic chanting heard in the background.' The plunge will be too sudden for the listener. The music, local to time and place, will not be sufficient to suggest it. In the theatre the audience is helped. There is the description of the scene in the programme. Then the curtain rises on the period-setting and the actors in costume. But in radio it is all coming down the same old spout, and the listener is stuck in front of the same old art-wood receiving set that was staring back at him early this morning for Food Facts and Kitchen Notes. Lead the listener gently by the ear. Prepare him. Best of all, start with the present day—a historian discussing the theme—and lead back to your scene in the past by the simplest device which will serve your purpose.

Using the medium, it must be said as strongly as possible, does not mean using sound. More precisely, it does not mean indulging in an orgy of sound effects. Inexperienced script-writers almost always hamper the producer by putting in an immense number of noises. 'Sound of V-type engine . . . feet rustling through sand . . . a room full of typewriters . . . muffled oars . . . man running down a spiral staircase . . . six-week-old baby, wanting mother' are some recent suggestions from rejected manuscripts. Sound effects are sometimes useful. Some reproduce much better than others, but instructions in the script for an effect of 'Punt approaching a weir' would never be put in if it were realised that all possible kinds of flowing water when reproduced on the radio sound precisely alike, and that they never sound even damp, much less like flowing water. Percussion sounds, whether typewriters or road drills, always sound like Sten guns. Irregular percussion is much better—almost all the sounds connected with steam-engines and railways, for instance, sound correct, and truly atmospheric. But even the most splendidly evocative sound effect—and here is an important point of technique—must never be made the cue for a change of scene.   Noises off must be supplementary, never controlling the text.

The mistake is to have the ear too much in mind when writing for the radio.   Paradoxically, it is the eye which one should remember.   The fact that nothing but sound comes down the spout makes it all the more important that visual pictures, visual writing, should be made as much use of as possible.   Here is another limitation which can be turned to exciting advantage. Radio is back in the glorious days of the Elizabethan stage, when without the use of scenery the set was made vivid for the audience by the descriptive writing for the actors.   'Think, when we speak of horses, that you *see* them printing their proud hooves in the receiving earth.'   And then Shakespeare, in the text of *Henry V*, makes us see them : the proud stallions, the tired jades before Agincourt as well, with the 'gum down-roping from their dim dead eyes.'   Like the Elizabethan dramatists, the radio script-writer must supply the place of scenery by the sharpness and accuracy not of his sound effects but of his vision.

When you arise, Critic, we do not expect you to agree with these three Commandments, nor do we suggest that all producers and broadcasters agree on their wording.   But you will have to make up your mind about the problems involved in them. Three Commandments—and shall we add one awful warning, even though this is a purely personal judgment and one on which no two radio experts ever agree ?   It is : beware actuality.

'Actuality' is the radio slang for the kind of super-realism which involves bringing to the microphone, in documentary work, the actual people who live in their own lives the documentary theme.   It means getting real fruit-growers to speak the lines in the documentary programme on market-gardening, real North-countrymen to speak the lines in the programme on industrial Lancashire, Sir A. B. himself in the reconstruction of the account of the light car industry.   There are advantages in this technique.   Many listeners feel their interest heightened by the sense that 'this is the voice of the people themselves.'   The accent, at any rate, will be authentic : and if an actor is representing a fruit merchant the fact that he has never been nearer Covent Garden than the east wall of the Garrick club is some-

K

times too apparent in his voice.   But is the real man truly more real ?   Can he be real at all when he is speaking into a microphone ?   He who in real life is the most rich and rounded character, the spontaneously flowing Devonshire farmer, finds it extremely difficult to be rich and rounded into a microphone, down the spout, in the extravagantly unpub-like atmosphere of a BBC studio.   When this kind of presentation comes off it is because the farmer or the North-countryman or whoever it is can summon up his normal character in extraordinary circumstances.   He can, in fact, assume a character.   He is, in fact, an actor.   So, whether he is a professional or an amateur, if the thing is to sound real it is an actor, surely, who must be used.

My own practice is to use one of the dozen actors who have mastered the technique of this kind of microphone impersonation. Not those who 'put on a voice,' but those who can truly summon up characters and assume a frame of mind.   To name a few— James McKechnie, Gladys Young, Betty Hardy, Carleton Hobbes, Jonathan Field, Ronald Simpson, Joyce Grenfell.   The art of those specialists is exquisitely adapted to the kind of realism nicknamed 'documentary.'

How many critics will agree with me ?   And how many professional broadcasters ?   My chief hope is that the listener will find in such scraps of broadcasting theory as this something which will help him to discriminate, help him to realise the limits of the medium, encourage him to appreciate the scraps of artistry, to decide what for him is 'good radio,' to select his programme, and avoid listening by the yard, so that he may really listen by the pre-selected inch—to help him above all, that is to say, not only to listen but to hear.   Active intelligence is as necessary at the listening end of the spout as it is at the other, particularly as this kind of disjointed comment, by writer-broadcasters and working radio journalists, is all he has to help him.   All, that is, until the advent of the Unknown Critic.

The Curtained World

By Sean O'Casey

What is the theatre, where is it, and what does it do? Some few years ago, sitting at a round table of a big film association, while he was engaged on the production of *Call It a Day*, Mr Basil Dean, according to a famous Sunday journal, told us that 'going back into the theatre horrifies him. It was like watching little black ants crawling about the grass. The theatre will soon be as specialised and old-fashioned as chamber-music is to-day. It isn't in touch with the audience any longer ; it's not a medium that can say anything to the mass of the people. The film medium is so much finer and more precise. You can get so much nearer your actors with the camera, and tell your story more intimately.' Then Mr Dean talked of film versions of Shakespeare, and said his next production would be Eleanor Smith's *Ballerina*.

That's the first lesson from the filmic gospel, and here followeth the second lesson from the theatric gospel, taken from a famous Sunday journal, and appearing in the same year as the first one : 'The Soviet Union has, probably the only theatre of its kind in theatrical history. It is called the Polar Theatre, and in 1935 has just rung down the curtain on a successful session of seventy performances given in the Arctic fishing villages, on ice-breakers and barges, and in the dining-rooms of the many scientific outposts and industrial settlements of the far north. The fourteen men and women, comprising the group, carried with them complete stage sets, costumes, and a collapsible stage. After long uncomfortable trips in open boats, often through stormy seas, and under a deluge of cold rain, they had to unload their equipment, often wading knee-deep in the icy waters. They played, it might be, on the shifty deck of an ice-breaker anchored off Wrangel Island, or in the small meeting-hall of a village, near the mouth of the Obi River in Siberia. The hall was crammed with the strangest audience the Polar Group had ever played before, and with rapt attention they followed a performance of Molière's *Tartuffe*.

'When it was over not a handclap came, and the players were puzzled and a little frightened till they learned that hand-clapping was unknown there as a sign of approbation, and the dead silence was their sign of profound respect and appreciation.'

If the drama dies in one place it springs to life in another, for drama was the first child given to the first man and woman born to the world. Wherever two or three of them are gathered together, there is the theatre. Wherever we sit down, stand up, lie stretched ; wherever we sing, dance, work, weep, curse and swear, or play games ; wherever a child be born, or a man or woman dies, there the theatre is, and ever will be. And now, wherever a soldier's camp is fixed, a gun goes off, or a bonny young airman flies upwards or crashes down to death ; wherever a field is tilled, or machines rush round in a factory, there is the stuff that drama and dreams are made on. As high as we can reach to heaven, as low down as we may get to hell, and all between, is the theatre proper and the theatre grand. It is gun-peal and slogan-cry, woe and wantonness and laughter, in the midst of the grace of God. It is more than a mirror, for if what be conceived there be conceived with fierceness, joy, grace, and exultation it will split the mirror from top to bottom as reality cracked the glass and scattered the threads by which the Lady of Shallot wove her pretty patterns from the coloured shadows that passed her window by. It is a big, wide, wonderful world of treasures for the young dramatists, if only they can banish fear of new things from their minds and the minds of their audience, and keep their anxious heads from being held in tight chancery inside a box-office window.

To-day young dramatists have a chance that few have had, for the winds of war are blowing open the gates of a newer and a stranger day. To-day all dramatists, he who has already blown a tune on the trumpet, and he who holds an unblown trumpet in his hand, find themselves in the midst of turbulent life and death, for everywhere is the centre of the storm of war that has swept us into its indifferent clutches. The last war carried the dramatist about, more or less at his ease, round and round the edge of it ; this one has sucked him into its centre. The stone-walled castle, no less than the gracious ivory tower, has been split to its foundations, and left both naked to the blast of anxiety and much and grievous tribulation ; so that life which was select and gracious, full of refined security, is to-day abroad on the wind-swept heath, without a cloak, abiding the pelting lightning-rent storm. Tinker, tailor, soldier, sailor, richman, poorman, beggarman, thief; silk, satin, cotton, and rags are all there, unhooded in the horrid hurlyburly. To-day the King's major audience sport no plumes, carry no gold lace on shoulder or sleeve, but are smoke-begrimed or asweat with labour, and he is oriflammed in the ruins of his people's buildings and his people's homes.

Here we all are actors in a fight more frenzied than a world ever saw before, touching only, if it touches anything, the fight between Michael and his angels with the hosts of evil. The mirror of nature has become a huge magnifying-glass, showing us ourselves as we never saw ourselves before. We have stood up to all that has happened with brave hearts and steady hands, so it can't be too much to hope that we shall stand up to welcome a widening, deepening, and intensifying of our theatre. Life can never be what it has been before ; changes have come, and many more are heralded. As it will be with us, so shall it be with our theatre ; and it will no longer be a decked-out place in which trivial objects glide in before the eye and glide out again to disappear for ever ; but it will be an honoured place where fine things are spoken, and where great names move and live and have their being.

The English theatre to-day is nothing to be proud about ; indeed, by and large, it is a thing of poor shreds and patches, with an odd one having a tint of colour. It is no more a part of the life of England than are the penguins in the Zoo. Indeed, the penguins, especially the King Penguin, are more interesting to the people than are the vital treasures of English dramatic art. Down where I am now, in Devon, among a good-natured, intelligent, hard-working people, many have never seen the inside of a theatre, much less the performance of a Shakespeare play. Reckoning her wealth and vigour, concerning the theatre England is a Cain among the nations—wearing the mark of God's condemnation on her brow through thinking she parades her dramatic glory in a suit of sackcloth. It is wonderful, too, how many are anxious to keep the theatre closed on Sunday though they never stir a finger to keep it open any other day of the week.

Where I lived for four years, in Buckinghamshire, the theatre to many of the people was still the house of Satan

and to many everywhere it is still a thing that makes God
close His eyes and shudder. In this county with a population of a quarter of a million, and three big towns, there is,
as far as I know, but one theatre holding 238 persons ; a theatre
but a few years old, and still in childish bib and tucker. And
this theatre has to work night and day to keep going, putting on a
new play weekly, mauling the unfortunate members with ceaseless
work to give this little corner of England a glimpse of what the
British drama is like. The one concession given to this activity
by the mass of wealth and vigour that is England is that the
theatre isn't required to pay the Entertainments Tax : for this
relief, much thanks. Here are a few words, spoken without
malice, by the present producer of the theatre in Amersham :
'The conditions under which repertory theatres work in England'
(England, mind you—wealthy, arrogant England) 'are, from a
theatre point of view, almost unspeakable. Rehearsals all day as
well as playing far into the night.' This little theatre holds fewer
than half those fitting into the Abbey, Dublin, and, to give a
spare living to its members, has to give a twice-nightly performance.

And, I dare say, the tale told here is the tale to be told of
all, or almost all, the other man-forsaken repertories in England.
There isn't a repertory in England whose greatest thrill isn't the
agonising uncertainty of what is going to happen to it to-morrow ;
and that is a mean aggravation against which no little theatre (or
big one either) can struggle towards a fine, fierce, or graceful
expression of its art. Brave and all as these tiny theatres are,
they aren't numerous enough to give any importance to their connection with the outer and inner life of the English people.

It is a parlous thing this, to associate contempt and indifference
with our grand achievement in dramatic literature ; and we are
all to blame for it, particularly our leaders, political and religious
and labour ; right, left, and centre. The Church, ever active
in her own sacred theatre, drenched in her own dramatic liturgy,
never now bothers her head about the theatre profane, unless on
an occasion when this theatre does something which some impul-
sive ecclesiastic thinks is bound to be a means of stirring up the
souls of her people, like a Bishop of Gunnersbury strutting on to the
stage after the first performance of *The Tents of Israel* to tell an

astonished audience that 'this was a great play because it showed a whole people kneeling on their knees.' That was the Bishop of Gunnersbury for you ! Perhaps it would have been a greater play still if it had shown a whole people standing on their heads ! To help to promote an interest in the theatre, we may rule the Bishops out, though they sit in the House of Lords, influence a mass of people, and rule in an effective way over many fair demesnes in this fair land. It is a pity they don't take an odd hour off to learn a little about a play. Surely this potent and widespread organisation could form a permanent dramatic group, say in each cathedral city, from among the members of her Young Men's and Young Women's Christian Associations, the Church Army, Church Lads' Brigade, and Bible classes, so that the dioceses might, at least, hear an echo of Shakespeare's voice speak brave and gay for England still.

In the old time before us the Church took a keener interest in the drama, and even touched drama into some of her most reverential rites. In the more dewy days of Christianity we find a record of a dramatically performed rite celebrating the coming of the three women to the tomb of the buried Saviour, called *Quem Quaeritis in Sepulchro Christicolæ*. It is set out in an MS. attributed to St Gall (an Irish Saint, by the way), and this is how it goes : 'While the third lesson is being said, let four brethren vest themselves. Let one of them, vested in an alb, enter as though to take part in the service, and let him approach the sepulcre without attracting attention, and sit there quietly with a palm in his hand. While the third response is chanted, let the other three follow, and let them all, vested in copes, stepping delicately as those who seek something, approach the sepulcre. These things are done in imitation of the angel sitting in the monument, and the women bearing spices coming to anoint the body of their Lord. When he who sits there beholds the three approach him, like folks lost and seeking something, let him begin in a dulcet voice of medium pitch to sing, *Whom seek ye in the sepulcre, O Christians ?* Then let the three reply in unison, *We seek Jesus of Nazareth who was crucified, O Heavenly One.* Then he who imitates the angel, chants, *He is not here ; He is risen even as He said before. Go ; proclaim He has risen from the grave !* At this, let the three turn to the quoir, and say, *Alleluia ! The Lord is risen !* Then let the one sitting there, and as if recalling them,

say the anthem, *Come, and see the place where He lay*. And saying
this, let him rise and lift the veil, showing the place bare of the
Cross, and only the clothes there in which the Cross was wrapped.
And when they have seen this, let them lay down the thuribles, and
take the cloth, and hold it up in the face of the clergy, as if to
demonstrate that the Lord has risen, and is no longer wrapped
therein ; then shall they sing the anthem, *Christ has risen from the
grave*, laying the cloth on the altar as they sing. When the anthem
is done, let the Prior, sharing in their gladness at the triumph of
our King, in that, having vanquished death, He rose again, begin
the hymn, *Te Deum Laudamus*. And this begun, all the bells chime
out together.'

Well played, boys ! As neat as any, and much more graceful
and exultant, that has ever appeared on the present-day stage.
We need more of this grace and exultation, more dulcet voices
of a medium pitch, of delicate movement without attracting
attention, of sitting quietly with, or without, a palm in the hand,
in our play-acting on the stage to-day. The above little ecclesi-
astically-made drama was bound to set up a quietly-clamorous
emotion in the breasts who saw and heard it, convincing them for
ever that God was in His heaven and all was well with the world.
The world lost a dramatist in St. Gall, disciple of St Columba, or
in whichever monk who wrote it. So we see—there are many
other instances—the Church not only gave the kiss of peace to
the drama without her walls, but added it to give added effect
and beauty to some of her own particular rites. Perhaps the
Church may stir herself again, some day, though I think the
chance has passed for ever now. Canterbury has, I believe,
given some pageants, and has done T. S. Eliot's *The Rock* ; but
these have but touched the stone walls, and have never got within
sight of the altar. It seemed to me there was a touch, more, an
embrace, of make-believe about these things, showing the Church
good-naturedly tolerant rather than affording a welcome to the
alleluias, amens, and glorias of the theatre which were and are
and are to come, *in saeculo saeculorum*. The plays given over the
wireless were, to me, an effort to dance the story of the Gospels
into the minds of the young to the sound of castanets. Recently
a civic luncheon was given to Mr J. B. Priestley because of a new
play of his to get production in Bradford, and the Bishop spoke
kind words over the tables ; but I'm afraid that the honour was

meant, not for the play, but for Mr Priestley because he was a son of the city.

No, it won't do : the Church must be ruled out of it.

Then there are the two premier Universities that lift, it may be, once a year, a play by Shakespeare, or Jonson, or Euripides in original Greek, out on to the lawn for an airing, then put it back into a warm cupboard for a rest for the rest of the year. There is, too, the plump and self-satisfied Conservative party, anxious now about putting on a little too much weight, and sensitive now of shoulders stooping, to the right to-day, to the left to-morrow ; speaking, governing, and acting as if the theatre didn't exist.

Following very close behind now is the brawny Labour party, many of its officials pressing forward to the heaven of bowler hats, respectable suits, and neatly folded umbrellas, regarding the theatre as a place for ninnies of leisure and levity, forgetful that without a vision the people perish, and that a facet of this vision should be aglow in a theatre that they and the mass members of the Trades Unions should set firmly upon its feet. It was left to a few Communists and fewer sympathisers to set about bringing the theatre back to the people, building with much labour and hard going a little theatre to bring colour and a laugh and an occasional tightening of the spine to the common people in the form of play and pantomime. But to England as England the drama is as if it never had been, and never will hang out on her battlements the masks of tragedy and comedy again.

Why has the colourful, vivacious, tragic life of the theatre faded from the ken of the English people ? It had a big life and a gorgeous time when the Trades Guilds went about in their wagons doing the Mystery and the Morality Plays, showing the goodness of God and the evil of Satan to the gaping crowds, clapping their hands and shouting for more, so that one couldn't get stir nor breath. Again, in Elizabethan times the gayest of colours swam before the eyes of the people, and the loveliest of language fell musically into outstretched ears ; to become scented and clever, but a gift for the few only, in the golden days of good King Charles ; to burst melodramatically out into paper bloom again, and then, finally, to be shepherded with golden whips into the toy-lighted corner of London's West End, along which faintly blows Mr Priestley's whispered appeal of 'don't desert a man because a graver note creeps into his work ; don't stay out of the theatre because the realities of life have crept into it.'

Some will blame the cinema, but it goes down deeper than that. The decay of the theatre, I think, began when the nationality of England began to grow pale in the rush and roar of the Industrial Revolution. Then all flocked to the towns, and the country's lore was lost, buried in the fields like the man hiding his talent in a napkin, though this was the talent of a nation. When all the spring and harvest festivals, the customs, the dances, the natural songs, the blossoms of folklore and folk music faded into forgetfulness and disrepute, a lot of theatrical inspiration went out of England's soul. They still flourish in Scotland, Wales, and Eire, and even in some of the more remote English counties ; but among the masses of the people they have been swallowed up in their Daisy Bell give me your answer do's and It's a long way to Tipperaries. One has only to listen to Workers' Playtime and Works' Wonders, this let the people sing business, to see what tremendous advances England has made in her own national loss. A few folk societies have tried to give these things life again, but have never got anywhere near the people, and seem to preserve these treasures as national ikons rather than to hand them out to the people as gorgeous and inspiring playthings.

We are far too ignorant of, and careless about, this great national wealth lying well outside of our national banks. Some time ago our great Prime Minister, speaking in Edinburgh, referred to Mr Harry Lauder as Scotland's national bard, thereby giving, unintentionally, a knock on Scotland's nose. Rabbie Burns, Dunbar, MacDiarmid, yes, but not Mr Lauder. In my opinion, England's older customs, her songs and dances, her folklore must be, and should be, familiar to us before a sprightly and serious native drama can spring into vigorous being. I don't, of course, mean the there'll always be an England stunt—that's as bad as the Irish wrap the green flag round me boys tomfoolery. I mean the deeper things that spring from the experience and credulity of life ; for simple as these may be, each has the glint of colour, touch of poetry, sigh of pathos, and the ray of imagination that give a glow to song, to story, and to drama.

Only in the Children's Hour do we sometimes hear a few of

these lovely things—recently I listened to a stirring Cumberland March that I never heard before and, maybe, will never hear again. England must sing more about herself; not of her Empire, but of herself. That will shake her shyness off, and make her more audible on the stage. And get the young dramatists away, too, from the curious heresy that nowhere is silence more golden than when it appears on the stage. For now there is a monastic awe for silence on the stage so that actors and actresses are losing the power of speech, and mutter and mumble their way about behind the footlights and the curtain, keeping all their secrets to themselves. Mr John Palmer in one of his critical books claims as bold and adventurous the dramatist who said that 'above all, the theatre is the art of the unexpressed, and has no worse enemy than literature.' And Mr Palmer, applauding this, says, 'this "theory of silence" should be sure of welcome and sympathy among ourselves, for it is a sacred postulate that the more poignant emotions are too deep for words. English lovers are expected to be incoherent ; English heroes are expected to be silent. In English drama the strong silent man will never die. Kill him in the plays of Alfred Sutro and he will appear, strong and silent as ever, in the plays of John Galsworthy.' Mr Palmer makes haste to excuse Shakespeare's *Romeo and Juliet*, saying, 'We must scrupulously beware of using the theory of silence as a cover for mere literary incompetence or neglect, and some of us may suspect that men are silent because they have nothing to say.' Quite so. A lot of these dramatists hide a personality within a mumble because they haven't a personality that can be lifted into a shout. Shakespeare's O what a rogue and peasant slave am I ! would silence every strong silent man of the stage into a silent pillar of salt.

But the first apparent change to come, already beginning to come, will be the physical method and manner of the theatre. As the war has set our buildings tumbling so it has set our needs tumbling into new ways of living, and our minds tumbling into new ways of thought. The big professional theatres of the West End have had their day, on the whole, a dog's day, and that day is now in its twilight, for the half-gods are getting ready to go ; and when the half-gods go, the gods arrive. Plays are being performed where they have never been performed before, and, by-and-by, the provincial cities and towns will not rest quiet without theatrical activities of their own. This has started more quickly in the United States than it has here, and a Congress of the National Theatre Conference has begun to set things moving. They have asked playwrights to give them an equal chance with the professional part of the theatre. Saroyan gave them *Jim Dandy*, and last year this play was done in forty-four centres, and is still being performed. Maxwell Anderson's *Eve of St. Mark* was performed in seventy cities before it came to Broadway ; and now a musical comedy has been written for production by the numerous centres of this National Theatre Conference. This outspread of interest and self-determination in the theatre will come to us, and will form new and fine endeavours, inflicting new trials on older actors and actresses staggering out of the art of acting under the burden of a huge weekly salary. It will give us a new theatre, imagination will supersede the dressmaker's shop, and show us that man doth not live by bread alone, but by every word out of the mouth of God ; by every word, mind you, and not only the word repeated by Nonconformist, Anglican, Roman Catholic, or Mohammedan ; but also the glowing word spoken by every fine building, statue, poem, picture, and play. This theatre will cordially send out to show its achievement to India, to Australia, over the sea to Skye, to St Helena, or whatever may be the ultima thule of the British Commonwealth.

It will be a theatre preserving all the delicate grace, beauty, and majesty of line that have been born before us, adding the sturdiness and lusty life of the presentday descendants of coopers, fullers, armourers, bow-makers, and all of a bygone generation, so that the theatre may become a passionate, graceful and colourful part of English life, giving us a vision of the whole earth, not as a mourning man in the fork of a dying tree gazing over a waste land, but like unto Pushkin's beautiful princess with the moon in her hair and a star on her forehead.

Evans : Photographer
By Alex Strasser

One day back in the nineties a visitor was announced to the Dean of a well-known English cathedral. The card showed the name and address of a bookseller in the City of London. Admitting the caller, the Dean saw a small, fragile-looking gentleman wearing an outlandish silk collar, a blue tie and a crushed soft hat. 'I have come to ask for permission to photograph your cathedral.' The Dean, after a momentary hesitation, agreed that this could be done. 'I shall start on such and such a day,' calmly continued the visitor, 'and, by the way, the rows of chairs in the nave would disturb the composition of the picture. Will you please have them removed before my arrival ?' Miracles seemed to happen even in the nineteenth century. The many hundred chairs had vanished at the appointed hour.

This episode was told by Bernard Shaw in an article written many years ago, and the spirited little bookseller referred to was Frederick Henry Evans, to-day recognised as one of the few great figures in English architectural photography.

To be an outstanding photographer means, on the face of it, to be consummate in this special field. But there is usually more to it than that. Photography in its early stage was certainly an eccentric form of craft. Not only did the camera obscura seem 'obscure' to the uninitiated, but everything to do with it was for him full of optical and mechanical mysteries, smelling partly of horrible chemicals and partly of downright black magic. No wonder that photography as an occupation attracted for a long time not so much the respectable, level-headed citizen, but either the quack who tried to make capital out of these 'mysteries' or the man of sufficient imagination and foresight who was aware that the camera was not a mere conjuring tool to make fun with, but an instrument which carried in it the seed of a truly new art. Hill, Cameron, Nadar and many other pioneer photographers, later Coburn, Steichen, Sutcliffe, to mention only a few of the following generation—they all show an unmistakable affinity as regards antecedents and general background ; all are striking and often picturesque characters ; all are not photographers in the sense of a chosen profession, but artists, scientists or journalists who turned to photography because, somehow or other, this strange and intriguing medium became essential—and even indispensable—to the pursuit of their aims. ·

Evans is no exception. A survey of his life and work reveals a picture which is, indeed, typical of the relationship between so many camera artists and photography—typical also in its reciprocal effects—but which at the same time is certainly unique in all aspects arising from personal disposition and circumstances.

Evans, who is nearly ninety years old to-day, started life as a clerk in the counting-house of a big London business, and a rather sick clerk he was. His health, always indifferent, became from time to time so bad that he was compelled to take long holidays. Thus at twenty or thereabouts he made a voyage to America for reasons of health. After his return to England he struggled on as a clerk, intermittently taking his enforced and prolonged vacations. Among the hills of the Lake District, in the rolling Devonshire country, his eyes opened to the loveliness of nature. He was always inspired by the beautiful, whether a grand landscape or building or a minute sea creature. Poring over a Ross microscope which he had purchased out of his savings, spellbound by the miracles of form and shape which the instrument revealed, he would speculate : ' Why should these lovely images be lost for ever ?' It was the same question which Fox Talbot, some forty-five years before him, had wistfully pondered while glancing at the 'fairy images' on the ground glass of his Camera Lucida. Talbot had answered this question by inventing photography ; and photography having been invented, Evans solved *his* problem by deciding to put photography tò the service of art.

He was then in his middle twenties. 'I was a late developer,' he says, perhaps not very seriously, 'always ten years behind.' Ross at that time used to give exhibitions of the wonders of the microscope for which he had built up a collection of his best slides. Some of the microscopic slides not quite good enough for exhibition were given to Evans by one of Ross's assistants, and one day, examining the spine of a sea-urchin, Evans became particularly entranced. He tried and succeeded in making a photograph of this slide. The result seemed to him so promising that he sent the picture to the Royal Photographic Society's exhibition, where it was awarded a medal for the best work of the year. That was his first practical step as a photographer.

In these years his health suffered again seriously, and ultimately it broke down completely. It is a strange feature of Evans's life that the mainspring of his energetic activities and achievements in various fields was his very ill-health, as it led to repeated changes of occupation. This time he had to give up his clerkship for good and think of something else. He was considering photography and would perhaps have taken it up professionally then and there had not an unexpected opportunity presented itself. Every Wednesday evening he would take a Turkish bath for his rheumatic fever, calling on his way at a bookshop in Queen Street, Cheapside, for the weekly literary supplement of the *Athenaeum*, which he read from cover to cover. The owner of this not very prosperous shop, one Jones, became interested in him and grew into the habit of referring inquiries about books which he could not settle himself to the knowledgeable young man. After a bit the unofficial assistant came to occupy an official position ; he borrowed some money from his father and became a partner in the business. But in a surprisingly short time this new capital was swallowed up, and the shop was nearly on the rocks. Jones died suddenly, leaving the venture under the control of Evans, who rapidly pulled it round.

One day, Bernard Shaw, surprised to see one of his books in the window (this seems to have been a rare sight in those days), entered the shop and found Evans lurking in the darkest corner of the dark establishment. 'You are selling my books,' he said. 'Why not ?' answered Evans, and they became friends. Evans had, and still has, the greatest admiration for Shaw. 'We who have read every word he has written,' he says with pride, implying that to have read Shaw is the highest of intellectual distinctions. Shaw, for his part, recognised in Evans the artist of marked ability and bizarre character that he is.

'Evans,' he wrote once, 'is a man of fragile health to whom an exciting performance of a Beethoven symphony was as disastrous as a railway collision to an ordinary philistine. . . . But his condition never prevented him from doing anything he really wanted to do, and the things he wanted to do and did would have worn out a navvy in three weeks.'

Shaw was not the only star in England's intellectual sky whom Evans knew not merely through the books which he read and sold. There was William Morris. Evans still keeps amongst his treasures a number of Kelmscott books with Morris's signature, which he points out to his visitors with great pride. And there was a young insurance clerk by the name of Beardsley, who used to rummage in the bookshop during his luncheon hour so as to forget for a while the drudgery of his existence. Evans took a liking to the young man and soon found out that Beardsley also was possessed of a passionate love of beauty and music. Beardsley felt that he could trust Evans, and showed him, rather embarrassed, some drawings he had made in his spare time. That Evans believed in Beardsley's talent from the very beginning is proved by the fact that he often swopped books which Beardsley wanted for some of his first drawings.

Evans remained Beardsley's friend and counsellor, and remembers many small incidents. Once Beardsley showed him a drawing of Madame Réjane which he had made for the *Yellow Book*. 'Fine work. How much is it worth?' asked Evans. 'A fiver,' replied Beardsley. E. gave him a five-pound note and B. tucked it into his handkerchief pocket. E. : 'It will get lost.' B. : 'It won't.' On the following morning Evans received a postcard from Beardsley : 'Where is that note?' Evans replied, 'That's the sort of lost property no one ever returns.' He sold this Réjane drawing later for £100.

Evans continued selling books in Queen Street for a long time, but at last his health forced him again to a decision. 'Every morning I opened the bookshop with the fear how much less of me would come out of it in the evening.' He was afraid that he himself would be swallowed up by his shop. So, at the turn of the century, Evans, exhausted, renounced his career as a bookseller and moved out of London to Epping Forest to take up, at last, photography on a large and unhampered scale.

To speak of him as a photographer, and to show his work in the right place and perspective, one needs briefly to explain the position of photography in general between, say, 1890 and 1914. This period is characterised by several distinct features. There was a rapid advance on the technical side, there was a steady decline in professional portraiture brought about by a glut of inferior studios, and there were renewed attempts on the part of intelligent photographers, mainly amateurs, to lift photography

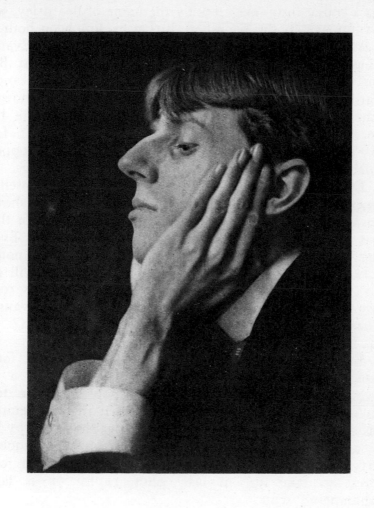

Aubrey Beardsley

George Bernard Shaw

from the plane of a mere mechanical craft to an acknowledged art. These attempts were natural and logical developments, but a strange confusion arose as regards the ways and means by which to attain this end.

Two distinct schools are discernible. The first regarded it as perfectly legitimate to draw on extraneous resources, such as pigments, for the achievements of their ends. The technique of 'controlled' printing was their mainstay, and there is no doubt that very artistic effects can be obtained by the gum process, the gum-bichromate process and the oil and bromoil processes. The doubt comes in over the question whether these artistic effects are *art* or any nearer to it than a photograph pure and simple. The question has never been, and probably never will be, 'officially' decided. But the followers of group two maintain stoutly that photographic art can only spring from pure photographic reactions, physical and chemical, and that the *negative* is decisive, not the print which, in their eyes, is secondary in importance. Be that as it may, one fact is certain : a good print can never be obtained from a bad negative by straight printing methods, whereas quite impressive pictures can be wangled from almost hopeless negatives by the pigment technique. In other words, the 'pure' photographer must be a good *photographer*, the adept of controlled printing must be clever with his pots of pigments, glue and oil.

Evans is, and takes a great pride in being, a 'pure' photographer. He never reduced, intensified or retouched his plates. If he was not satisfied with a negative he smashed it. He printed on platinum paper. 'We artists are at the mercy of our material. If I had not had double-coated plates and the platinoprint, I would not have touched photography again.' He attributed to this combination his ability to express himself as he wished, to combine in one picture strongest high-lights and darkest shadows without losing any of the delicate half-tones which are so characteristic of his work.

Evans was, as in all his other pursuits, entirely self-taught. He proceeded by observation, self-criticism and boundless energy. His cathedral pictures are a good case in point. During one of his sojourns in Devonshire he said to himself : 'I'll return by way of Salisbury and see what a cathedral looks like.' This visit was decisive. It prompted him to engage in photographing cathe-

L

drals. He emphasises that this had nothing to do with any devotional feeling—it was simply the appeal of beauty which actuated him, in this case mainly the beauty of stone texture. He studied the problem and, somewhat facetiously, remarks that 'cathedrals are very good subjects for students—they don't walk about.' From this period of studies and observation he went on to the next stage of self-criticism.

In an article written exactly forty years ago he speaks of his thoughts and conceptions about the photography of ecclesiastical architecture. He starts by describing how Turner's small water-colours impressed him by their 'superb sense of height, bigness, light, atmosphere and grandeur.' When, some time later, he started his cathedral studies, he recalled these little masterpieces and wondered 'whether anything photography might ever do could merit a little of the praise so justly lavished on the incomparable Turner.' He goes on : 'After a while I took heart a little, for, seeing that my subjects did not call for colour in their rendering ; that the chief things needed were extreme care and taste in composition ; faultless drawing (in the sense of correct choice of lens, etc.) ; adequate treatment of the fine details such subjects abound in ; and exhaustive studies of the conditions making for the best effects of light and shade and atmosphere ; it seemed to me that cathedral pictures were well within the camera's special field of work. . . . If success be to convey to another the vital aspect and feeling of the original subject, so to translate one's own enjoyment of a scene into a visible record as to affect the critic with the very quality of one's own original emotion, then surely it matters not in what form or method of art it be achieved, it will be as vitally valuable : and if it be possible by way of the condemned "box with a glass in it," so much the more credit to the worker who uses that despised tool to so good an end.'

Having made up his mind about the fundamental questions, Evans began his work. Shaw's story, told at the beginning of this contribution, gives a fair idea of the way Evans set about a problem. The difficulties which confront photographers in the architectural field, and especially in churches, are considerable. Evans had often to wait for weeks until everything was as he wanted it : the balance of light and shade just right, the sunlight

Ely Cathedral

Dirge in Woods

Steps to Chapter House, Wells

Lincoln Cathedral

streaming through a window in the desired intensity, the atmospheric conditions creating a right perspective, and obstacles,
where possible, put out of the way.

Even then many problems remained, such as local difficulties
and the question as to how to establish the grandeur of a large
composition without distortion or magnification of near portions.
The use of long-focus lenses was often impossible because of limited
space. Ladder-tripods had to be used for getting nearer to
details high up the walls. Evans used to take his first pictures
with a tiny hand camera for plates 3¼ in. square. While lament-
ing this fact he felt consoled by his recollection of Turner's small
water-colours, which proved that 'acreage has nothing to do with
art.' Later on, he used cameras from half-plate to 10/8 in. size
and a variety of lenses ranging from 6 in. focal length to the
telephoto lens. His greatest care was directed to the exposure
times ; they varied between several seconds and several hours,
and he always used the largest aperture possible. 'Wrong expo-
sures lead to trying the impossible task of improving a bad negative into a good one.' For certain purposes, such as the interiors
of Westminster Abbey which he made in 1911, he used specially
prepared emulsions, all double-coated. No available plates
would have given him the necessary control over such lighting
extremes as prevail in the Abbey.

He took countless photographs in most of England's important
cathedrals ; in some cases he was commissioned, but mostly he
worked on his own accord. All his work shows his supreme
technical skill and uncommon gift of 'seeing.' Although his
name is mainly associated with the photography of cathedrals
he was a master also in other fields. Three times he went to
France on special commissions and photographed the majority
of her famous chateaux. He liked landscape photography and
was very much attracted by wood scenes. The tall uprights of
the trees in his picture 'Dirge in Woods' are strikingly akin to
the pillars in the picture of Ely Cathedral. Evans took also,
though to a lesser degree, photographs of his friends. His best
known portrait is that of Beardsley. He was at first puzzled to
know how to tackle him. 'There's not much to be done with a
face like yours,' he told him. 'You're only a gargoyle, you
know.' Beardsley at once put his hands up to his face in the
attitude made famous by the subsequent photograph. 'That's it !

A gargoyle on Notre Dame,' exclaimed Evans excitedly, and made the exposure.

Evans was, of course, paid when he was commissioned, but he never took on any work for the sake of payment. He declined many attractive offers. 'I always had my bread and butter. I wanted to be free.' And free he remained, an independent but modest and retiring sort of man. Although a member, and later an Honorary Fellow, of the Royal Photographic Society, he never took any great part in its activities. Shortly after the last War, when it became more and more difficult and costly to obtain platinum papers, he gradually, and probably mournfully, gave up his beloved photography.

Thus and thus has Evans become the nonagenarian that he is, to-day. That is almost an achievement in itself, but he does not seem to take much notice of it. He is mentally as active as ever. In his neat house in Acton, with his wife and daughter, he leads a quiet but still rich and full life. Small, gnome-like, a fringe of white hair covering cheeks and chin, wearing a black velvet jacket, a blue silk tie, slippers and, occasionally, a skull cap, he skips round his room with immense agility, busying himself with many things. He is still interested in current literature, but for real relaxation he turns to his pianola, for which he has himself cut 1500 rolls of music. His rooms are filled with numerous treasures which constitute his links with the past. Paintings, drawings and photographs crowd the walls. A strange-looking mechanical contraption of uncertain purpose in one corner and the roll-cutting machine in the other are puzzling to the casual visitor.

Evans regards his photographs as his greatest treasures. And he is right. As things are, the cathedrals of England are in danger. His pictures will forever reflect their beauty. They are the contribution of a true artist to his country's culture.

EDITOR'S NOTE: *While this book was in preparation Mr Evans died: on June 24, 1943, two days before his ninetieth birthday. All his friends, and they range over three generations, mourn the loss of a remarkable and endearing personality who brought to the twentieth century the essential qualities of the great Victorians.*

The Attics at Kelmscott Manor

Paysage Fantastique

Animals Courting
By Julian S. Huxley

The trouble about acquiring knowledge is that it reveals fresh ignorance : the more facts, the more questions. Thanks to observant hunters, gamekeepers, amateur naturalists, and professional biologists, we are now in possession of an immense body of facts about the peculiarities of behaviour and structure connected with the securing of a mate in animals. But the facts immediately turn themselves into a series of insistent questions—why, why, why ?

Why do stags not have beautiful tails (or rather trains, for let us be accurate) like Peacocks ; or vice versa, why do not Peacocks have bony excrescences on their heads like stags ? Why are male dogs or horses not provided with bright-coloured adornments like cock Pheasants or Sage Grouse ; why don't they sing like Nightingales or mocking birds ? Why are male Elephant-seals or Bustards much bigger than females, while in most creatures the sexes are approximately equal in size ? Why are most mammals restricted to blacks, whites and greys, browns, russets and yellows, while monkeys, like birds (and fish) run the gamut of colour ? Why does the human species not possess gaudily-coloured posteriors like so many apes and monkeys ?

Within the one group of birds, why are some conspicuous in both sexes (like Crows or Loons), some inconspicuous in both sexes (like Sparrows or Skylarks), some again conspicuous in the male sex but inconspicuous in the female (like most Ducks and some Finches) ? When there are special plumes or ornaments used for display, why are these sometimes restricted to the males (as in Pheasants, Grouse, or Birds of Paradise), but in other species found in both sexes (as in Herons, Grebes, Auks, or the English Robin) ? Why is song almost entirely confined to one group of

165

M

birds ? And why do birds sing anyhow ? Why do Skylarks and Pipits sing in the air, while most birds sing from a perch ?

Why do so many birds, like Prairie Chicken, Ruff, Birds of Paradise, or Oystercatchers, have special communal courting-grounds, or at least perform their courtship while in flocks or groups ? How is it possible for evolution to have produced adornments which are actually a hindrance to their possessor in the ordinary affairs of life, like the train of the Peacock or the plumes of some Birds of Paradise ?

Do reptiles indulge in courtship ? or fish ? or insects ? or worms ? and if not, why not ? Why do female spiders sometimes eat their mates ? Why do male fiddler-crabs have one claw enlarged until it is nearly as big as the rest of their body, while the females have two tiny claws like the males' small one ? Why, when there is a difference in brilliance of adornment between the sexes, is it almost invariably in favour of the male in lower animals, while the reverse is true in the human species ?

That is a selection of the questions which the facts insist on asking. Curiously enough, no one bothered very much about answering this kind of question until after the middle of the last century. This was mainly because the theory of Special Creation still held the field in biology. The thousands of different species of animals were supposed to have been created once and for all, with all their peculiarities of construction and behaviour as we observe them to-day. No particular explanation was required, beyond that of an all-wise Creator : if we could not fathom the purpose of a particular organ or instinct, so much the worse for us. Furthermore, even biologists had scarcely begun to interpret animal behaviour except in human terms, so that all kinds of human interpretations were uncritically accepted. In the field we are here considering, this anthropomorphic tendency showed itself by thinking of animal display in terms of human courtships—bird song was some sort of a serenade, bright plumage was the equivalent of putting on your best suit, fighting was a duel for possession of a bride, and so on.

With the acceptance of the idea of evolution, however, all this was changed. Animals had not always been what we see today. They had gradually become their modern selves, and all their characteristics demanded an explanation, for nothing could have evolved without some biological reason. Darwin himself was the first to tackle the kind of question I have been posing, and propounded a special theory to account for special masculine weapons, such as deer antlers or stag-beetle jaws, and for special masculine adornments, such as the peacock's train, or the bright colours of certain male lizards. According to him, such characteristics owed their evolution to what he called Sexual Selection—selection based on a struggle or competition between rival males for the possession of a mate. The successful males would reproduce themselves, the others not ; and so the characters making for success in this sexual struggle would be inherited and progressively developed generation by generation.

This was a reasonable hypothesis at the time it was propounded, in 1871 ; but gradually new facts came to light which it did not meet or cover. There were the numerous cases, apparently unknown to Darwin, of special adornments developed by both sexes and used in mutual display. There was the fact that many kinds of bright masculine colours are not used in display towards females at all, but only in threat against rival males. And there was the difficulty that in most song-birds the males are not only monogamous, but do not begin their courtship display until *after* they are mated for the season, so that the display could have nothing to do with the choice of mates.

For these and other reasons, Darwin's theory of Sexual Selection fell into disrepute in the early years of the present century. However, the facts remained, and continued to pose their questions. Gradually, as the result of a great deal of patient observation and a certain amount of experiment, the answers began to shape themselves, until today we can at least make general sense of the situation. Masculine weapons and bright display characters do owe their evolution to selection, though it is not Sexual Selection in the diagrammatic sense in which Darwin employed the term.

With regard to obvious weapons, the position is much as Darwin stated it. They have been evolved to fight for the possession of mates. Furthermore, as is to be expected, they are more striking when the battle is for a whole harem of females, for then the selective advantage to the victor, in the shape of having more descendants, is multiplied many times. The antlers of stags, the mane and heavy forequarters of the male bison, the huge size of the male elephant-seal are cases in point. But there was a further subtlety that has only come to light since Darwin's day. Fighting is exhausting and dangerous : so, while it will pay, biologically speaking, to fight for mates if fighting is necessary, it will pay still better if you can secure your object without a fight. Thus characters are evolved which serve for threat, as symbols of fighting strength, or even for bluff, in lieu of fighting strength.

Sometimes the weapons themselves are also threat-symbols. This is so, for instance, with stags' antlers. An unmated stag will not challenge a stag in possession of a harem if his rival's antlers are too big compared to his own. Similarly a baboon will bare his great canine dog-teeth to overawe an approaching rival. Sometimes, on the other hand, the threat-character has the special function of accentuating the general impression of size and strength, or giving a more horrific appearance. The male elephant-seal when angry inflates his proboscis ; the male mandrill has brilliant patches of colour on his cheeks, which serve the same purpose as the war-paint of savages ; the male bison and lion have size-enhancing manes.

And this may pass over into bluff. Male lizards will often fight, and various of them have bright colours which they display as threat-characters to save fighting. The most elaborate threats are found in the species which fight least. Thus one American lizard, when its territory is invaded by a rival, turns broadside on, thus showing its brilliant blue colouration, and compresses its body sideways so that it appears nearly twice its normal height. So successful is the bluff that in this species actual fighting hardly ever occurs.

Finally, there is another kind of threat which is very common in birds, being specially developed where the males stake out a large territory, as is the case in most song-birds. Round this territory the whole business of reproduction later centres. The females will only mate with males that are in possession of a territory ; the nest is built there, and in the territory the parents find food for their young. Males will fight each other viciously for the possession of a territory ; but they prefer not to have to fight, and so a male without a territory will often choose to go on in search of an unclaimed area rather than run the risks of battle. Accordingly it is biologically important to advertise the fact of being a territorial owner : it may keep a number of rivals from trespassing, and so obviate the need for fighting. At the same time, the advertisement has to be directed at the other sex also—here is a territory complete with husband, at the service of the first hen bird to take up her quarters there. As the advertisement has to serve two purposes at once—attraction to mates as well as warning to rivals—it must not be all threat, as with the elephant-seal's proboscis : it must be a mere symbol of possession, and concentrate on conspicuousness.

This appears to provide the origin of bird song, and also of some of the conspicuous colours of male song-birds. The yearly business of reproduction begins with the males staking out their territories : in migratory species, the males migrate first, and may be in possession of a territory for several days before there are any hen birds in the country at all. Once in possession, the males spend a considerable part of each day singing, which they generally do from one or other of a few conspicuous perches (or, in birds of open country, on the wing like a lark). The male's song is usually at its best before he has been joined by a female. Thus full song is a sign of a male in occupation of his territory. Another male will normally not wish to risk a serious fight by invading the territory, but will pass on, warned by the song, until he finds an unoccupied area. Conversely, the hen birds will be attracted by the song, for it advertises a potential home complete with husband. If there is another hen already in possession, a new-comer will have to fight ; if not, she simply settles in, and the pair is then normally mated up for the season.

Of course, everyone knows that birds may sing at other times of the year (as after the autumn moult) or in other circumstances (for instance, as a result of anger) ; it is also doubtless true that the individual bird usually sings because it 'feels good.' But this does not contradict the idea that song owes its evolutionary origin to the need for male conspicuousness on the territory ; and this indeed is the only view that will fit the facts.

The conspicuous colours of so many male song-birds, like Goldfinch or Cardinal or Blackbird, serve the same sort of purpose—they advertise the presence of the cock bird as prominently as possible.

Such is the broad general theory of the biological meaning of song and male conspicuousness in song-birds. When, however, we explore the detailed differences between different species, we run up against a great many other interesting points and prin-

N

ciples. One of the most striking things about song-birds (though it is one which naturalists do not seem to have bothered about until quite recently) is the degree of difference which we often find between the males of closely related species. In the thrush family, for instance, the primitive colouration is brown with spotted breast and underparts. But the American Robin has a chestnut red breast ; the European Blackbird is jet black all over, with golden bill ; the Ring Ouzel has a white neck-crescent on a chocolate ground-colour ; and so on. Or again, almost every species of finch and bunting is distinctively coloured in the male.

It is the word *distinctive* which gives us the key. The cock bird on its territory needs to be conspicuous ; but he needs also to be different from the cock birds of other species, especially those of closely related species, so that there shall be as little biological wastage as possible, through hybridisation, through hens of another species presenting themselves as potential mates, or through battles with other males which are not really rivals.

Distinctiveness to the ear is demanded as much as to the eye ; and accordingly we find that on the average related species differ as much in their songs as in their plumages. However, when we go into details, we are confronted with some cases where related species look very alike but have highly distinct songs. Why is this ? Such birds generally look alike because they need to escape detection, and have developed a colouration which matches their background—mottled brown for the pipits of our moors ; pale green for the leaf-warblers of our deciduous trees. The need for visual protection has overridden the need for visual distinctiveness. All the more reason, then, for accentuating the distinctiveness of what is left—namely song. In some cases most remarkable results have been effected by evolution. Thus the two European leaf-warblers, the Chiffchaff and the Willow-warbler, are almost exactly alike to look at, and often overlap in the same area. But while the latter has a typical warbler song, the Chiffchaff has a song of two repeated notes (from which it takes its name). Sometimes, however, it gives a brief and faint warble at the close of its chiff-chaffing, revealing that its song has been evolved from one like the Willow-warbler's—and evolved as it has just in order to be as different as possible.

Something of the reverse sort has taken place in birds in which visual protection is not so necessary—the Stonechat as against the Whinchat, for instance, the Yellow Bunting as against other buntings. Since, however, there is here no reason for special auditory protection, the songs may still be conspicuous, and will therefore still need to be fairly distinct.

However, all these elaborate characters of song and distinctive colouration, combining warning to rivals with attraction to mates, are territory advertisements, and not display or courtship in the usual sense. Territorial birds do have a real display, but this does not begin until *after* a female has settled in an occupied territory, and the pair is therefore mated up for the season or the brood. So obviously Darwin's original idea, that courtship had something to do with the selection of mates, will not work here. Yet the male's displays may be elaborate and often-repeated, with drooping of wings, fanning of tail, raising of crest, strange posturings and antics, and sometimes with the presentation of nest-material to the hen ; and when bright plumage is present they actually show it off to special advantage. They could not have been evolved unless they had some biological meaning and advantage. For a long time this puzzle remained unsolved. In the last few decades, however, we seem to have reached the solution. For one thing, they stimulate the female's readiness to mate ; and for another, they have a physiological effect on the reproductive organs and help to ripen and activate them.

Readiness to mate may be determined mainly by purely physiological agencies, such as the discharge into the bloodstream of hormones from the gland part of the reproductive organs : this is what happens to female cats or dogs or other lower mammals 'on heat.' In this state they are not only ready but eager for mating ; accordingly, no display by the male is needed—and none is to be found.

In birds, however, this does not happen ; there is no such special discharge of 'mating-readiness' hormones over a brief period, and readiness to mate is largely a psychological and emotional matter. Male display in birds is thus a device for stimulating the hen's emotions to a pitch at which she is ready to mate. Sometimes, as when one sees a peacock displaying all his magnificence before an apparently quite indifferent hen, this may seem a trifle far-fetched. However, we can remind ourselves that male display can be looked on as an advertisement, and in human

affairs manufacturers are willing to pay large amounts of hard
cash for advertisements, even though these may have no effect
on 99 people out of a hundred, or on 99 occasions out of a hundred. The only question that matters, both for the human
advertiser and the male bird, is whether the expenditure produces
results.

That is one point ; but there is another. It is now well-estab-
lished that in birds emotional stimuli, apparently acting through
the nervous system and the ductless glands, may help in the
ripening of the eggs. In doves, an isolated hen may even ripen
and lay eggs (though these, of course, are sterile) as the result of
seeing a male in another cage display at her. So a great deal of
the apparently fruitless display of male birds (as of cock sparrows
before the hens) is really serving to ripen the eggs in the female's
ovaries.

This would be of particular biological advantage in bad
seasons. It is well known that inclement weather may discourage
birds from breeding. When the weather has been cold and wet,
the number of eggs in a clutch is on the average lower than in good
seasons. So any stimulating effect of display on reproduction
would be of biological advantage both to the individual male,
through his leaving more descendants, and to the species.

There is a good deal of evidence that something of the same
sort happens in the males too, though here it is more the successful
rivalry with other males, coupled with the general excitement of
the breeding season, which produces the result.

Quite recently, a further interesting fact has come to light :
this effect of display and general emotional excitement on the
reproductive organs can spill over from the individual to the
group. In other words, if a number of birds are closely congre-
gated together in the breeding seasons, the effect of a male
courting his mate may have a stimulating effect on other females,
and in general the excitement caused by display is shared by the
group as a whole. In gulls, this has the effect of making egg-
laying a little earlier in large than in small colonies, and in con-
centrating it into a shorter time, which reduces the total toll of eggs
and young birds taken by enemies. In Fulmar Petrels it even
appears that when a new colony is established it must contain
more than a certain minimum number of birds before breeding
can occur : many very small new colonies have been observed

where the birds return year after year to their nesting ledges, go through their courtship, but do not lay—more mass stimulus is needed.

This group-stimulating effect at once accounts for the fact that so many birds conduct their display publicly, in crowded groups—either at the nest in various gregarious breeders, or at special places used for nothing else. These communal display-grounds are found in all kinds of birds, from Grouse to Birds of Paradise, from waders like the Ruff to song-birds like Manakins.

There are two other quite different kinds of bird courtship that must be mentioned, since they show so clearly the connection of type of display with mode of life. One is the exaggeration of purely masculine display, which we find in birds that are polygamous or promiscuous in their mating habits, instead of practising monogamy, at any rate for each breeding season, like those so far described. Pheasants, Peacocks, various Grouse, Birds of Paradise, Ruffs—in all these the females alone brood the eggs and look after the young, and therefore must be dull and inconspicuous, while the function of the males in reproduction is confined to securing as many mates as possible. Thus the males are accordingly very conspicuous, with an elaborate display. In the most striking examples, as in Ruffs, Blackcock, Sage Grouse, or some Birds of Paradise, the cock birds gather each spring on special display-grounds, where they spar and fight with each other and display at any female who visits the mating-ground. In these cases Darwin's original idea apparently holds good, and there is a real sexual selection, a hen choosing her mate according to her fancy, the males merely endeavouring to stimulate her to choose them by means of their display.

At the other end of the scale are those numerous kinds of birds where both cock and hen play equal or almost equal parts in all reproductive activities, both helping in building the nest, in brooding the eggs, and in feeding and looking after the young birds. In most of these birds, this equality is reflected in appearance and in display—both sexes having special bright plumage, and using it to show off to each other in displays which are mutual, both birds playing similar roles, instead of one-sidedly masculine, as in the courtship of a Bird of Paradise or a barnyard rooster.

Apparently in Darwin's time these mutual displays had not

been described. Yet they are very widely distributed. Great Crested Grebes pose in the most extraordinary ceremonies, showing off their handsome ruffs ; Fulmar Petrels shake their heads with mouths open wide, displaying a delicate mauve interior ; Puffins nod and nibble with their huge and brilliantly coloured outer beaks, which are grown specially each spring ; Egrets pose before each other in a mutual display of filmy lace aigrettes ; Dabchicks indulge in a loud duet ; Loons run races side by side in strangest poses.

The biological meaning of mutual display is in the main the same as that of one-sided display in territory birds—to stimulate readiness to mate and to ripen the reproductive organs. But it appears to have another function too. The mutual ceremonies seem to give great emotional satisfaction to the pair, and to act as a bond between them, helping to keep them together throughout the breeding season. This is biologically important, since the co-operation of both birds is necessary if the brood is to be hatched and reared. In confirmation of this, we find that mutual displays, instead of coming to an end when the eggs are laid, are often continued right through the breeding season, until the young can fend for themselves.

The same kind of thing, but extending through a lifetime instead of a season, and on a higher emotional plane, is to be seen in happy marriages in our own species.

I have already said something of the need for escaping notice (by enemies) against the need for attracting notice (from rivals and mates). This has led to a number of very interesting results. The two needs make contradictory biological demands—the one for inconspicuousness, the other for conspicuousness. The contradiction is reconciled in various quite different ways, according to the circumstances of the case. When the species is defenceless and lives in open surroundings where it is in urgent need of concealment from enemies, then, as with Skylarks, the colouration may be entirely protective in both sexes, and masculine display may be reduced to posturing, with drooping of wings and spreading of tail, without any brilliance to set it off. Or species that need protection may have some bright sexual plumage, and yet keep it hidden most of the time, flashing it out only for display, as with the yellow crest of the Goldcrest, or the white of the Bustard, or the orange pouches of the Prairie Chicken.

In most territorial birds, however, the need for concealment does not seem so great, and the males are generally brightly or strikingly coloured, as with finches, buntings, or blackbirds. As the hen has to brood the eggs, she is in greater need of concealment, and her plumage is correspondingly duller. Exceptions to this are found in birds which nest in holes, where the brooding female cannot be seen ; here, as in Nuthatches, the force of heredity can work unopposed by selection, and the bright plumage of the males is much more completely transferred to the females.

In ducks, the males neither brood the eggs nor help in looking after the young, and are therefore of much less value to the next generation than the females. Hence, if enemies are going to take a certain toll of the species, it is better that the males should suffer, and so, while the ducks must be made as inconspicuous as possible, it will be an advantage to the species (though not to the individual males !) for the drakes to be conspicuous. This is probably one reason for the bright colours of so many kinds of male ducks, which make their possessors conspicuous all the time, and not only for purposes of threat or courtship.

Finally, we reach a point where we can give quantitative expression to the forces working for conspicuousness. In monogamous territory birds, courtship display characters will have what we may call a fractional reproductive advantage—for instance, they may counteract the depressing effects of bad weather and stimulate the hen to lay rather more eggs than she otherwise would have done. But the advertisement characters which warn rivals off an occupied territory and attract a mate to it—these may have a whole unit of reproductive advantage : either a bird secures a territory and a mate, or it does not, while the display characters only come into play when a mate has already been secured. So, as their advantage is larger, it will override the need for concealment to a greater extent ; and in point of fact we find that the most conspicuous male characters, both of plumage and voice, are concerned with territorial advertisement, while those used exclusively in display are less conspicuous, or are only revealed during display itself.

Finally, when the species is polygamous or promiscuous, the unit reproductive advantage may be multiplied a number of times, if the male secures several mates. Nature here is playing for very high stakes, and we find that display characters (which are those that count in such cases) may be developed to such an extent that not merely is there little room left for concealment, but that they may actually hinder the cock bird in its day-to-day struggle for existence. The train of the Peacock is a hindrance ; and the wings of the male Argus Pheasant have become so entirely devoted to purposes of display that they are almost useless for flight.

I have spent so much of my space on birds because courtship is better developed in them than in any other group of animals, and also has been more thoroughly studied. But there are other kinds of animals with some sort of courtship display, and the type of display differs with the type of animal.

In the first place, we clearly shall not find anything in the nature of courtship in sedentary creatures like sea-anemones or sea-squirts ; nor in brainless and headless and eyeless creatures like jellyfish or sea-urchins ; nor, indeed, in any of those many types which loose their eggs and sperms at random to consummate their microscopic marriages in the waters of the sea. All these depend at best on some simple chemical stimulus : for instance, the discharge of eggs by one sea-urchin causes all other sea-urchins in the neighbourhood to liberate their sexual cells.

This, however, is a very wasteful process : an average sea-urchin has to produce some five or six million eggs every season. The first approach to courtship is seen in some sea-worms, in an attempt to reduce this wastage. The worms gather in swarms, and the males wriggle and contort themselves, probably also releasing some chemical substance. This primitive dance is a stimulus to the females to shed their eggs, which in its turn stimulates the males to release their sperm.

However, this can hardly be called courtship in any proper sense of the word. As we ascend the scale of animal life, the first performance meriting the name is found among the highest form of crustaceans, the crabs. Most even of these have no courtship —the males merely search lumberingly for a mate, approaching any smaller individual indiscriminately, and succeeding only by trial and error. But in one small family, the Fiddler-crabs, while the females have two tiny claws which act as spoons in feeding, the males have to be content with one, the other being enormously enlarged (sometimes weighing almost as much as the rest of the body) and often brightly coloured. These 'sex-claws,' as we may call them, are not primarily weapons ; the males use them in a form of display, rising on tip-toe and lifting and brandishing the giant claw. As one observer put it, 'they seem to be advertising their maleness.' Often several distinct species of Fiddler-crab may live in the same area ; but the colour of their claws and the precise method of brandishing them are then very different.

Crabs have very rudimentary eyes and brains. They seem to be able to recognise only a very limited number of different situations—food, danger, sex, and a few others. What the waving of the giant claw does is to advertise, in the simplest possible way, the existence of a sex-situation. And the difference between the claw-display of different crabs is to emphasise the separateness of the sex-situation for each species. In other words, we have here the beginnings, but in very rudimentary form, of the type of advertisement-display connected with territory in birds, with its conspicuousness on the one hand, its distinctiveness on the other.

Our next group up the scale is the spiders ; and here the value to the male of advertising a sex-situation is particularly high— because otherwise he may be mistaken for a food-situation and eaten, since the female is much bigger than he, and equipped with a brain which cannot go much beyond treating any small moving object of an animal nature as prey to be captured. There is one group of spiders that stalks its prey by sight, and another, of course, which is virtually blind and traps insects in a web. In the stalkers the male display is visual—an elaborate dance, made more conspicuous by patches of bright colour on some of his limbs, and as different as possible from the behaviour of a fly or other small insect. As he approaches, gesticulating, the female will often rush at him as if to seize him, and he will retreat. So the display goes on, until at last the female is persuaded that this is a sex-situation and not a food-situation. In the web-spiders it is no use appealing to sight : it is touch which is the master-sense. So here the males crawl up to the edge of the web and vibrate one of the strands—again in a special way, quite unlike the vibration caused by the struggles of a trapped insect. Spider courtship is thus unique—it is concerned not only with stimulating the female's readiness to mate, but with masculine self-preservation.

Next we reach the insects, that astonishing group which includes more than three quarters of all animal species, and lives by elaborate instincts, hardly complicated by intelligence. It is among insects that the most bizarre specialisations of life and behaviour are to be found, and their courtships are no exception. Male grasshoppers of one family advertise a sex-situation by means of sound—but they do it with their legs. A kind of cricket anticipates the human male by presenting candy to the object of his attentions—but he produces it himself, in the shape of the sweet secretion of a special gland on his back. This is normally covered with a flap ; but when he approaches a potential mate he lifts this lid and invites her to partake. Another insect called Hepialus resorts to perfume. Under his body the male has two little pockets lined with glands that produce a sweet scent. His front legs have ceased to be legs, and their feet have been converted into a sort of brush or powder-puff. In courting a female, he puts these 'hands' into his pockets, thus covering them with scent, and then vibrates them at the female, so as to dust her with the perfume. Then there are the strange little flies called Empids. These are carnivorous, eating other insects, and in some of them the males present a captured prey to their mates. In certain species the gift is made more conspicuous by being embedded in a large 'balloon' of glistening bubbles, secreted by a special gland : this conspicuousness doubtless serves to advertise the fact of a sexual situation, complete with potential husband and juicy gift, to the females. Finally, in some species the advertisement is all that is left. The male flies parade their glistening balloons without any captured prey ; but sometimes they make them more conspicuous by inserting a flower-petal or other bright object. If you scatter little bits of coloured paper, the males will pounce on these and use them to adorn their balloons.

Sometimes it is the female which advertises the sexual situation by a special odour : and then the males may evolve amazing organs of smell, like the huge branched antennæ of certain moths like the Oak-eggar, far more sensitive even than the nose of a dog, by which they can discover the females at a distance of miles.

In the little fruit-flies called Drosophila (famous because of their employment in research in Genetics) there is a stimulati : display by the males, which vibrate their wings in a special way before their mates. That this stimulates the females to a general readiness to mate, rather than leading to a real selection of one male rather than another, was shown by an ingenious experiment of Professor Sturtevant's. When he cut off males' wings and put the males singly in bottles with a female apiece, the number of successful matings was reduced, and the time before mating happened much lengthened. But when he put a wing-clipped male in a bottle with a female and a normal male, not only was the time before mating quite short, but the wing-clipped male was successful almost as often as his intact rival. In other words, the wing-display of the normal male had induced in the female a general readiness to mate, and then it was more or less a matter of accident which male she mated with.

But now we must get back to the vertebrates. There are a few fish with male display—all of them, as might be expected, species which have internal fertilisation, instead of discharging eggs and sperms into the water. Male Newts have large and brightly coloured crests, and an elaborate display, in which a stimulating scent is wafted at the female by movements of the tail. Frogs and toads advertise a sexual situation by sound—the first employment of true voice in the evolutionary history of life. Little is known of the display of reptiles : in lizards, as I have already mentioned, it seems to be entirely concerned with threat or bluff towards rivals of the same sex.

Finally, we come to our own group—the Mammals. From our point of view they fall into three groups of very different size : —our own species ; the primates, or apes and monkeys ; and all the rest. Beginning with the third group, the lower mammals, we have first the fact, already mentioned, that their sexual life is much more directly under physiological control, less under psychological control, than that of birds. Of course, birds have hormones just as mammals have emotions ; but the relative importance of emotions is greater in birds, of hormones in mammals.

Thus (if I may over-simplify the question a little) while in birds elaborate displays are required as an external stimulus to induce readiness to mate, in mammals this is not necessary since the stimulus is provided from within by the periodic turning on of the tap, so to speak, of the female sex-hormone. Accordingly emotionally stimulating display is reduced to a minimum and all that is left for the males to do is to mate—or to fight, threaten or bluff for the possession of mates. The evolutionary result appears in such grotesques as the male Warthog. In nocturnal mammals, the males often advertise their presence vocally. The most familiar example, as town-dwellers know only too well, is the cat ; but there are many other examples, such as Bush-babies and Hyenas.

I have already given examples of organs of combat, threat and bluff in lower mammals. When we come to the monkeys and apes, we find these in great profusion. Many male primates have their faces rendered conspicuous and impressive and indeed horrific in one way or another—by mustachios ; beards ; ruffs ; great fleshy folds as in the orang-utan ; ivory white gums and patches above the eyes which are revealed only when the animal is angry, as with Gelada baboons ; coloured fur, as with the Diana monkey ; or coloured skin, as in the horrifying Mandrill, with his blue and scarlet cheeks and nose. The male Mandrill is of some psychological interest, for apparently no one has ever witnessed in him any expression of emotion which could be construed as tender—nothing but rage, anger, and hostility ; he is also about twice as heavy as the female. This is the logical outcome of an evolution stressing combat at the expense of courtship.

There is another fact of considerable interest about the primates ; whereas the colours of lower mammals are entirely restricted to shades between black and white, and between yellow, russet and brown, in primates we find blues, violets, greens and true reds as well. This is without question to be correlated with the fact that all lower mammals (if we may judge from all those which have been investigated) are colour-blind, whereas primates can see in colour. If birds were colour-blind, all their display plumage would be in pigments which made striking tone-contrasts with each other ; we should never have witnessed such gorgeous productions of nature as the Peacock's train or the glories of the Birds of Paradise, which depend mainly on true colour-contrast.

Finally, as scientific observers interested in fact and undeterred by ugliness, we must note the frequent presence in lower primates of strikingly conspicuous posteriors. Sometimes these are found in the males, as with the pastel shades of the Mandrill ; more frequently in the females, as in Chimps. The absence of this particular type of sex-character in the human species is one of the major differences between man and lower primates. The change is correlated with man's adoption of the erect posture, which in its turn has focused sexual interest on the face and the front of the body. As J. B. S. Haldane has stressed, this was one of the most far-reaching changes in our evolution—a new mental attitude growing out of a new physical attitude, and leading to a long new chain of consequences in our behaviour and our standards of beauty.

Indeed, man, though so closely related in structure to the apes, differs radically from all lower animals in his sexual life. For one thing, he is fully sexed throughout the whole of his adult life. Birds and all other vertebrates, for instance, pass through one or more neuter periods each year, during which their interest in sex is *nil*, or at best very minor. In monkeys and apes there is a tendency to extend the periods of emotional interest in sex ; and in man this tendency has been pushed to its limit.

As regards sex-characters, two curious trends have appeared in the later stages of human evolution. One is the tendency for the male human being to shave, even if shaving involves immense discomfort. There can be no doubt that the human beard (including under that term mustachios and whiskers), like that of monkeys, originated as a masculine threat-character, concerned solely or primarily with warning, intimidating, or bluffing rivals, and scarcely at all with any stimulative effect on the female. The tendency to its artificial removal is an indication of a decreased importance of sexual threat in our human affairs, and of an increased importance of personal choice of mates, and in general of the finer shades of personality and their expression. When beards or portions thereof have survived, they have often been cultivated as the expression or symbol of some non-sexual characteristic—a Vandyck beard for the artist, a long grey beard for the sage, a moustache for the soldier, and so forth.

The other and biologically even more remarkable tendency is that towards the enhancement and advertisement of feminine more than of masculine beauty—a tendency the exact opposite of that found in almost all lower animals in which the sexes differ

in their adornments. This tendency has been effected partly
through heredity—in woman's long hair, delicacy of feature, and
beauty of figure—but has been since time immemorial reinforced
by art.   Art has accentuated in the woman features which she
shares with men, like prominence of eyes, or colour of lips and
cheeks and nails ; or it has accentuated her inherited differences
of figure, as by tight-lacing, or bustles, bodices or brassières ; or
it has provided new distinctive beauty and conspicuousness, as in
so many features of women's dress throughout all history.

This seems to be the result of another unique feature of human
reproduction.   In all lower animals the only measure of success
in mating is the number of offspring produced.   But in our own
species there is, in addition to and sometimes in virtual exclusion
of this biological measure, a social measure of mating success, in
the shape of social position, wealth, comfort to be gained during
the individual's lifetime, or transmissible to his or her children
by social inheritance.   Not only this, but during most of human
evolution, especially in its later stages, women have stood to gain
more by a 'good marriage' than have men.   Men inherit the
family name, men can carve out their own futures, and so when
it comes to finding a mate, men can rely more on their position or
their prestige, their abilities or their achievements ; women have
in general been the selected, not the selectors, and have had to
rely more on their immediate attractiveness and their beauty,
natural or artificial.   It will be interesting to see what effect in
the long run will be exerted by the economic emancipation of
women : human nature is so complex that prophecy is difficult,
but probably it will tend towards less difference between men and
women in the matter of sexual adornment—but whether this will
be brought about by less finery and attention to appearance for
women, or more for men, is hard to say.   Perhaps we can hazard
that this too will depend on economic factors, and that if we get
real economic equality between the sexes, and also real prosperity
and plenty for all, we shall find both men and women blossoming
out in beautiful clothes.

Display, whether courtship-display before mates or threat-display
against rivals, is biologically speaking a product of two different
components—reproduction by means of separate sexes, together
with a psychological development that has reached beyond a

certain minimum level of sense-organs and brain. All these posturings, these songs, this gorgeous plumage, this distinctiveness of voice or appearance, these expressions of hostile excitement—they are all devices for projecting into the mind of another individual the fact that a sexual situation exists. At the lowest level the devices are the simplest and crudest symbols—an exciting odour, a huge claw brandished aloft. But as sense-organs become more elaborate and emotional life more complex, the display devices follow suit, until they come to constitute a large fraction of the beauty and the exciting strangeness of life. All the most elaborate beauty of birds, all their songs ; the antlers of deer, with their recurrent growth and shedding, which if they were not familiar would be one of the most astonishing facts of nature; the masculine grandeur of lion or bison ; the cheerful music of frogs and toads, of grasshoppers and crickets ; the bizarre faces of our monkey cousins ; *haute couture* and the huge cosmetics industry—these are all in their various ways the product of this trend of evolution to project this or that aspect of a sexual situation into the consciousness of potential or actual mate or rival.

The type of display varies with the kind of sexual situation and the animal's general way of life. The Peacock or the Bird of Paradise reminds us that in certain conditions beauty is of more avail than brutality ; the mutual courtship of Grebe or Egret, with pleasures shared by both sexes, shows that one-sided masculinity is not an evolutionary necessity, and that sex-equality can be in some conditions the correct biological solution. It is at least entertaining to speculate as to what possible new beauties and shared delights sex-display, if sublimated and consciously guided, and rooted in economic prosperity and equality, may have in store for the human species, which is still in the very early stages of its evolutionary career.

Le Plus Bel Amour de Don Juan

By J. Barbey d'Aurevilly

Translated for the Saturday Book by Gerard Hopkins

[Jules Barbey d'Aurevilly was born in 1808 and died in 1889. More than in the lives of most literary men these terminal dates are important for a consideration of his work. He spanned almost a century of artistic revolution, and in his single person exemplified tendencies that waxed and waned through several generations. Balzac was the passion of his youth, Bourget the friend of his old age. Throughout his working career he was dominated by two strong tendencies which are to be found isolated in other writers. The romanticism of the early nineteenth century—and especially the Satanic romanticism of Byron—continued to be an influence upon his imagination to the very end. Nowhere is it more strongly marked than in the collection of short stories entitled *Les Diaboliques* (from which *Don Juan* is taken), which was not published until 1874. Parallel with this romantic mood there runs another, of intellectual interest in, and analysis of, character and conduct.

The chief weakness in his not inconsiderable achievement as a writer of fiction derived from a failure to find the perfect balance between these primary sources of his inspiration, a failure which was accentuated by the increasing identification of his work with the Normandy of his birth. The great 'regional' novels of his prime, *L'Ensorcelée*, *Le Chevalier des Touches*, *Un Prêtre Marié* and *Ce Qui Ne Meurt Pas*, treat psychological problems against a background of dark and mysterious natural forces, and in them, as in most of what he wrote, the central theme tends to be swamped by the tumultuous setting. The story here presented in an English dress is a very fair example of this danger. The scene is built up with enormous and encrusted care, but the incident which is

designed to give it point seems, when at last it emerges, almost too
slight to bear the huge weight of 'atmosphere' upon which
d'Aurevilly has lavished so much conscientious labour. Still,
he occupied an important minor place in French nineteenth
century literature, and if this story succeeds in awakening interest
in a novelist who is scarcely known on this side of the Channel, it
will have served a useful purpose.   GERARD HOPKINS.]

> *An innocent heart is the*
> *Devil's choicest morsel.*

I

'D'you mean to say the monster isn't dead ?'
     'He's far, God knows, from being that !' I answered, and
added hurriedly, remembering her churchgoing proclivities, 'it
is, indeed, by God's own ordinance that he lives on, dear lady.
Yes, he is still with us and, what is more, has elected to settle
down in the parish of Sainte-Clotilde, that most aristocratic of all
neighbourhoods.   The King is dead !   Long live the King !—as
we used to say before the fragile porcelain of our ancient Mon-
archy was shattered.   Don Juan is a king whose throne no
democrats will ever shake !'
     'I had forgotten for a moment,' she replied, as though to
prove her own sagacity, 'that Satan never dies.'
     'He even . . .'
   - 'Who, Satan ? . . .'
     'No, Don Juan . . . made one in a charming supper-party
not longer than three days ago . . . but where, you'll never
guess. . . .'
     'Doubtless, at your wicked Maison d'Or.'
     'Oh come, dear lady !—it is many years since such a place
could provide diversion for His Mightiness.   The great Don
Juan has always somewhat resembled that notorious monk
Arnaud of Brescia who, so say the chroniclers, lived only on the
life-blood of men's souls.   With such scarlet does our friend of
choice give colour to his wine, and it is long since vintage of that
quality could be found in a mere haunt of the frail and gay !'
     'I suspect,' said she, with irony, 'that he found his entertain-
ment in a Convent of the Benedictine nuns, those ladies who . . .'
     'Are vowed to a life of Perpetual Adoration ? . . . and in
o

that conviction you are right. For the adoration which our Satanic gentleman inspires is, indeed, something that knows no end.'

'I find you, for a Catholic, not a little prone to blasphemy,' she answered slowly, and in her words there was a tone of modesty affronted. 'Spare me, I beg, the details of the party if, as I imagine, this story of Don Juan is but a pretext to discuss your flaunting hussies.'

'No pretext, I swear. The hussies in question, if hussies they be, are none of mine . . . alas !'

'Have done, sir !'

'Permit me in all modesty : they were . . ."

'The *mille è tre* ?' she interrupted with a sudden change of mood all curious now for what I had to tell and, once again, almost her charming self.

'Not all of them, not all . . . a bare dozen only. In such numbers, you will see, was safety . . .'

'. . . And danger too !'

'You know, as well as I, how few will over-fill the boudoir of the Comtesse de Chiffrevas. Great dramas have been played upon that stage—but it is small !'

"What !' cried she, all wonder: "and was this supper, then, served in a boudoir ?"

'Yes, dear lady, and why not ? Soldiers eat with a good appetite on the field of battle. This party for My Lord Don Juan was designed to be no ordinary festival, and what worthier setting could it have than the scene of his past triumphs, made sweet with memories instead of orange flowers ? A pretty conceit, surely ; rich with a tender melancholy ! No ball for those awaiting execution, this, but a supper for their entertainment. . . .'

'And Don Juan ?' she asked, much as Orgon exclaims 'and Tartuffe ?' in the play.

'Don Juan was delighted, and supped well : *Himself alone, watched by their many eyes !* . . . Don Juan in the person of one well known to you . . . of, indeed, no less a hero than Comte Jules-Amédée-Hector de Ravila de Raviles.'

'That man !' she cried ; 'you do well to name him thus !'

And though she was of an age to have outdistanced dreams she fell, this fiery daughter of the Church, to dreaming of Comte

Jules-Amédée-Hector—that man of Juan's race, the race that never dies, to which, though God gives not the world, he has permitted Satan to give it in His stead.

2

What I had just told the aged Marquise Guy de Ruy was no more than the literal truth. Scarcely three days had passed since twelve ladies of the virtuous Faubourg Saint-Germain (have no fear, I shall not name you !) not one of whom, if one may credit gossip of the drawing-room, but had granted her highest favours (to use a charming, if outmoded phrase) to Comte Ravila de Raviles, had been moved by the singular idea of inviting him to a supper—*at which there should compete no other man*—in celebration, well . . . of what ? On that point they were silent. In such a scheme there was a note of dash and daring. Though, taken singly, women may be cowards, they can, united, brave the greatest dangers. Alone, not one of all those present would probably have ventured on an hour of intimacy with Comte Jules-Amédée-Hector ; yet now, together, in their phalanx ranked, they thought nothing of forming a Mesmer's chain about the dangerous electric charge stored up in Ravila de Raviles. . . .

'What a name ! . . .'

'A name, dear lady, writ in the stars !'

The Comte de Ravila de Raviles—who, let me add by way of parenthesis, had ever lived a life in keeping with the high, Imperial sound of that great natal heritage—seemed to incarnate the sum of all seducers known to us in history or romance ; and the Marquise Guy de Ruy—an old, embittered woman whose blue eyes were less cold only than her heart, less piercing only than her wit—knew well that in an age when women count, each day, for less, she, of all the world, could fairly claim to hold Don Juan in her memory. But the Don Juan she had known had been, alas, only the hero of Act Five. The Prince de Ligne, for all his bright intelligence, could not envisage Alcibiades at fifty and, in this matter of age, the mantle of Alcibiades seemed like to fall upon the shoulders of the Comte de Ravila. Like d'Orsay, that dandy who recalled a bronze by Michael Angelo and kept his beauty till his dying day, he had been blessed with just those looks which mark the race of Juan and do not descend, as with the ruck of

mortals, from sire to son, but flower here and there, often at long
intervals, in one or other of the human family.

His was Beauty's self—insolent, gay, Imperial—in short,
Juanesque. That word alone expresses it beyond all need of mere
description ; and—had he made some compact with the Devil ?
—it still was his. Yet God would not be cheated, and already
life's tiger-claws had seamed the Olympian brow rose-garlanded
by many lips ; already on the pagan head there showed the first
white hairs, dread heralds of the onset of Barbarian hordes, fore-
shadowing the death-throes of the Empire. He wore them with
a high serenity born of a pride that fed upon the consciousness of
power. But to the hearts of all those women who had loved him,
the sight of them struck sometimes with a sense of searing melancholy. Who knows but what they read upon his face the tale of
their own mounting years ?—a tale that for them all would end
in that last fearsome supper with the cold Commander relentless
in his marble whiteness, after which naught would remain for
them but Hell—the Hell of age which marks the threshold of
eternal nothingness ! And so, perhaps, before they had to share
with him that last and bitter meal, they planned to offer him
another, of their own supreme confection.

For supreme it was, exquisite in taste and delicacy, redolent
of patrician luxury, a thing of carefully devised surprise, ingenious
fantasy ; the most charming, the most delicious, the most appe-
tising, the most intoxicating, and, above all, the most original
supper that had ever been concocted. That it was original who
could doubt ? Most feasts are an expression of gay hearts, of a
desire to find excuses for enjoyment ; but this was born of
memories, regrets, almost, one might say, of irremediable despair
—but of despair in full dress, hiding its tormented face behind a
mask of laughter, of despair which had deliberately willed this
festive night, this one last act of madness, this final flutter of the
wings of youth, this ultimate debauch without a morrow.

And those who offered it, so little marked by the modesty of
that high Society to which they all belonged, must have felt as
did Sardanapalus on his pyre, when round his couch were piled,
to die with him, his women and his slaves, his horses and his
jewels and all the splendour of his wanton life. They, too, had
heaped upon the brazier of this feast all the full opulence of theirs.
To it they brought what store they had of beauty, wit and skill,

their panoplies of gems, the trophies of their power, pouring all out in one last ecstasy upon the mounting flames.

The man at whose feet they glowed and glittered was more to them than Asia to the Eastern king. For him they exercised their every wile, as women never had for any man, for any roomful of assembled brilliance ; flaunting a jealousy which, in the world, they hid and now need hide no longer, knowing—how could they not—that each of them had owned him once, seeing in shared and parcelled shame no cause for blushing. . . . None there but struggled to outdo her sisters in carving, for all to see, his name upon her heart.

To him that evening brought a pleasure full and rounded, the very sum of all delight. For was he not at once a Sultan and a priest confessing these fair nuns ? Half way down the board he sat, a king, and master of his slaves, with, facing him, the Comtesse de Chiffrevas—in that boudoir of the peach-silk walls which, could they have 'peached' in very truth, might have had such strange, bad tales to tell—and looked, with eyes whose colour was the icy blue of Hell—though more than one poor soul had fancied it the blue of Heaven—upon the glittering twelve. Adorned with all the skill their woman's genius could devise, with, there before them, crystal and flowers and lighted candles, they ran the gamut of life's full-blown charms, sounding all the notes of opulence, from the scarlet of the opened rose to the dull gold of sweet and pendent grapes.

In such a company was no green tenderness of youth, nothing to call to mind those 'misses' whom Byron loathed, smelling of bread and butter, with figures yet unformed. None there but showed in curve and colour the mellow wealth of autumn, the rich glow and savour of the ripened fruit ; full, gracious bosoms regally displayed, great cameo clasps and bare, resplendent shoulders, arms superbly formed yet lacking naught of strength, muscled as those of Sabine mothers who struggled with the men of Rome and might have grasped and stayed the moving wheels of life's great chariot.

I have spoken much of fantasies. Not the least charming was that which had ordained a staff of women servers only, that no discordant note might mar the harmony of an event where women ruled alone and did the honours of the feast. . . . Thus might My Lord Don Juan—of the branch of Ravila—plunge his hot

glances in a sea of flesh which glowed with all the life that may
be found in Rubens's rich and virile canvases. But not alone his
eyes found ravishment. His pride, as well, could play at will
within the ether, limpid yet suffused, exhaled by all those gathered
hearts. For deep down, in despite of those who may think otherwise, Don Juan is a man who loves the spirit, resembling in that
the great Satanic Majesty who ranks souls higher even than bodies,
and makes of them the chosen merchandise of Hell.

Brilliant, aristocratic, representative of all that is best in the
Faubourg Saint-Germain, though, on this night of nights, as
impudent as pages at the Court of France—when France still had
a Court and pages to adorn it—these ladies played with verve
and nimbleness a game of wit incomparable. Never, they felt,
even in the happiest moments of their past, had they so shone.
They knew a sense of power beyond what they had ever thought
to have. The joy of it, the consciousness of heightened living,
and, too, the havoc wrought on high-strung nerves by all the
adjuncts of the scene—the gleam of lights, the penetrating scent
of flowers swooning in the rising warmth of perfumed bodies,
the stimulus of heady wines, the thought of the strange feast
which did not lack that spice of sinfulness demanded by a famous
lady, once of Naples, to make exquisite her iced champagne, the
dizzying thought that they had planned and plotted to make real
a festival which had, for all its lovely shamelessness, no touch of
coarse or crude, but stayed in every detail true to the mannered
foibles of their age, a festival where not a gown was disarranged
though hearts might beat with joy of ancient fires renewed—all
these things combined at once to stretch, though not to break, the
harp-strings of their singing hearts, so that they sounded notes of
heavenly sweetness, and chords that bettered words. . . . Surely
no stranger sight could be imagined ? Will Ravila one day write
out in full this curious chapter in the memoirs of his past ? . . .
Who knows ? . . . but sure it is no other pen could compass
it. . . .

I was not—as I told the Marquise Guy de Ruy—myself a
guest, and if I can narrate some details of what happened, that
is because I had them from no less a person than Ravila who,
with the indiscretion which, as the world knows, marks the whole
race of Juan, was at pains one evening to recount them.

3

It was late—or rather, early. Dawn was breaking. High on the ceiling, and at one point of the curtains of rose silk that hung hermetically closed against the light, a spot of opal radiance formed and glowed, an eye, it seemed, all curious to see what strangeness was afoot within the shut and brilliant room. Weariness had laid its hands upon the female guardians of that Table Round, those revellers who, but an hour ago, had shone and sparkled. Inevitably, to every feast there come such moments when exhaustion, bred of emotion and long hours of pleasure, touches the tousled heads, the flushed and pallid cheeks, the heaviness of shadowed eyes, nor spares the thickened, guttering flames of all the many candles which look, for all the world, like flowers overblown on sculptured stalks of gilt and bronze.

For long the conversation had been general and full of life, struck, like a tennis ball, about the table. But now it eddied, broken in flecks and fragments, so that few words were audible in the tuneful hum of high-bred voices twittering in the sweet confusion of a choir of birds at dawn upon the confines of a wood. But one rose suddenly above the din—high-pitched, imperious, a shade impertinent, as befits a Duchess. To Ravila it spoke in words that must have been the sequel and the end of some hushed talk between them, which none of all the ladies there had heard, so deep was each in conversation with her neighbour.

'You, the Don Juan of these times, should really tell which of your many loves has flattered most your pride as one much sought of women, the love which, looking back on all your life, seems now its fine perfection. . . .'

The question, and the voice which carried it, cut sharply through the scattered talk, and a quick silence fell.

She who spoke was Duchess of *****—let the mask of asterisks remain unraised, though you may know her whom I mean when I say that in all the Faubourg Saint-Germain no woman has a paler skin, nor hair more gold, nor blacker eyes, nor pencilled brows more amber-sweet. . . . At the Count's right hand she sat, as might a just man at the Throne of God ; for was he not the god of this great feast, though not this evening had he made his enemies his footstool ? Slim she was, and dreamlike as a flowing arabesque, or fairy queen in velvet robe of green and shimmering silver, whose long train curled about her chair like the serpent's tail of fairest Melusine.

'Yes, indeed !' said the Comtesse de Chiffrevas, as though as mistress of that house she wished to urge compliance with the wish. 'Tell us which of all the loves you have inspired or felt, you most would like—if time could be reversed—to live again !'

'Which would I not !' said Ravila, speaking as might a Roman Emperor whom long indulgences had left insatiate. He raised his glass—not one of those silly barbarous objects which nowadays we are content to use, but a long, slim crystal of old days, fit chalice for great wine, of the kind known as a *flûte*, perhaps by reason of the heavenly melodies it sets a-singing in our hearts. Then with a glance he gathered all the eyes that gemmed the board's fair girdle, and :

'Still,' he said, and set it down again with an air of melancholy strange to see in a Nebuchadnezzar whose only grass so far had been the seasoned salads of the Café Anglais—'still, you are right to say that there is always *one* among the emotions of a lifetime which shines more brightly in the memory as age advances ; one, which is worth the sum of all the rest !'

'The diamond of price,' remarked the Comtesse de Chiffrevas dreamily. Maybe she was reading secrets in the flashing brilliance of her own.

'And the story of my country,' murmured the Princesse Jablé . . . who had been born in the foothills of the Urals. 'I mean that famous, legendary stone which turned from pink to black, yet was a diamond still, and shone with brighter radiance when its colour changed.' This she said with a flash of that gypsy charm which so becomes her—for gypsy she is, even though for love the handsomest Prince of all the Polish emigration married her ; even though she wears the royal air as surely as though the blood of the Jagellons flowed in her veins.

There was a clamour of raised voices : 'Yes !' they cried, one and all ; 'tell us of that, dear Count !' and passion sounded in their suppliant tones, while expectation set their bodies tingling. They sat, a close-packed pyramid of beauty, some cheek in hand, their elbows on the table, some leaning backward in their chairs, their lips concealed by spreading fans. From the gay battery of their speaking eyes they riddled him with questions.

'If that, then, be your will,' replied the Count, using the careless elegance of one who knows that waiting spurs desire.

'It is,' announced the Duchess, keeping her gaze upon the sharp edge of her golden fruit-knife, as some Turkish despot might have looked upon a scimitar.

'Listen, then, to my story,' said he, still with his air of quiet indifference.

They watched him, and they waited. They devoured him with their eyes. All women thrill to a tale of love ; but who knows—the peculiar charm of what he was to tell may have lain, for each of them, in the thought that perhaps this story might turn out to be her own. . . . They knew him for too great a gentleman, bred in too high a world, to name the lady of his narrative, to stress, where secrecy should rule, the tell-tale points of evidence. And this certain knowledge served but to inflame their curiosity. Hope even more than eagerness now made them hang upon his lips.

Vain, they feared a rival in this record of what had been the fairest exploit in a life made bright by many ! . . . Once more the ageing Sultan was to throw his kerchief. . . . No hand would pick it up, but she who knew it for her own would treasure silent happiness within her heart.

Buoyed by this hidden faith, they listened, and what they heard came with a shock of thunder to them all.

4

'I have often heard it maintained, by many moralists of wide reading in the book of life,' began the Comte de Ravila, 'that the love which most strongly holds a man is not his first, is not his last, as many would affirm ; it is his second. But all general views of love are true, and all are false. What I have just said does not hold in my own experience. . . . The story you have asked of me, and which I am about to tell, belongs to the happiest period of my youth. At that time I was no longer what is generally termed a young man, though I was a man still young who—to use a phrase much loved by my uncle, the Knight of Malta—had 'closed his years of wandering.' At that time, in the full flower of my manhood, I enjoyed the most intimate of relationships—for that is how, in Italy, they would so charmingly describe the fact—wit' a lady who is known to, and admired by, all of you. . . ."

Impossible to describe to those who did not see it the glance which, as he spoke, passed between the ladies as they sat drinking in the tempter's words.

'She was,' continued Ravila, 'blessed with all qualities. She was young, she was rich, she came of a great family ; she had beauty, wit, the sensitiveness of the artist, and, with it all, she was as natural as only those born in your world can be. . . . What she hoped for, what she sought, was to please and serve me, to be at once the best of friends, the most kind of mistresses.

'I was not, I think, the first man she had loved. Once already she had given her heart—and not to her husband had she made the gift ! But that affair had been all virtue and rapture, all high ideals and platonic affection, a thing more violent than satisfying, a preparation merely for the love which, always, in such cases, treads upon its heels : an experiment, as it were, in passion, analogous to that "white Mass" said by young priests to ensure they shall make no mistake when first they come to celebrate in sober truth and with the Consecrated Elements. . . . At the time that I came into her life this white Mass was the sum of her experience. I was to be the true Celebration, and she conducted it, like a Cardinal, with all the pomp of Rites.'

At these words a smile fluttered round the listening circle, a delicious flicker of the lips, like the spreading ripple on the glassy surface of a lake. . . . It came, it passed, the lovely tribute of a moment.

'Truly, she was a being apart,' went on the Count : 'rarely have I known such true goodness, such gentleness of spirit, such delicacy of mind. They showed, these qualities, even in her passion—and passion, as you know, is not always either kind or gentle. . . . Never have I seen a woman less given to intrigue, less influenced by considerations either of prudishness or coquetry —both of them weaknesses too often seen commingled in her sex, like the double strands of a skein which a cat has tangled. No, there was nothing of the cat in her. Hers was what the damned tribe of scribblers, who debauch us with their phrases, would call a primitive nature with a patina of civilisation, of which she displayed, however, only the charming gewgaws and never those small corruptions which we are tempted, sometimes, to find still more attractive. . . .'

'Was she dark ?'—the Duchess, who was growing impatient at this splitting of metaphysical hairs, put the question abruptly.

'You betray a certain lack of subtlety,' replied Ravila, intent upon a fine distinction. 'Yes, you might call her dark, for never have I seen hair of such pure jet, so ebon-bright, clothing the lovely curve of any woman's head. Yet her skin was fair, and'— added the master-critic who had studied womankind to other ends than those of portraiture, 'it is the skin and not the hair which determines the category of complexion. She was fair, let us say, though with hair that was as black as night. . . .'

The golden heads of those about the table, whose claim to fairness lay but in their locks, moved imperceptibly. It was obvious that their owners were already losing interest in the tale.

'As black as night,' he repeated : 'brooding above the radiance of dawn. For in her cheeks there showed that freshness of pure pink and white so rarely seen ; nor had it taken harm from the Paris life of darkened rooms wherein for many years her ways had lain, a life that burns, so often, natural roses in its candle flames. Hers had but caught the glow and shone, as did her lips, with a full-blooded red. The double splendour well accorded with the rubies which she wore upon her brow, for those were days when women set tiaras in their hair. The effect was ever of three sanguine jewels, for such was the burning ardour of her eyes that none might tell their colour. Slim, yet strongly built, her noble figure might have graced the wife of some colonel of cuirassiers—her husband, at the time, commanded but a squadron of light cavalry—and she had, for all her air of breeding, the healthy vigour of a peasant girl who drinks the sun in through her skin ; and in her soul, as in her veins, that sunlight pulsed, for ever ready to shine through. . . . But now comes the strange part of my tale. With all her strength and her simplicity, her nature purpurine and pure as was the blood that flooded through her cheeks and tinged her arms, she was—who could have guessed ?—a blunderer in the arts of love. . . .'

At this a few eyes fell, to be raised a moment later bright with mischief.

'As much a blunderer in the arts of love as she was careless in

her life'—Ravila said, but satisfied their curiosity no further.
'The man she loved had, therefore, to be for ever impressing on
her two great lessons she had never learned . . . to keep from
lowering her shield before a world ceaselessly armed and ignorant
of mercy, and in the intimacy of love to practise that great art
by which love lives. Love she knew, but not the art of love,
differing in this from most women whose knowledge is but of the
art. To understand and use aright the lessons of *The Prince*, one
must, in the first place, be a Borgia. Borgia came first and
Machiavelli later ; one was the poet the other the critic. And
she was no Borgia, but an honest woman in love, and as simple,
for all her staggering beauty, as any little girl who scoops up
water in her hand when she is thirsty and, in her haste, lets all
escape. . . .

'There was something almost charming in the contrast
between this shy awkwardness of hers and the deep passion of
her woman's heart. None, seeing her in the great world, would
have suspected this difference, would have dreamed that one
who loved as she and knew the happiness of love so lacked the
power to give back what she took. But at that time I was not
sufficiently a detached observer to rest contented with an artist's
contemplation, and that, I think, was the reason why at times
she was restless, violent and jealous—as a woman tends to be in
love, as she was then. But restlessness and violence and jealousy
were all swallowed in the bottomless goodness of her heart so
often as she willed or thought to do an act of harm, for she was
awkward in her wounding as in her caressing. She was like a
lioness of some unknown breed, thinking she had claws, though
when she sought to flesh them she found that there was nothing
there but splendid velvet pads ! When she scratched it was with
velvet that she did so !'

'To what end is this tale ?' said the Comtesse de Chiffrevas to
her neighbour. 'This was surely not Don Juan's happiest love ?'

How could such complex minds believe in such simplicity ?

'And so we lived,' said Ravila, 'in a sweet intimacy which,
for all afflicting storms, was never torn and broken. Nor, in this
country town which men call Paris, was our state a mystery to
any. . . . The Marquise—for that was her rank . . .'

There were three such at the table, and their hair was dark :
but they gave no sign, knowing well that it was not of them he

spoke. . . . Among them was but a single hint of velvet, and that the down which showed upon the lip of one . . . a lip superbly moulded, which, you may well believe, curled now with not a little scorn.

'And thrice a Marquise, too, as a Pasha may, with three tails, triple his rank,' went on Ravila, whose wit was waking. 'She was of those who can hide nothing, even should they will to do so. Her daughter, a child barely thirteen, saw at once, despite her innocence, the feeling that her mother had for me. What poet, I wonder, has ever thought to ask how we appear to little girls whose mothers we have loved ? Such a question goes deep, and often I asked it of myself when I caught that spying glance, so dark and threatening, fixed on me. There were sombre depths in her large eyes, and she was fiercely secret. Most often when I came she left the room, and, when she had to stay, left as wide a space as possible between us. She had of me a sort of nervous horror which, though she tried to hide it, was too strong and, willy-nilly, showed. It was revealed in tiny details, not one of which escaped me. The Marquise who, as a rule, noticed but little, was never tired of saying : "You must be careful, dear ; I think the child is jealous."

'I was a great deal more careful than she. Had that girl been the Devil in person I would have defied her to read my mind. . . . But her mother's was as open as a book. In the flushed mirror of her face, so often clouded, each thought was seen reflected. Such was the child's fierce hatred that I thought she had surprised her mother's secret, had read it by the light of something said, some look, too tender, caught and weighed. She was a little weakling—though to know that can be of little interest to you—unworthy of the splendid mould in which she had been formed : and ugly too, as even her mother knew, though loving her no less for that ; a flawed topaz, or, shall I say, a figurine of bronze with jet-black eyes . . . a talisman of power ! . . . And so it went on, until . . .'

With this sudden outburst he fell silent . . . as though he wished to deaden its effect, realising, perchance, that he had said too much. But interest showed again on all the listening faces, an interest tense and not to be disguised. At last the Countess, as in a flash of sudden vision, said between closed teeth :

'Well, until . . . ?'

5

'While our love was still in its early stages,' went on the Comte de Ravila, 'I was in the habit of petting her as one always does pet children. I brought her bags of sweets, I called her "little mask," and often, while talking to her mother, would caress her hair—that sickly, blackish hair which, where the light fell, had the colour of dead wood. Her wide mouth which broadened readily for others into smiles grew sulky in my presence. An ugly frown would form between her eyes, and all her face grew hard, so that the "little mask" became mask-like in good earnest, deep-etched with lines of suffering, until it resembled that of some caryatid in a sculptured servitude, as though the touch of my hand were some weighty cornice she was doomed to bear upon her head.

'So marked was this ill-humour, so hostile did she show herself, so certain was she to shrink back at the barest hint of some endearment, that soon I left her quite alone, and ceased even to speak with her. "She takes you for a thief," her mother said ; "and knows by instinct that you steal some part of the affection which is rightly hers." And sometimes, in a mood of rigid moralism, added : "She is, you see, my conscience. Her jealousy but speaks my sense of guilt." One day she questioned her about this lack of friendliness to me. She got no answer, but only mulish silence or some broken words. When children will not speak, you know, one has to ask and ask again, drawing out responses as others draw a bottle's cork. "It's nothing. . . . I don't know," the girl would say, until, at last, checked by the hardness of that face of bronze, her mother ceased and turned away in weariness. . . .

'I should have told you that this curious creature was sombrely devout, a very Spaniard of the Middle Ages, and super-stitious too. Her thin body was plastered with scapulars, and on her chest, flat as her hand, and round her brownish neck, she wore a multitude of crosses, images of the Virgin and medals of the Holy Spirit. "You, alas, are without Faith," the Marquise said ; "and it may be that some words of yours have scandalised her. Be careful what you say before her, please. God knows I am much to blame already : do not make me worse in her eyes than I already am !" And, seeing that her daughter's attitude remained unchanged, her enmity unsoftened, "Soon you will grow to hate her, nor could I blame you if you did." But she was wrong. In face of such continued sulkiness I was indifferent, showing, at worst, impatience now and then.

'We treated one another with the cold politeness of grown persons out of love. I kept with her a careful ceremony. Though she was no taller than my arm I called her "Mademoiselle," and she, with icy distance said "Monsieur." She would never, in my presence, do anything to draw approval, nor strive to conquer her self-consciousness. Her mother could not make her let me see her drawings, or play for me upon the piano. If, by chance, I came upon her while she practised, her earnest concentration would stop short, and she would rise from her stool, refusing to continue. . . . Once only, when her mother had insisted (there was company that day) did she consent to take her place at the open instrument. She did so with a martyred look, in which, I can assure you, there was no hint of kindliness, and played some little piece with clumsy fingers. She was turned from me, nor was there any mirror in which she could see that I was watching. . . . Suddenly her back (she always held herself badly, so that her mother would say : "If you sit like that you will end by having a weak chest"), her back, I say, straightened, for all the world as though my gaze had been a bullet in her spine. She slammed the piano shut, making a terrible noise, and rushed from the room. . . . Someone was sent after her, but for the rest of the evening she did not reappear.

'No man, it seems, can ever be too vain. There was nothing in the behaviour of this mysterious child, in whom I took so small an interest, to hint at what she felt for me. Nor did her mother guess. Though she was jealous of all the women whom she knew, she remained, in this, as little jealous as I was fatuous. What finally occurred to show the truth, she was fool enough— still pale from the terror she had felt, though laughing that she should have been so moved—to tell me in our privacy.'

He stressed the word *fool*—no actor could have done it better —as though he knew that all the interest in his story hung upon that vocable.

And seemingly it was enough, for the twelve fair faces flamed with intense emotion till they shone like those of Cherubims before the Throne of God. And who shall say that woman's curiosity is not a feeling every whit as strong as the Adoration of the Angelic host ? . . . But they, unlike the Cherubims, did not end at the neck, and, as he looked at them he saw, no doubt, that they were in the mood to hear what more he had to tell : for he continued, making no further pause :—

'Yes, she was laughing. Each time, she told me later, that she called the scene to mind she laughed again. But there had been a moment when her mood was not so gay.

' "I was sitting," she said—and I shall try to use her very words—"just where I am now." (It was on one of those seats called "back-to-back sociables," of all seats yet devised the best for quarrelling and making quarrels up without so much as moving.)

' "But luckily you were not there, as you are now. For suddenly, who do you think was announced ? . . . you'll never guess . . . the Curé of Saint-Germain-des-Prés. He is a man, I think, whom you have never met. . . . You do not go to Mass —the more's the pity—and how then should you know that old and saint-like priest who visits no woman of his parish unless it be to beg alms for his poor or money for his Church ? I thought, at first, that such was now his object.

' "He had given my child her first Communion, and she, for loyalty, had made him her confessor. As such I had often invited him to dine, but never with success. As he entered the room I could see that he was deeply troubled. His features, as a rule so calm, showed now an awkwardness he failed to hide. It was more, I thought, than simple shyness, and some anxiety must have sounded in my words.

' "My dear, dear sir," I said, "what is the matter ?" " It is . . . It is . . . madame, that you see before you the most embarrassed man in all the world ! Never, in all the fifty years of my sacred charge of souls, have I been entrusted with so delicate a mission, nor one that I less understand."

' "He sat down, but asked me first to close the door, to keep it closed, while he should tell me what he had come to say. Such solemnity, as you may well imagine, frightened me, and this he noticed.

' "Do not unduly terrify yourself, madame," he said ; "you will need to keep your wits about you if, when you have heard my story, you are to make me understand this incredible event which, in truth, I cannot take as serious. . . . Your daughter, on whose behalf I stand before you, is, as you know, an angel of purity and grace. I know her soul ; I have held it, so to say, in these two hands, since she was seven years old, and am convinced she is mistaken . . . doubtless by reason of her innocence. . . . But this very morning she told me in Confession that she is—you will credit it no more than I, madame—with child ! . . .''

' "I gave a cry.

' "You do, madame, as I did, hearing her, for she spoke in tones of terrible despair, and there was no doubting her sincerity. I, who can see into her heart, dare swear that she knows nothing of the world or of its sins . . . I would answer for her at the Throne of God, as for none other of the young girls whom I confess. I can tell you no more. We priests are the surgeons of the soul, and it is our duty to bring our penitents to bed of every shameful secret, no matter how they may struggle to conceal the truth. But our hands must be gentle : they must not wound nor soil. Most carefully, then, I urged and questioned her. But, having told her tale, avowed her fault—her crime, she calls it—confessed herself damned to eternity, for she believes, poor child, that she has incurred irretrievable damnation—she would say no more, but kept a stubborn silence. This she broke only to beg that I would see you and explain her guilt . . . for, 'Mamma must know,' she said, 'and I could never have the strength to tell her.'

' "I listened to the Curé of Saint-Germain-des-Prés : with what mingled amazement and anxiety you may imagine. Even more than he did, I believed in my daughter's innocence. . . . What she had told her confessor was not, it is true, impossible, yet I refused to credit it . . . I *would* not : still, it *could* have been. For all her thirteen years she is a woman . . . and there have been times when her precocity dismayed me . . . I was seized by a fever of curiosity. . . .

' "I must know all . . . I *will* know all," I said to the good man who, in his stupefied embarrassment, was fumbling with his hat. "She will not speak while you are here but I am sure that she will tell me all . . . that I can succeed in forcing the truth from her, and then we shall understand what now seems to us incomprehensible !"

' "At that he left me—and, as soon as he had gone, I went

P

upstairs to my daughter, having no patience to send for her and to wait until she came. I found her, not kneeling but prostrate, before the crucifix which hangs above her bed, pale as a corpse, her eyes quite dry but rimmed with red, as though she had wept much.

' "I took her in my arms, set her by my side at first, then on my knees, and told her I could not believe what I had just learned from her priest. But she broke in upon my words, assuring me with trembling voice and looks of terrible distress that he had told the truth. It was then that, in a mood of mounting pain and wonder, I asked for the name of the man who . . .

' "But I could not finish the question. . . . The horror of that moment is indescribable. She buried her head on my shoulder, hiding her face . . . but I could see that the back of her neck was the colour of flame, and I could feel her tremble. She maintained with me the same silence which she had opposed to her confessor. I was faced by a blank wall.

' "He must be someone far beneath you in station, for otherwise you would not be so deeply shamed"—and this I said, knowing her pride, and hoping to shock her into speech.

' "But still she said nothing, still kept her face buried in my shoulder. And so we sat for what seemed an endless age. Then suddenly, without changing her position, she said : 'Swear, Mamma, that you will forgive me !'

' "I swore all that she asked of me, even at the risk of perjuring myself a hundredfold. I was filled, I was boiling, with impatience . . . I felt as though my head would burst and my brains spill out.

' "It was . . .' she said, 'it was . . . Monsieur de Ravila !'— and lay unmoving in my arms.

' "You can picture, Amédée, the effect upon me of your name ! At a single blow my heart received full punishment for the great sin of my life. You are, where women are concerned, a dangerous man. I have always feared a host of rivals, and often there have formed within my mind those horrible words—'why not ?'—which spring to the lips of every woman when she thinks of the man she loves yet cannot wholly trust. . . . But I kept my thoughts concealed from the cruel child who doubtless had divined where lay her mother's heart.

' "Monsieur de Ravila," I said—and felt that all my secret

sounded in my voice. "But you never speak to him, you run from him, always." I was about to add—for I could feel within my heart a rising anger—"then both of you are false to me !"—but I bit back the words, Whatever happened, I must know the details, one by one, of this most horrible seduction ! . . . With a gentleness which I thought would be my death, I questioned her, when suddenly I felt the awful pressure slacken, the agony relax, as, with an air of perfect innocence, she said : 'It was one evening, Mamma. He was sitting in the big armchair which stands at the corner of the hearth, opposite the sofa. He stayed there a long while but finally got up, and I . . . I . . . was prompted miserably to go and sit where he had sat . . . and oh, Mamma, it was as though I had fallen into flames ! I tried to rise, but could not . . . my heart failed me . . . and . . . I felt, Mamma, that there within me . . . was a child !" '

The Marquise had laughed, Ravila said, telling that story, but not one of the twelve women round the table so much as smiled . . . nor he.

'And that, ladies, I ask you to believe,' he concluded, 'was the loveliest passion that in all my life I have inspired.'

He stopped, and no one broke the silence. The ladies of his audience sat deep in thought. . . . Had they seized the full meaning of the tale ?

When Joseph was a slave in the house of Madame Potiphar, he was so beautiful, the Koran says, that the ladies whom he served at table fell a-dreaming, so that they cut their fingers with their knives because their eyes would never leave his face. But our times are not his, and our emotions at dessert are less deeply stirred.

'Yes, your Marquise must have been a fool, for all her wit, to tell you such a thing !' said the Duchess. She liked to play the cynic, and was cutting nothing at all with the golden knife which never left her hand. The Comtesse de Chiffrevas gazed at the Rhine wine in its emerald glass which glowed mysterious as her thoughts.

'And—the little mask ?' she asked.

'Oh, she married and went to live in the country,' answered Ravila. 'By the time her mother told the tale to me she was already dead.'

'And but for that ! . . .' the Duchess said, and brooded still.

Table Talk

By Peter de Polnay

I'd been waiting more than half an hour. It wasn't fun waiting. The valley was bleak and cold. The slag heaps were abomination itself. And the wind. I hated the wind. I called myself a fool for having come with Trevor. And on my leave too. But I wanted that fiver back.

So this was Corris. Two women walked past me talking in Welsh. It sounded like a long-drawn-out angry quarrel. Then two boys came. Speaking Welsh too. They must be angry, I thought. The houses were as bleak as the valley. Then an officer came. A one-pipper. I looked away not to have to salute him. Then a drizzle started and that clinched matters. My pipe went out, and an Army lorry drove through the narrow twisting street, and I just had room to stand against the wall of a house. On the hillside there was all the slag in the world. My pipe went out because of the drizzle. I started to walk up and down. Battledress is the best camouflage of your person. Nobody notices you, and your own person is overlooked. That was as it should be. I hate being noticed, especially in a Welsh village waiting for a man who was doing God knows what.

At last Trevor came. He came whistling and called to me. 'Sorry, old bird, to have kept you waiting so long. But it's all right.'

That was good. I'd have my fiver back.

'Now we got to walk back to Machynlleth,' he said. 'Then we'll catch the train to Shrewsbury. We'll celebrate. A nice early dinner and we'll be back in town before midnight. I know a place in Shrewsbury where we can get a smacking good dinner, war or no war.'

. Since he was called-up Trevor had become more vulgar. He'd been all his life a pretty vulgar sort of chap, but he'd had pretensions and had been annoyingly 'refained.' Now that was gone. In the pre-war world you never quite knew whether he was a tout or a Hoover salesman. At present you knew he was a tout. Or worse. Perhaps much worse.

'How much ?' I asked.

'Eighty smackers,' he said.

'That's a lot,' I said.

'More than I expected,' he said.

The Dovey was trickling along beside the road. Fine trout pools, and the road turned, and the dark valley was opening up. The landscape became more generous.

'So you pulled it off,' I said. 'She really believed that you are getting a commission?' I laughed. Trevor was walking fast and his red face was very red. A red suet pudding and the small dirty forage cap made his face even more red and suet-like.

'I don't know why you're laughing,' he said. 'If they gave me a commission at least they'd have an officer who is a gentleman too. And none of your nonsense. I thank you.' He started to swing his arms, and I looked away and sniggered. It started to rain hard. Luck was with us. A lorry came up from behind. It stopped and we asked for a lift. The driver said, 'Jump in behind.' It was riotously funny to watch Trevor heaving his heavy body into the lorry. It was dark inside the lorry and it smelt badly. The lorry started off with a jerk and Trevor sat down on his behind. I don't think he liked that.

'What a lousy thing this is,' he said. 'But I can tell you, my friend, that in the not so distant future you'll see me travelling in state again. And you won't see me in this bloody uniform for long, either.'

Very obligingly the lorry driver took us to the station. I said 'Thank you' to him, but Trevor didn't thank him. That sort of thing was beneath his dignity. We, definitely, had luck. There was a train leaving for Shrewsbury. We got into a third-class compartment. Another soldier sat in the corner.

'Going on leave, mate?' he asked.

'Mind your business,' Trevor said. 'Who the hell gave you permission to address me? I don't know you, my man, and I don't want to know you.' I felt uncomfortable; the pale little soldier in the corner was squashed. He muttered something under his breath, and thereafter didn't even dare to look at Trevor.

'I don't like this part of the world,' I said to him.

'Awful,' Trevor said. 'Though, mind you, there's good fishing here. I used to come down in my Rolls before the war and fish the river. I thought of buying a large estate with a castle or something.' He spoke in a reproachful voice to make, I suppose, the soldier realise that he was in the presence of one of his far betters, and therefore repent of his impertinence. In fact *lèse-majesté*.

'Was she nice to you?' I asked.

'I'll tell you all about it in Shrewsbury. There are things one doesn't discuss in public.' So I was properly ticked off. 'But,' he went on, 'you'll have a good dinner, my boy. A corking good dinner.'

At Shrewsbury we went straight to a posh hotel. The private bar was full of officers. I didn't care for it and I don't think they cared for our presence either. Trevor swaggered up to the bar.

'Pardon me,' he said to two officers, and got between them, and in a loud voice ordered two double Scotches and ginger beer.

'We don't serve doubles,' the barmaid said.

'Quite right too,' he said. 'There is a war on, so they say. Give us four singles, and what will you have, queen of my heart?'

I was quietly blushing in the background.

'I could do with a Guinness,' the barmaid said.

'And good for you too,' he said. The barmaid laughed. I heaved a sigh of relief. I thought we'd be kicked out.

'I don't like coming up too often to the bar,' Trevor said. 'So make it eight singles and two Guinnesses. And very nice too. And you want money. Here's a fiver. Nice and white like your soul, God bless your heart.'

'Did you kill somebody?' the barmaid asked.

'That's a good one,' he laughed. 'I killed my mother-in-law.'

He came to the table with the drinks. He suddenly looked lugubrious. 'Killed,' he said. 'And a very good thing it would be too. Come on, drink it up. It's just poison.'

I offered to pay for a round, but he refused.

'You're my guest, laddie,' he said. 'By and by we'll settle that fiver.'

'No hurry,' I said.

'You're the only pal I got left,' he said. 'I won't forget you. You'll see I'll stand by you. And you know, laddie, I am as good as my word. We'll have another round and then food. They used to do you very well here before the war.'

He was tall and fleshy. His skin was the colour of a baby's

soap advertisement. He'd no hair to speak of. Generally speaking, he looked repellent. A fatted-up reptile. I knew him well. Years ago I tried to make money on horses. I didn't ; but I met Trevor in a pub to which touts and such-like people went. He always knew which horse would win. At times he was right, more often he was wrong. Then I'd no money and didn't see him for ages. Then I ran into him and I suppose I looked pretty down and out. He looked prosperous. He wore a Brigade of Guards tie and a neat dark blue serge suit. A white collar too. He was working in a bucket shop. He got me a job with his firm. I wasn't a success and they gave me the sack. He stayed on and the bucket shop got into trouble and I read about it in the paper. Trevor's name figured in the case but he didn't go to jail. I saw him again and things were rather bad for him. The serge suit and the white collar were gone. He wore once more his shabby sporting clothes and his customary Old Etonian tie. Anyway, he was free. The war came and I was called up and I forgot him. That was nearly three years ago. A long time. And he still owed me five quid. A lot of money for a private. So I was pleasantly surprised yesterday when he came to see me. That was the second day of my leave and the sixth day of his. He hated soldiering, and his battledress was creased and dirty. His large belly stuck out as if it were something independent and detached. He was glad to see me.

'I never expected to find you here at the old address, laddie,' he said. 'How's the wife ?' I said she was away on munitions in the Midlands, so he immediately volunteered the information that she must be earning six or seven smackers a week, and six or seven smackers was not a sum to be laughed at. I assured him I didn't laugh.

It was unnecessary for him to tell me he was completely broke. I said you didn't need money in the Army. He brushed that aside and said that he slept in Salvation Army hostels since he was on leave ; and what a terrible way of spending one's leave. He was mighty upset about it. He was on the rocks and whined because the rocks were hard and cold. He was one of those men who can't hide their misfortunes : not even in battledress. I took him out for a drink. We went to a pub and there was hardly any swagger left in him.

After the second double Scotch he somewhat revived. He told

me he'd been to the Glasshouse. He said he hit his major on parade. Just to show, he explained, that he, Trevor, was a better man and was afraid of nobody. I didn't believe him. He was rather vague about the Glasshouse, and since I'd had a twenty-eight days' session at Chatham I knew he must be lying. After the third drink he admitted that he'd been handed over to the civilian police and had served a short term. It was still on account of the bucket shop. Or something worse. But I didn't say that to him.

I remembered he spoke a lot about his mother-in-law who'd money but since the death of his wife had refused to have anything to do with him. I asked him why didn't he go to her and ask her to help him. She wouldn't, he was certain of that. I persisted and suggested, as an alternative, that he should, as the saying goes, sit down on his haunches and live on his Army pay as most of us have to. He said that was out of the question and he needed money for a damned good thing which would bring him in thousands. And he must think of after the war. What would become of him if he'd no money whatsoever ? Eventually he said he'd go if I went with him ; moreover, he was afraid of her.

What with the wife being away, and being short of cash too, I consented to accompany him to Wales. To doctor our railway warrants was child's play for us. And I wanted that fiver back. So we went down by the night train, and a very uncomfortable journey that was. Now as I watched him in the bar I congratulated myself on having given him the right advice.

'Lucky I went to see you yesterday,' he said, and his nondescript eyes tried to look grateful. We went in to have our dinner. He swaggered into the dining-room. His belly led the way. His battle blouse was covered with ash. His head was thrown back, the lights shone on his bald crown, and I wouldn't have been surprised had he sung the song about the man who broke the bank at Monte Carlo. The dining-room was packed with officers.

'The bastards,' he said. 'If there were fair play in this country I ought to be a major by now.'

'Well, according to your mother-in-law, you're getting a commission,' I said, and sniggered a little.

'Stop that,' he said. Then he said, 'Now, laddie, we'll do ourselves proud.'

We didn't. The soup was water and the frozen imported meat was like all the frozen imported meat. And that is saying very little. But he ordered a bottle of wine. I told him not to, much too expensive and probably it would be muck. It was muck.

'Never mind,' he said. 'We'll have a second bottle if we feel like it. Poverty and the rest of it are left far behind. I'm telling you, far behind.'

He didn't order a second bottle. We had coffee in the lounge and he told the waiter he wanted two liqueur brandies.

'I don't know what you're saying,' the waiter said.

'Liqueur brandies,' Trevor repeated, and his face was crimson.

'Never heard of it,' the waiter said. He was a sort of wartime waiter and had never heard of liqueur brandies before ; or, as a matter of fact, of anything else either. You could see that in his face and on the saucers : for he'd spilled the coffee and it was embedded in the saucers.

'Send me the manager,' Trevor said. The officers were glaring.

'And call me sir, my man,' he added. The officers were near apoplexy. The manager came, and Trevor shouted, and the result was two tiny drops of methylated spirit, and he paid six bob for each. There was still half an hour left to catch the train to town.

'I wish I hadn't sold all my civvies when I was broke,' Trevor said. 'I'll have to get some black market coupons.' He wagged his head. 'Lots of money in the black market.'

'Now tell me how it went,' I said.

'It was simple, old bird. The old woman was surprised to see me. I haven't seen her for six years. My wife died six years ago. She's a swine and she always said that my wife died because I broke her heart. That's rubbish. Have you ever seen a broken heart lying on the roadside ? I haven't.' He laughed. 'But you know what old women are like. My mother-in-law is a witch. Well, I asked her if she remembered me. She said she didn't. So I told her I was recommended for a commission and I needed money for that. That tickled her vanity and so she forked out eighty smackers.' He finished his coffee by pouring the contents of the saucer into the cup. There was a good deal of ash in the saucer. 'Look at that girl over there. Looks okay to me.'

'Go on,' I said.

'There isn't much more to tell. She thought it is a grand thing to be an officer, and I promised her to come down and see her when I got my pip, and she smiled and giggled at the thought of parading me in front of her neighbours, God curse her.' He ordered two cigars and lit one. He puffed most conspicuously.

'I don't want to be an officer,' he said. He corrected himself. 'I wouldn't be an officer if they paid me. I want to get out. I'm going to desert. Yes, sir.'

'You'll be caught,' I said.

'You'll be surprised,' he said.

We talked of all sorts of things, and then his voice grew heavy, and he leaned forward and said to me :

'If I'd guts I ought to have killed her.'

'Why ?'

'Because she's an old witch.'

'You don't kill people who give you eighty quid.'

'I should have killed her. Listen.' He put his head close to mine. Nasty little veins were all over his cheeks. They were bluish red, and now it wasn't a soap advertisement any more but just those veins trying to break through the bloated skin. 'I want to tell you how I'd have done it.' He used to be full of all sorts of stories how he should have done it. It was usually backing the wrong horse. I remember an evening before the war when we supped on a bar of chocolate on his bed, and he told me how he should have cleared at Sandown, of all places, two hundred thousand pounds ; and so convincing it was that hungry though I was I left half of the bar of chocolate : for we were going half and half.

'I rang the bell,' he said, his eyes almost popping past the eyebrows, 'and nobody answered. So I rang again. Then I heard a distant noise. Not for nothing have I been a salesman in my time. I knew the parlour door was opened and the old witch was coming down the stairs. So I stood against the wall and when she opened it she couldn't see me. I pushed past her and was in the damp passage with old coats hanging all over the place, and umbrellas that never got dry. No light, of course. The bally house smelt of stinginess. You know stinginess has a special smell of its own. She never kept drinks in the house. Well, she called out in Welsh who I was. I said it was me and you ought to have heard her. She just screamed and screamed. In Welsh too.'

'That must have been frightening,' I said. 'Is this how it happened ?' I asked.

'Fool,' he said. 'This is how it should have happened. As a matter of fact she kissed me when I came in.' He laughed. 'Don't interrupt me. It's a good yarn.'

I said I wouldn't and he went on.

'Then she stopped shrieking and I said I wanted to speak to her. So we went upstairs. I climbed those steep stairs behind her. She puffed and her bones squeaked, and honestly I thought she might fall to bits half-way up the stairs. Well, we went into the parlour and there was an old mangy cat. Had that cat for years. I hate cats. What I like is horses, though you know, laddie, one can lose a nice bit of money on them. Well, I said I was broke, I'd been to jug, the Army is killing me, so what about some money to make things easy ? She cursed and said I killed her daughter and I was an un-Godly swine and I never went to Salems and Tabernacles and Bethels and the rest of it. Then I asked her again and she said, no, not a penny, and the quicker I went the better. She . . .'

'Now is this true or not ?'

'Of course it isn't. I told you what happened. But who's telling this story, you or me ? So I started to whine and I said she was my wife's mother and why shouldn't she help me and make life bearable. She went out of the room and I thought I'd moved her and got my pigeon. But the old witch came back after a few minutes and gave me a ten bob note, crumpled it was, and said that I should get out. She took it from her purse and I saw there was small change in it, not much, and a key. I took the money and said good-bye to her and she went to the door with me. She was wheezing. Getting that money had tired her. She opened the door for me and I said I couldn't find my way in the dark, and she went out to switch on the light. As she passed me I grabbed her neck with my left hand and with my right fist I hit her as hard as I could.' He banged his fist on the table and the saucers rattled and danced. 'It's damned easy to hit such an old woman. Went down surprisingly quickly. I dragged her upstairs and then went to the bedroom. The key fitted to

the top drawer of a chest that stood beside her bed.   There was a
lot of junk in it and woollen things she wore over her bally bones.
I rummaged there and found the money.   Eighty quid in fivers.
What fools old women are.   Anybody could have found it.'

'This isn't worthy of your other stories,' I said.   'You should
have made it more complicated.'

There was a clock in the lounge.   We had ten minutes left.   He
beckoned to the waiter, who came over slowly, impertinently.

'Two double Scotches,' Trevor said.   'And make it snappy,
my man.'

The waiter walked away.

'Worthy or not worthy,' Trevor said, 'let me finish it.   So I
took the money and thought I should look for her cheque book,
but that wasn't a good idea.   Probably hadn't a bank account
at all.   They're old-fashioned in that valley.   I went back and,
imagine my surprise, she'd crawled to the settee and was trying
to get up.   Like an old tom she looked.   A tom somebody had
kicked because it was mewing too much.'

'Much better,' I said.   But where were our drinks ?

'First I pushed her back on to the floor.   I was rough with her,
I can assure you.   She lay very quiet and didn't even wheeze.
Then I gave her a piece of my mind.   I told her what a witch she
had been.   Never did anything to help me, and here she was
rotting away and holding on to her money, and I haven't even
money for fags and she just sits on her bally money and lets me
starve.   I told her all that.   Then I said if she ever breathed a
word that I'd been there I'd come back and ring her old neck.
She looked at me and I didn't like her look, so I gave her a kick
in the ribs ; I hope I broke one.   Then I went.   I opened the
front door, but I heard a noise overhead.   So I banged the door
and went up on tiptoes.   There she was crawling towards the
door of her bedroom.   On all fours she was.   It fascinated me.
She didn't hear me.   I tiptoed behind her.   It was difficult for
her to open the door.   But Christ, she worked hard.   Put up her
hand, didn't reach the knob, put it up again, with the other hand
tried to raise herself higher, the hand gave way, and I stood and
watched her and she was like a snail you've trod on.   When I
was a kid I always trod on snails.   Funny how they wriggle.   At
last the door was open.   She crawled into the bedroom and
stopped at the wall.   Then she began to knock on it.   She knocked

hard. And a voice from the other side shouted, "Anything the matter, Mrs Llewellyn?" So she was going to give the alarm. Wanted me to be caught. That made me mad and I grabbed her neck with one hand and squeaked like her, "Nothing, thank you ; just wanted to know if you're in." Thank God, I haven't forgotten my Welsh. The voice shouted, "All right, Mrs Llewellyn, you know we're always here, if you need anything just knock." "I know, dearie," I squeaked. The other woman had a young voice.'

'That's an excellent touch,' I said. 'You know how to spin a yarn. But we'd better go. It's time.'

'Where's the drink?' he said. But the waiter was invisible. Trevor wanted to go in search of him but I didn't let him. I didn't want to lose the train. So we left without the drinks.

'I'll write to the manager,' Trevor said in the dark street. 'I'll have him sacked. Don't worry. We'll have one at Birmingham.'

We got into an empty compartment. I asked him to go on with his yarn.

'Don't you worry,' he darkly said. 'You'll hear the end of it. Well, then I lifted the old witch and carried her back to the parlour. Dropped her and told her that she'd never get the police after me because I was going to kill her that very minute. She didn't flinch. Those old eyes were just hating me and were sorry she couldn't get the police at me. I put my hands round her neck. She tried to scratch me. Think of that ! But I finished her off. Believe me or not, it took me something like ten minutes. She'd nine lives if a cat ever had. But it was good to kill her, rotten old thing that she was.'

'Pretty good story,' I said. He grunted.

'Not a bad story at all,' he said, and there was something queer in his voice. The train stopped. It was Birmingham. We went into the refreshment room and they only had beer. So he drank three pints, but I couldn't manage more than two. When we returned to our compartment we found it full. I was wedged in between a gunner and an R.A.F. bloke. There was little room for a large bloated man like Trevor. Nevertheless he fell asleep. I couldn't sleep. I thought of his story and all of a sudden I realised he'd told me the truth. There was nothing out of the ordinary about it. I often heard that you start as a minor crook and then you go on till you do something really wicked, and then that's that. Of course, a thing like that couldn't happen to me because I'm a careful bloke and I know when to stop. But it was different with Trevor, and besides he'd no wife to earn good money on munitions. I got rather frightened. He'd been seen in my company, and the villagers in that God-forsaken valley must have noticed me and surely would remember me once the thing is known. I had a good mind to sneak out of the train at Banbury. I felt cold.

He was sleeping with his head jerking with the train. He was hideous to look at. His long arms were crossed on his chest. The murderer, I said to myself, and wished from the very bottom of my heart that I hadn't gone to Wales with him. And that made me think of the fiver. If he returned me my fiver that would be plenty of evidence for the police to rope me in as an accomplice. Thank God I hadn't asked for it. And he said, too, that those eighty quid were in fivers. I started to perspire : I shook him. He didn't wake up, so I kicked his leg with my heavy Army boot. He opened his eyes and looked at me sheepishly.

'What is it, laddie ?' he asked.

'Look here, Trevor,' I quickly said, 'I was thinking of it, and things, you know, are going well with me. The wife ; and in the Army one doesn't need much money. Anyway, not a bloke like me. You know I have simple tastes . . . so, well, I think you'd better hang on to that fiver. We'll see after the war.' And by then you'll be hanged, I said to myself. He was grateful and then fell asleep.

In a village like that, I mused, they wouldn't discover the crime before next morning. Well, I must do something about it. The best thing for me would be to go to the police and tell them what he told me. That would clear me. I felt better. The train chased on and the compartment was hot and smelly, and there were snores of every variety. At last Paddington. We got out.

'Look here, laddie,' Trevor said on the platform, 'that was very handsome of you about the fiver. I am very grateful. I won't forget it, I'll always stand by you. To-morrow, you know, my leave is up. To be quite frank with you, I blew to-night the whole fiver that old cat gave me. What about lending me a dollar to see me back to my unit ?'

I was flabbergasted and immensely relieved. I couldn't utter a word. Nobody likes to give away a pal, and I always stick by my pals. He misunderstood my silence.

'Don't be mean, old bird,' he said. 'We had a good dinner, what ? Come on, give us that sub of a dollar. You'll get it back.' I gave him five bob.

In the Tube I said to him, 'Do you know I almost believed your yarn.' He wasn't interested. He looked round the carriage with evident disgust.

'We should have taken a taxi,' he said. 'I hate Tubes.'

He rattled the two half-crowns in his pocket.

CRIME ALBUM

It Takes Two to Make a Hero
By Francis Iles

This is the story that was told me by a complete stranger one wet morning at the Dodo Club.

I do not know what are the qualifications for membership of the Dodo, but I believe the club was founded as a kind of carry-over on a permanent basis of one of those ephemeral clublets which contribute so much to the charm of social life at the older universities. At any rate, most of the members were youngish—that is to say, on the undeveloped side of forty—their number was small, and, according to George Pidcock, each of them was a distinguished man in some modest way of his own : though what claim to distinction George himself could have put forward, beyond being a first cousin of mine, I could never imagine.

In any case, it was to lunch with George that I was there on that morning, and it was because the day was wet that I arrived more than an hour early. For the hall porter at the Dodo knows me ; the morning-room into which they show visitors is well provided with those more obscure periodicals, to be seen only in clubs, which have a peculiar fascination for me ; and in short I looked forward to quite a pleasant hour of relaxation before the exacting job of being entertained by George for lunch.

But my luck was out.

The very first magazine I sought was missing, *Retrogressional Advancement,* my own particular favourite : the organ of a Society which seeks to prove that just as the human eye in reality sees things upside down, so human life is really lived backwards and we are born into it at such a stage of unnatural development as suits our individual egos, proceed reverse-ways through it for the purpose of discarding all useless knowledge, attain the False Amnesia as infants, and finally the True Amnesia, leading to the Blissful Disintegration, when we retire at last into the wombs of

216

those whom we wrongly believe to be our mothers but who are really our daughters. . . . This magazine was missing.

Apparently I must have vented my chagrin aloud, for the next moment I was horrified to see an enquiring head come into view round the wing of an arm-chair and fix on me the usual baleful eye of the Disturbed Member. I had a wild impulse to explain that by all the precedents the morning room of the Dodo should be uninhabited at noon, or I would never have broken so many of clubland's most sacred rules as that one mild exclamation had managed to shatter—disturbing a Sitting Member, implying criticism on the part of a Non-member in the presence of a Member, failing to comport oneself humbly and reverently as befitting a Non-member in the presence of a Member, breaking a Silence although not a Member, frequenting the club at Unreasonable Hours although not a Member, and, of course, Not Being a Member. As it was, however, I could only blush painfully and grab at *Darkness is Life*, the organ of a Society which seeks to prove that only by living permanently underground can mankind hope . . .

'Were you looking for anything?' asked the head.

'No,' I said. 'No, no. Oh, no. Not at all. Nothing. Oh, no. No.'

He got up, and I saw with incredulity that his eye was not baleful at all, but concerned, with the concern of a host for a guest. 'I'm afraid you were looking for something. What was it?'

'*Retrogressional Advancement*,' I said.

With a peculiarly attractive look of guilt he indicated the copy in his own hand. 'I'm so sorry,' he was beginning, when suddenly his expression changed and he looked quite startled. 'Good God, are you really a Retrogressional Advancer? They positively do exist, then? 'Pon my word, I thought the whole thing must be a leg-pull. I say, I didn't mean that. Of course . . . most extraordinarily interesting . . . quite see there may be something in it . . . h'm. . . .'

I put him out of his agony.

And then, of course, he ordered sherry, and asked whom I was waiting for, ordered more sherry on hearing that it was George Pidcock, confessed to never having heard of George Pidcock, and finally ordered more sherry as a penance for never having heard of me either. (I should explain that this happened after the war, when sherry was beginning to get into circulation again.)   In short, within a very short time we were getting ready to tell each other the stories of our lives : which for two complete strangers, and members of a normally reticent race, was remarkable enough.   It was, however, not until he learned that I was a writer that this excellent man began to show signs of human weakness.   They were signs I knew too well.   I had fled from them at cocktail-parties, at Lord's, in the drawing-rooms even of elderly relatives.   They were indications that the signmaker has a 'plot' for one :   either 'just a little thing, you probably won't think much of it, came to me in my bath this morning,' or 'and absolutely true, you'd hardly need to alter it, honestly someone ought to write it up.'

Usually, I say, the only thing to do is to flee (unless you happen to be particularly good at the glassy smile, the mandarin nod, and all the rest of it) ;   but this time things were different.   After all, this man had not savaged me, as he had been entitled to do ;   instead he had fed me with kindness and gladdened me with sherry.   Besides, I liked the look of his long, restless legs and his small round English head with the fair clipped moustache of his caste.   So I did as never before since the days of my apprenticeship :   I encouraged him.

Curiously, it needed encouragement to bring his tale out of him.   When it came to the point, he showed diffidence.   I encouraged him further.

'No, no,' he said.   'It's not that.   I was just wondering whether I haven't been a bit—what's the word ?—precipitate. After all, it's rather . . . what's the word again ?   I'm afraid you'll think me only half-educated.   I suppose *you* can hit on the right word every time.'   I assured him I cannot.   'Well, "confidential," then.   No, not "confidential."   "Intimate," that's more like it.   Yes, it's a bit intimate.   Rather gives a fellow away, I mean.   Not that the . . . the chap who told me put me under any injunction not to repeat it.   I mean, there's no seal of secrecy, but . . . anyhow, I'll tell you what I'll do.   I'll tell you the story exactly as it happened . . . that is, as it was told to me, of course . . . and if it's any use to you, it's up to you to twist things round a bit so that it's not too absolutely obvious.   How's that ?'

'Admirable,' I said.   'And you must give your informant a fictitious name, mustn't you ?'

'By Jove, yes. That's an idea. Of course I must. I say, that's worth a couple more sherries, don't you think?' He got up and rang the bell. ' "Smith"! That's what we'll call him. Smith, yes. Jolly good. Smith!

'Well, it was in the war. About the middle of the war. This chap Smith had got a spot of leave. He was a young subaltern then in . . . oh, well, better not mention his regiment, but his battalion was quartered at the time in one of the more deadly regions of Yorkshire ; and believe me, Yorkshire-lover as I am, some bits can be grim.'

'I've been stationed in Catterick Camp myself,' I told him.

'Ah, well, you can sympathise with Smith. You see, his leave came at just the wrong time. He was engaged to a girl in London . . . grand girl and all that, much too good for him (so Smith says, of course!) . . . but she was some sort of big noise in the W.R.N.S. and was going to be up to the eyebrows in it all that week : couldn't give the poor chap two minutes in all his eight days. Then, his father was with some Government Mission over in the U.S. at the time ; he didn't feel much like planting himself on any of his other relatives ; and, in short, poor old Smith just hadn't got anyone he wanted to see or anywhere he wanted to go. So what do you think the poor boob did? He went to Brighton. You see, he'd got some pretty good memories of Brighton before the war. For instance . . . oh, well, no need to go into that. Point is, he went to Brighton. And, believe me, to go to Brighton in war-time was asking for trouble. Well . . . he got it.

'He put up at the good old Cosmopolitan, and there wasn't anything wrong with *that*, except that all the waiters were ninety years old and could only just about crawl on their hands and knees, and the food restrictions were too much even for their chef, and the fuel orders left the place freezing. But outside it really was . . . well, poor old Smith could hardly recognise the place as Brighton at all. Dead, damned and deserted. A few giddy whirls of barbed wire along the front, practically all the hotels and boarding-houses closed, no life in the place, nothing but rain, wind, and general misery, and all the general foulness of an early English spring. I mean, you can see this chap Smith looking out of his hotel bedroom (the lounge being too cold to sit in), over a grey sea, with the gulls screeching dismally past his window and Smith feeling he could screech with them and wondering what the blazes had made him come to such a god-forsaken place and how the blazes he was going to stick it for six more whole days. Ever see Brighton during the war ? Well, believe me, it was a bit grim. Poor old Brighton !

'Anyhow, there's always the flicks. So Smith put on his greatcoat and went downstairs to get hold of a local paper and find out what was on. And, of course, when he did find the list, there wasn't a film that he hadn't seen before—and thought pretty poorly of when he did see it ! That was how it would be, of course. It was that sort of leave.

'So Smith falls back on the last resource of the utterly bored. He reads the local paper. And when he'd read what there was to read, dash it if he didn't read the advertisements too. I mean, you can judge what his state was by then. So when he saw a rather amusing advertisement in that local rag, you'll understand that he was in the right frame of mind to do something about it.

'Now look here, I hold no particular brief for friend Smith, or whatever the phrase is, but in view of what's coming I must impress on you that, so far as I can judge, he'd always considered himself just about an ordinary sort of chap. I mean, ordinarily decent, I suppose, though no plaster saint ; and with the ordinary amount of guts, if no plaster hero. At least, that's what Smith himself thought ; and I shouldn't be surprised if his friends would have thought so too—if they'd ever thought about it at all. But that just shows how difficult it is to judge : difficult even to judge oneself. Because, you see, Smith hadn't been tested then. When he was . . . I say, I'm telling this very badly. I haven't told you about the advertisement yet, have I ?

'Well, so far as I can remember . . . I mean, so far as I remember Smith's words, the advertisement went something like this : "Young Lady has Sporting Prints for Sale. No. something-or-other, such-and-such street." Something like that, anyhow.

'Now for some reason this made Smith prick his ears up. It sounded . . . well, why "sporting prints" ? And why go out of the way to rub in "young lady" ? Smith couldn't help feeling there was something queer about it. And he remembered there's some kind of American joke about "etchings" ; never been able to make out quite what it is, but you find it in any American comic paper you pick up. And the more Smith turned it over, the more it seemed to him that this young lady, with her sporting prints, ought to be investigated. Even "young lady" sounded pretty good to him, in that ghastly boredom and not knowing a soul for fifty miles round and no one to talk to but old waiters brushing up the crumbs with their long white beards. Of course there wasn't a thought of disloyalty to his fiancée. Smith, as I say, was an ordinarily decent chap. Besides, he knew she couldn't help not being available : Duty before Devotion, and all that. But just a pleasant chat or so, and perhaps a personable face to share a bit of war-food with . . . there couldn't be any harm in that. Though I can't deny that those Sporting Prints, and their Etching cousins, did strike friend Smith as definitely something to be followed up.

'Anyhow, he didn't think too much about it. He just grabbed his cap and left. I can tell you, he was in the mood.

'Well, he found the street all right. It ran back from the front and Smith didn't think it was much of a street for a young lady to live in ; a sort of mixture of cheap little shops, cheap boarding-houses, and pubs. The number given in the advertisement didn't impress Smith either. At first he thought it was a tobacconist's shop. Then he saw there was a side-door, half-open to show a glimpse of a flight of dark, steep and rather dirty stairs. Evidently the young lady lived in the maisonette above the shop, and Smith was beginning to wonder if she were really a very nice young lady. He didn't care much for the occupant of the shop either. In fact it gave him quite a nasty jar, as he was hesitating outside the door, to see a fat little Jew squatting behind the counter like . . . like a kind of frog, you know, and watching him with beady bright eyes that never winked. I mean, it quite put Smith off his stroke. Perhaps he had a bit of a guilty conscience already. I don't know. Anyhow . . .

'Smith had one queer . . . what's the word ? . . . "foible," I think. I mean, if there was anything he didn't like, or that frightened him, he . . . well, he sort of went for it bald-headed. You know . . . without giving himself time to think. It was a form of funk, really, though Smith didn't know it then. Anyhow, that's what he did. He marched straight into the shop, and asked for twenty cigarettes. His case was full, but that was how it had taken him. The tobacconist gave them to him without a word, and then Smith remembered that he wanted a new flint for his lighter, and he handed it over to be fitted. It was rather a special lighter, I ought to tell you : gold, and all that. In fact, it was a present from his fiancée. Smith saw the man's eyes open a bit when he saw it, and he muttered something about it being a nice instrument. Smith only grunted. He'd taken quite a sizable dislike to the man. You know how it is. Probably quite unreasonable . . . excellent husband and father and all that. Still, there it was, and Smith just leaned his back against the counter and stared out of the door until the flint had been fitted. However, he'd got his nerve back, and that was the main thing. So as soon as the job was done he just said to himself, "What the hell !" and marched straight from the shop into the doorway next to it, and didn't care a damn that the Jew's eyes were on his back all the way. After all, why should he ?'

My stranger paused and sipped his sherry. In his eyes was a curious look which I couldn't quite define.

'And Smith went up those stairs ?' I prompted him, for I was really eager to know.

'Oh, yes, Smith went up those stairs,' he smiled. 'There was the usual wooden partition of the converted maisonette at the top : you know—before you reach the landing, so that you have to ring the bell from a stair below. Very awkward, I always think. Anyhow, Smith rang—and waited. He was really quite a bit excited now, you'll understand. Those "sporting prints" were looking even more significant to him now that he'd seen the young lady's surroundings. And he was excited because he wasn't used to this sort of thing—I mean, calling on strange "young ladies" in dingy maisonettes. It was definitely an Adventure, with a capital A.

'So when his ring wasn't answered he felt quite disappointed. However, he thought he'd try again—and was surprised to find what a lot of courage it takes to ring a second time at a strange bell when one isn't sure of one's welcome. But this time he was luckier. He heard a door open inside, and then the flap of the letter-box was lifted and a girl's voice said, "Who is it ?"

'Smith explained hurriedly that he'd called in answer to the advertisement, and there was a pause. Then the girl inside said : "Oh ! Well . . . I'm just having a bath. Could you possibly come back in about half an hour ?"

'I told you Smith was a bit young in those days. It didn't

occur to him to offer to help with the bath, or get the towels warm, or anything. He just said he'd be delighted to come back in half an hour, and went downstairs again like a little gentleman. As a matter of fact, he was thinking what a charming voice it had been. He hadn't really expected that, and it put an edge on his curiosity. He wouldn't have missed his return visit now for wild horses.

'He stopped at the street-door to light a cigarette, and noticed that the little tobacconist wasn't in his shop ; and for some reason that pleased him. It would have looked as if the girl had turned him down, you see, and he didn't like the idea of the fat little frog chuckling over that.

'Well, Smith put in the half-hour on the front. He didn't think it was worth going back to the Cosmopolitan—unfortunately !—and . . .'

'Why "unfortunately" ?' I put in quickly.

'You'll see. And you'll see why it was unfortunate, too, that the front was practically deserted. It was just getting dusk, I ought to explain, and the day was bleak enough to keep people indoors in any case ; so you'll understand that the front wasn't just the most popular spot in Brighton at that moment. Smith spent some of the time striding along in the wind trying to get warm, and some of it huddling in an empty shelter trying to get out of the wind ; and he didn't know which was the lousier. So when his half-hour was up he wasted no time in getting back— and his keenness hadn't lost anything by the delay.

'It was past black-out time by now, and the shops were closed too. Smith noticed as he passed that the tobacconist had shut, and was glad those beady eyes wouldn't follow him through the doorway again this time. He positively jumped up those stairs in spite of the darkness, and you can be pretty sure that by this time Smith wasn't nearly so bored with Brighton as he had been.

'At the top of the stairs he pulled out his lighter to find the bell, and then he noticed a queer thing : the door just wasn't closed. Still, he couldn't walk in, of course, so he rang. No reply. He rang again. Still no reply. Then he wondered : Was it possible that the girl had had to run out for a few minutes, and had left the door ajar especially for him ?

'Now I ought to tell you—you'll find out soon enough in any case—that this chap Smith was rather a timid sort of cove. I mean, hated doing the wrong thing, or shoving himself forward, or making himself conspicuous in any way. Feeble, of course, but there you are ; that's how he was. So it took quite a bit of self-jolting before he could make up his mind to barge in through that open doorway and go on up the next flight of stairs. Probably it was only the thought of that cold, windy front, and the hardly less cold and draughty lounge at the Cosmopolitan that finally made up his mind for him. Like a good few of us, perhaps, Smith loved Adventures with capital A's in theory, but not quite so well in practice. Not an enterprising sort of bloke, you understand. Didn't pretend to be.

'Well, he didn't shut the door behind him, just pushed it to much as it had been. The landing light above was on, but it was too dim to show beyond the door, so there was nothing to worry about the black-out. The landing at the top of the next flight of stairs was furnished like a little hall. Smith hesitated there and gave a hoarse sort of croak by way of a *heil*, but there was no answer. There were two doors opening on to the landing, and one of them was ajar, with the light on inside. So Smith sidled in. He still wasn't quite sure whether he was doing the right thing or not, and was quite prepared to feel the biggest ass in Brighton if things turned out wrong.'

My friend paused and sipped again ; and this time I was careful to say nothing which might break his thread. His face, when he continued a moment or two later, was expressionless.

'It was a nice room. Quite large, but furnished to give an effect of a kind of solid cosiness ; shaded lights, big armchairs, and all that. I believe there was . . . I believe Smith said there was a divan too : it was the sort of room where there would be a divan, and lots of cushions on it too. But *not* a doll over the telephone. No, decidedly not dolls.

'The room brought Smith up with rather a jerk. It wasn't the kind of room he had been expecting, you see. He had expected dolls. He stood irresolute just inside the door, wondering whether to make a bolt for it while the going was good. He was pretty sure now that he had done the wrong thing.

'Then something caught his eye : a portfolio lying on a little rosewood table by one of the armchairs. His brain went click ! "Sporting prints !"

'Well, of course Smith *had* done the right thing. And of

course he'd known all the time really what those "sporting prints" would be. He'd just deliberately been kidding himself, because if the advertisement had said "feelthy pictures" he'd have known that no officer and gent, let alone the fiancé of an officer and lady (in the Wrens), could possibly go chasing after them.

'Mind you, they weren't the limit. Just rather charming nudes—but with that very definite difference, if you know what I mean.'

As a matter of fact I didn't, and murmured as much.

'Stockings,' said my friend succinctly. He paused and smiled. 'Ridiculous, really, isn't it?''

'Quite,' I agreed. 'But rather fun. And there has to be a difference, of course. So I suppose Smith, remembering he was an officer and gent, tiptoed away, and . . .'

'Eh?'

'I mean, everyone lived happily ever afterwards.' Frankly I was disappointed. The story had seemed to be leading up to something better than a glimpse of a few rude postcards. I wondered what all the fuss had been about.

'What?' My companion seemed puzzled.

'I mean, that's the end,' I explained patiently.

'The end? Good heavens, no. I say, I *am* telling this rottenly. Why, we haven't got to the really interesting bit yet.'

'We haven't? Then you're not telling it rottenly at all: you're telling it darned well. Carry on.'

'I say, do you really think so? I don't know anything about telling stories, you know. I'm only telling it exactly as it happened . . . that is, as Smith told me it happened, of course. You really want me to go on?'

I assured him I did want just that, and after ringing the bell again he resumed.

'Well, as a matter of fact you were right. Smith did remember that after all he was an officer and a little gent; and as the houri still didn't show herself, he prepared to depart—and I won't pretend he didn't feel he was doing a pretty noble job. In fact, I don't believe he'd absolutely made up his mind when he noticed a door which looked as if it ought to lead into the adjoining room, and he thought he might just as well take a peep in there before clearing out. No need for nice scruples now, you see. So he did. And . . . and . . .'

'Yes ?' I prompted him.

My companion studied the nails of his left hand with apparent nonchalance, but I could see that his whole arm was tensed. I wondered what on earth was coming.

'There was a naked girl lying on the floor, dead,' he said in a flat voice. 'Her throat had been cut. There was an awful lot of . . . blood.'

'Good Lord !'

'Yes. It gave Smith . . . rather a shock.'

'Well, naturally. What did he do ?'

'That's just the point. What did he do ? He beat it.'

'Beat it ?'

'Yes. Lost his head, I mean. Pretty rotten, don't you think ?'

'Well,' I said carefully, 'I don't know about that. After all, you say he was young, and . . ."

'Yes, but not so young as all that. He ought to have rung up the police there and then. Of course he ought. But . . . don't you see the difficulty ?'

I didn't quite. 'You mean, he didn't want, as an officer, to be mixed up in the murder of . . . ?'

'No, no ! The point was, that little Jew had seen him go in the first time, but he hadn't seen him come out five minutes later. He hadn't seen him come back half an hour afterwards. How was Smith going to prove that he hadn't been there all the time ? He hadn't been back to his hotel, there wasn't a soul who could swear to having seen him on the front. *How was Smith going to prove he hadn't cut the girl's throat himself?*'

'Oh, I see !' I exclaimed softly. 'Yes, of course.'

'As you say. Smith saw the point at once. And I can tell you, it made him sweat. After all, innocent men *have* been convicted . . . or haven't they ? And in any case, what could Smith do ? The girl was dead . . . perfectly dead ! Her murderer was probably with her when Smith first called. But Smith hadn't seen him. He couldn't tell the police anything useful. The case would have been just the same whether Smith had barged into the maisonette or not.

'Besides, there was more to it than that. I told you Smith's own father was a member of a Government Mission, and the girl he was engaged to had a big job in the Waafs . . .'

'As a matter of fact, you said the Wrens,' I murmured.

He looked at me. 'Did I? Well, really it was the Ats. Anyhow, her father was . . . well, I'll just say that to certain newspapers the news of his daughter's fiancé being mixed up in a scandal about a dead prostitute would have seemed just too good to be true. Or so Smith thought. So after sweating blood for a minute or two, trying to decide, he just grabbed up the portfolio and . . . beat it.'

'Ah, he collected the portfolio at all events.'

My tone was ironical, but the blue eyes my host turned on me were innocent. 'Of course,' he said simply. 'It had his finger-prints. Luckily he hadn't touched anything else except the doors, but he couldn't very well take them with him.'

Again I thought he had come to the end, for he paused and sipped thoughtfully at his sherry. But before I could make the appropriate comments he was off again.

'Well, that was that. Smith beat it back to the Cosmopolitan and ordered a couple of the biggest drinks war-time Brighton could manage. He was pretty badly shaken. The portfolio was under his arm, underneath his great-coat, and I can tell you it was burning a hole in his side. As soon as he'd finished his drinks he went up to his bedroom, cut the thing to ribbons with his razor, and burnt the strips in his empty fireplace. Have you ever tried to burn a few dozen shiny postcards? It's not so easy as it sounds. It seemed to Smith to take hours. And when it was done he got in a panic about the ashes, and daren't go down to dinner till he'd collected them all and put them down one of the lavatories and pulled the plug on them.

'Smith didn't enjoy his dinner much that evening.

'Perhaps it was stupid of him to get the wind up so vertically, but . . . I don't know. It seemed to him that a terrible lot hung on it. Not merely himself, you see, but all those other people. There'd be just hell to pay. He could see the headlines: "FIANCÉ OF MINISTER'S DAUGHTER HELD ON MURDER CHARGE," "FATHER IN GOVERNMENT—FIANCÉ IN GAOL." Oh, Lord, I've given it away now. Well, it doesn't matter. Anyhow, you see it *was* serious. And Smith couldn't be sure the police wouldn't trace him. He couldn't be sure that he hadn't done some damn silly thing that would lead the police straight to him. Lord, how he cursed that fat little frog of a tobacconist, with his cursed inquisitive, beady eyes.

"I needn't tell you what sort of an evening he spent. And the night ! It was just hell. Smith's had a sympathy for criminals ever since. Waiting for that touch on the shoulder, you know . . . well, it's true . . . even in one's sleep.

'He thought it all out—oh, half a million times ! And by the morning he'd decided what to do. The obvious thing, he thought, was to get away from Brighton. The police would have his description—bound to ! "Tall young officer, wearing military great-coat and peaked cap, fresh complexion, fair moustache," all the rest of it. So the first thing Smith did was to shave off his moustache ; then he dressed in civvies—luckily he'd brought a suit with him. Then he went down to breakfast . . . and I can tell you it took a bit of courage to do that. Then, as soon as he could manage it, he got out of that hotel. He had a notion that the police would be making a round of the hotels. He had a taxi, and drove to the station. Probably the police would be watching the station too, but he had to chance that.

'The funny thing was, he couldn't remember whether he'd shut the front door of the maisonette. It worried him like hell. If he had, you see, and the girl lived alone . . . well, the murder might not be discovered for days. But if he hadn't, and the lights burning inside . . . it worried poor old Smith to death.

'Anyhow, he got to London all right. There was just one moment of panic, in the train. He was lighting a cigarette, and suddenly he remembered that the Jew could identify his lighter. It would be one of the first things the police would know. For all he knew the two other blokes in his carriage had heard of it somewhere already, and were on the look-out for it. He just jumped up, barged down the corridor to the lavatory, and threw the thing down. It was a nice lighter too.

'There was nothing about the murder in the papers, and after a time Smith calmed down a bit. Perhaps he had left that door shut after all. He tried not to think of that poor girl lying there, all naked and cold, with the electric light burning overhead, just waiting for someone to come and find her . . . someone else, who wouldn't make such a mucker of it . . . someone else, in fact, who hadn't got other people to protect first.

"He put up at a hotel and spent the afternoon at his club. After tea he went to a theatre (remember what queer times the theatres used to keep during the war ?). And whom do you think he ran into in the first interval? No—not a Brighton policeman: his girl. She'd got twenty-four hours' leave, rung up the Cosmopolitan just after he left, and his club ditto. The porter was able to tell her where he'd gone, so it wasn't a coincidence. (You writer blokes don't like coincidences, I know.)

'Well, of course she took him off home for food after the show and wanted to know what had happened to his moustache. So it all came out. Well, not all. Smith managed to fake up some kind of a reason for calling on the girl without mentioning the sporting prints, and he didn't volunteer the information that she was a tart. But he told her all about the Jew, and the black-out being done in the flat (of course you spotted that more or less fixed the time of the murder), and the jam he was in over it all. As a matter of fact he wanted to tell her. She was a . . . well, frankly, she was twice the man poor old Smith was. Clear-headed, you know, sensible and intelligent and all that, a really capable girl ; one of the very best. God knows what she ever saw in poor old Smith."

'You knew her, then?' I could not help putting in maliciously.

'Eh? Oh! Well, yes ; as a matter of fact, I did. Slightly, you know. Just slightly.'

'Yes, and what did she say?'

'Oh, she took it very sensibly. Didn't ask any awkward questions. Quite saw it wasn't Smith's fault. Didn't blame him a bit for clearing out. Quite saw his point about her father, and herself. In fact, behaved exactly like the grand girl she was.'

'Good. So all ended happily?' I said, again conscious of disappointment. Dash it all, a fellow should not tell a murder story at all if it is going to end in a series of anti-climaxes. If a man gets mixed up in a murder, his life ought to be affected by it in some way. A murder, to be artistic, ought to behave like a bomb in the lives of law-abiding citizens, with its wounded as well as its slain.

'Happily? The devil it did !' exclaimed my host with energy. 'That's the whole point. You see, the girl took it for granted that Smith had only delayed going to the police until he had talked it all over with her. When she told him that it didn't matter a cuss about her father, or herself, she expected him to march straight off to the nearest police-station and spill the whole story.'

'Oh !'

'Yes. That's rather how Smith felt. Because he just didn't see it that way. He pointed out over and over again the harm it might do her father, he even let drop a hint or two as to the girl's real profession and the sort of unsavoury scandal it would mean. But it was no good. They argued the whole evening but the girl wouldn't budge an inch. It was his duty to go to the police, irrespective of the consequences to anyone, so go he must : and that was all there was to it.

'Well, I'm afraid you can see what's coming. Smith couldn't keep it up for ever. It was clear the girl meant what she said about her family, and gradually she pulled that line out of Smith's grasp. He had been clinging to it, you see. But when they came to the real show-down, they both had to face the truth. It hadn't been the girl's family Smith was really thinking of : it had been himself. And that was the moral problem Smith was driven in the end to face : either to go to the police, confess to what he'd done and what he'd left undone, and take the rap if it was coming to him, or . . . !' My host broke off, swallowed a sip or two of sherry, and then added quietly : 'Or admit himself to both of them a coward.' He looked me suddenly in the face. 'Which would you have done ?'

'God knows ! Which did Smith ?'

He twiddled the stem of his wine-glass. 'Smith *wanted* to do the right thing. I think we can say that for him. But when it came to the point . . . ! After all, there were so many factors. He was keen on his job in the Army ; doing well, too. And there was the girl's father : Smith couldn't brush him aside like his daughter had done. And his own father too. And after all, how could it help if he did go to the police ? He couldn't tell them anything they wouldn't know already. No ! It's no good making excuses. Smith just hadn't the guts. Not even when the girl made a personal matter of it. Finally she cut short his blethering and told him plainly that she couldn't marry a . . . a coward. Either he went to the police then and there, or their engagement was at an end. Smith felt like death, but . . . he couldn't go to the police and chance being arrested for a murder he hadn't done. So the girl pulled off her ring, Smith took it. . . .' He sighed. 'Smith never saw her again.'

There was silence.

At last I said : 'And that really was the end ?'

'Not quite.' An ironic little smile played round his mouth. 'There's just one more touch—quite a nice one. To get back to his hotel Smith had to go to an Underground Station. The bookstall was closed, but by it there was one of those blackboards they used for contents-bills in the war. Smith saw chalked up on it : "Girl Murdered at Brighton. Man Confesses." '

'Perfect !' I exclaimed. 'Of course I can use it. Why, it's a short story as it stands, twist in the tale and all.'

'I thought you might be interested,' said my host mildly. 'Er . . . you will wrap it up a bit, though, won't you ? I mean . . .'

'Oh, yes. It's only the essence I want. But what a climax ! Hero forced by heroine like a rat into corner ; heroine drawn up to her full height, relentless and contemptuous ; finger-of-scorn business ; hero slinks out into the snow (I hope it was snowing) . . . life shattered . . . empty future . . . the dishonour of the regiment . . . I suppose he did love her, by the way ? Yes, of course he did, or it would be a lousy story. And then that nasty jab under the ribs from the blackboard, showing that all his agony had been in vain and if the poor boob had only held his tongue like any sensible man . . .'

My host looked bewildered and not a little hurt. 'I don't quite understand ?'

'Why,' I said unmercifully, 'It's a good short story, sliced off just there. But Smith wasn't a short story. He was a man. And was Smith's life really shattered ?'

'Well, no, if you put it like that. I suppose it wasn't.'

'I do put it like that. You see, things work out a bit differently in real life. It doesn't stop, for instance, like a short story does. Now, is this Smith of yours married ?'

'Er . . . yes, he is.'

'Any children ?'

'Well, a couple . . .'

'Does he love his wife ?'

'Of course he does.'

'Good ! Then shall I tell you what I think ? I think Smith had the devil's own luck.'

'What on earth do you mean ?'

'Why, can't you see ? But for that little episode Smith might be married now to a cold, unemotional, steel-bar of a woman, without a spark of humanity or the decent femininity to love a man all the *more* for lacking a bit of moral guts once in a while— if indeed anybody but one of those death-or-duty fiends could call it moral guts to go and get oneself gratuitously arrested for a murder in which one had no concern at all. Take it from me, Smith was well out of that engagement. Don't you agree?'

'Well, I . . . Smith . . . I don't think Smith's ever looked at it that way,' he stammered.

'Oh, I've no doubt Smith will have thoroughly dramatised the episode,' I rubbed it in. After all, I owed him a good turn for the story, though he might not know I was doing him one. 'But you tell him from me that it's about time he saw it in its proper perspective. The whole problem was artificial, and to make it a test of true love was the act of an iceberg, not of a grand girl. Instead of helping Smith to increase his normal stock of courage, which a decent girl does by encouraging his *amour propre*. that smug little wretch did him a great deal of harm. It takes two to make a hero, you know. Instead it's obvious she gave him a bad inferiority complex, by the angle he stresses of his own story. Now look here, you take Smith aside and tell him from me that he's got just as much guts as the next man. It's all nonsense to go on looking on himself as a spineless sort of——'

A large hand suddenly descended on my shoulder and a large voice boomed in my ear. 'Hullo, old boy! Sorry I'm a bit late and all that. Someone been feeding you the odd spot of sherry? Good!'

'Yes, I don't know if . . .' I looked round for my late host, but his place was vacant. Behind me I heard a door quietly closing. I tried to keep the intense curiosity out of my voice. 'Yes, some complete stranger's been very kind. Did you happen to see him, George? I wish you could find out who he is.'

'Oh, I know who he is,' George said largely. 'New member. Name of Farquharson. 'S a matter of fact he's rather our star turn here.'

'Star turn?'

'Yes. Our one and only V.C.'

In Vino Veritas

By A. A. Milne

I am in a terrible predicament, as you will see directly. I don't know what to do. . . .

'One of the maxims which I have found most helpful in my career,' the Superintendent was saying, 'apart, of course, from employing a good Press agent, has been the simple one that appearances are not always deceptive. A crime may be committed exactly as it seems to have been committed, and exactly as it was intended to be committed.' He helped himself and passed the bottle.

'I don't think I follow you,' I said, hoping thus to lead him on.

I am a writer of detective stories. If you have never heard of me, it can only be because you don't read detective stories. I wrote *Murder on the Back Stairs* and *The Mystery of the Twisted Eglantine*, to mention only two of my successes. It was this fact, I think, which first interested Superintendent Frederick Mortimer in me, and, of course, me in him. He is a big fellow with the face of a Roman Emperor ; I am rather the small neat type. We gradually became friends, and so got into the habit of dining together once a month. He liked talking about his cases, and naturally I liked listening. I may say now that *Blood on the Eiderdown* was suggested to me by an experience of his at Crouch End. He also liked putting me right when I made mistakes, as so many of us do, over such technical matters as finger-prints and Scotland Yard procedure. I had always supposed, for instance, that you could get good finger-prints from butter. This, apparently, is not the case. From buttery fingers on other objects, yes, but not from the pat of butter itself, or, anyhow, not in hot weather. This, of course, was a foolish mistake of mine, as in any case Lady Sybil would not have handled the butter directly in this way, as my detective should have seen. My detective, by the way, is called Sherman Flagg, and is pretty well known by now. Not that this is germane to my present story.

'I don't think I follow you,' I said.

'I mean that the simple way of committing a murder is often the best way. This doesn't mean that the murderer is a man of simple mind. On the contrary. He is subtle enough to know that the simple solution is too simple to be credible.'

233

This sounded anything but simple, so I said, 'Give me an example.'

'Well, take the case of the magnum of Tokay which was sent to the Marquis of Hedingham on his lordship's birthday. Have I never told you about it?'

'Never,' I said, and I, too, helped myself and passed the bottle.

He filled his glass and considered. 'Give me a moment to get it clear,' he said, 'It was a long time ago.' While he closed his eyes, and let the past drift before him, I ordered up another bottle of the same; a Chateau Latour '78, of which I understand there is very little left in the country.

'Yes,' said Mortimer, opening his eyes, 'I've got it now.'

I leant forward, listening eagerly. This is the story he told me.

The first we heard of it at the Yard (said Mortimer) was a brief announcement over the telephone that the Marquis of Hedingham's butler had died suddenly at his lordship's town house in Brook Street, and that poison was suspected. This was at seven o'clock. We went round at once. Inspector Totman had been put in charge of the case; I was a young Detective Sergeant at the time, and I generally worked under Totman. He was a brisk, military sort of fellow, with a little prickly ginger moustache, good at his job in a showy, orthodox way, but he had no imagination, and he was thinking all the time of what Inspector Totman would get out of it. Quite frankly I didn't like him. Outwardly we kept friendly, for it doesn't do to quarrel with one's superiors; indeed, he was vain enough to think that I had a great admiration for him; but I knew that he was just using me for his own advantage, and I had a shrewd suspicion that I should have been promoted before this, if he hadn't wanted to keep me under him so that he could profit by my brains.

We found the butler in his pantry, stretched out on the floor. An open bottle of Tokay, a broken wine-glass with the dregs of the liquid still in it, the medical evidence of poisoning, all helped to build up the story for us. The wine had arrived about an hour before, with the card of Sir William Kelso attached to it. On the card was a typewritten message, saying, 'Bless you, Tommy, and here's something to celebrate it with.' I can't

knew that Sir William Kelso was a friend of his lordship's and called him Tommy, and that he might reasonably give him a bottle of wine on his birthday. He did *not* know that Sir William would be dining there that night ; that is to say, *even as late as six o'clock that evening, he did not know.* He was not likely, therefore, to be anyone at present employed or living in Lord Hedingham's house. Finally, he had had an opportunity, for what this was worth, to get hold of a card of Sir William's.

As it happened, there was somebody who fitted completely into this picture. It was a fellow called—wait a bit—Merrivale, Medley—oh, well, it doesn't matter. Merton, that was it, Merton. He had been his lordship's valet for six months, had been suspected of stealing, and dismissed without a character. Just the man we wanted. So for a fortnight we searched for Merton. And then, when at last we got on to him, we discovered that he had the most complete *alibi* imaginable. (*The Superintendent held up his hand, and it came into my mind that he must have stopped the traffic as a young man with just that gesture.*) Yes, I know what you're going to say, what you detective-story writers always say—the better an *alibi*, the worse it is. Well, sometimes, I admit ; but not in this case. For Merton was in gaol, under another name, and he had been inside for the last two months. And what do you think he was suspected of, and now waiting trial for ? Oh, well, of course you guess, I've as good as told you. He was on a charge of murder—and murder, mark you, by poison.

'Good heavens,' I interjected. I seized the opportunity to refill my friend's glass. He said, 'Exactly,' and took a long drink. I thought fancifully that he was drinking to drown that terrible disappointment of so many years ago.

You can't imagine (he went on) what a shock this was to us. You see, a certain sort of murder had been committed ; we had deduced that it was done by a certain man, without knowing whether he was in the least capable of such a crime ; and now, having proved to the hilt that he *was* capable of it, we had simultaneously proved that he didn't do it. We had proved ourselves right—and our case mud.

I said to Totman, 'Let's take a couple of days off, and each of us think it out, and then pool our ideas and start afresh.'

Totman frisked up his little moustache, and laughed in his

conceited way. 'You don't think I'm going to admit myself wrong, do you, when I've just proved I'm right?' Totman saying 'I,' when he had got everything from me! 'Merton's my man. He'd got the bottle ready, and somebody else delivered it for him. That's all. He had to wait for the birthday, you see, and when he found himself in prison, his wife or somebody——'

'—took round the bottle, all nicely labelled "Poison; not to be delivered till Christmas Day."' I had to say it, I was so annoyed with him.

'Don't be more of a damned fool than you can help,' he shouted, 'and don't be insolent, or you'll get into trouble.'

I apologized humbly, and told him how much I liked working with him. He forgave me—and we were friends again. He patted me on the shoulder.

'You take a day off,' he said kindly, 'you've been working too hard. Take a bus into the country and make up a good story for me; the story of that bottle, and how it came from Merton's lodging to Brook Street, and who took it and why. I admit I don't see it at present, but that's the bottle, you can bet your life. I'm going down to Leatherhead. Report here on Friday morning, and we'll see what we've got. My birthday, as it happens, and I feel I'm going to be lucky.' Leatherhead was where this old woman had been poisoned. That was the third time in a week he'd told me when his entirely misconceived birthday was. He was like that.

I took a bus to Hampstead Heath. I walked round the Leg of Mutton Pond twenty times. And each time that I went round, Totman's theory seemed sillier than the last time. And each time I felt more and more strongly that we were being *forced* into an entirely artificial interpretation of things. It sounds fantastic, I know, but I could almost feel the murderer behind us, pushing us along the way he wanted us to go.

I sat down on a seat, and I filled a pipe, and I said, 'Right! The murderer's a man who wanted me to believe all that I have believed. When I've told myself that the murderer intended to do so-and-so, he intended me to believe that, and therefore he didn't do so-and-so. When I've told myself that the murderer wanted to mislead me, he wanted me to think he wanted to mislead me, which meant that the truth was exactly as it seemed to be. Now then, Fred, you'll begin all over again, and you'll take things as

they are, and won't be too clever about them. Because the murderer expects you to be clever, and wants you to be clever, and from now on you aren't going to take your orders from *him*.'

And of course, the first thing which leaped to my mind was that the murderer *meant* to murder the butler !

It seemed incredible now that we could ever have missed it. Didn't every butler sample his master's wines ? Why, it was an absolute certainty that Perkins would be the first victim of a poisoned bottle of a very special vintage. What butler could resist pouring himself out a glass as he decanted it ?

Wait, though. Mustn't be in a hurry. Two objections. One : Perkins might be the one butler in a thousand who wasn't a wine-sampler. Two : Even if he were like any other butler, he might be out of sorts on that particular evening, and have put by a glass to drink later. Wouldn't it be much too risky for a murderer who only wanted to destroy Perkins, and had no grudge against Lord Hedingham's family, to depend so absolutely on the butler drinking first ?

For a little while this held me up, but not for long. Suddenly I saw the complete solution. It would *not* be risky if (*a*) the murderer had certain knowledge of the butler's habits ; and (*b*) could, if necessary, at the last moment, prevent the family from drinking. In other words, if he were an intimate of the family, were himself present at the party, and, without bringing suspicion on himself, could bring the wine under suspicion. In other words, and only, and finally, and definitely—if he were Sir William Kelso. For Sir William was the only man in the world who could say, 'Don't drink this wine. I'm supposed to have sent it to you, and I didn't, so that proves it's a fake.' The *only* man.

Why hadn't we suspected him from the beginning ? One reason, of course, was that we had supposed the intended victim to be one of the Hedingham family, and of Sir William's devotion to his sister, brother-in-law, nephew and nieces, there was never any doubt. But the chief reason was our assumption that the last thing a murderer would do would be to give himself away by sending his own card round with the poisoned bottle. 'The *last* thing a murderer would do'—and therefore the *first* thing a really clever murderer would do. For it couldn't be explained as 'the one mistake which every murderer makes' ; he couldn't send his own card accidentally. 'Impossible,' we said, that a murderer should do it deliberately ! But the correct answer was, Impossible that we should not be deceived if it were done deliberately—and therefore brilliantly clever.

To make my case complete to myself, for I had little hope as yet of converting Totman, I had to establish motive. Why should Sir William want to murder Perkins ? I gave myself the pleasure of having tea that afternoon with Lord Hedingham's cook-housekeeper. We had caught each other's eye on other occasions when I had been at the house, and—well, I suppose I can say it now—I had a way with the women in those days. When I left, I knew two things. Perkins had been generally unpopular, not only downstairs, but upstairs ; 'it was a wonder how they put up with him.' And her ladyship had been 'a different woman lately.'

'How different ?' I asked.

'So much younger, if you know what I mean, Sergeant Mortimer. Almost like a girl again, bless her heart.'

I did know. And that was that. Blackmail.

What was I to do ? What did my evidence amount to ? Nothing. It was all corroborative evidence. If Kelso had done one suspicious thing, or left one real clue, then the story I had made up would have convinced any jury. As it was, in the eyes of a jury he had done one completely unsuspicious thing, and left one real clue to his innocence—his visiting-card. Totman would just laugh at me.

I disliked the thought of being laughed at by Totman. I wondered how I could get the laugh of him. I took a bus to Baker Street, and walked into Regent's Park, not minding where I was going, but just thinking. And then, as I got opposite Hanover Terrace, who should I see but young Roberts.

'Hallo, young fellow, what have *you* been up to ?'

'Hallo, Sarge,' he grinned. 'Been calling on my old school-chum, Sir Woppity Wotsit—or rather, his valet. Tottie thought he might have known Merton. Speaking as one valet to another, so to speak.'

'Is Inspector Totman back ?' I asked.

Roberts stood to attention, and said, 'No, Sergeant Mortimer, Inspector Totman is not expected to return from Leatherhead, Surrey, until a late hour to-night.'

You couldn't be angry with the boy. At least I couldn't.

He had no respect for anybody, but he was a good lad. And he had an eye like a hawk. Saw everything and forgot none of it.

'I suppose by Sir Woppity Wotsit you mean Sir William Kelso,' I said. 'I didn't know he lived up this way.'

Roberts pointed across the road. 'Observe the august mansion. Five minutes ago you'd have found me in the basement, talking to a cock-eyed churchwarden who thought Merton was in Surrey. As it is, of course.'

I had a sudden crazy idea.

'Well, now you're going back there,' I said. 'I'm going to call on Sir William, and I want you handy. Would they let you in at the basement again, or are they sick of you ?'

'Sarge, they just love me. When I went, they said "Must you go ?" '

We say at the Yard, 'Once a murderer, always a murderer.' Perhaps that was why I had an absurd feeling that I should like young Roberts within call. Because I was going to tell Sir William Kelso what I'd been thinking about by the Leg of Mutton Pond. I'd only seen him once, but he gave me the idea of being the sort of man who wouldn't mind killing, but didn't like lying. I thought he would give himself away . . . and then —well, there might be a rough house, and young Roberts would be useful.

As we walked in at the gate together, I looked in my pocket-book for a card. Luckily I had one left, though it wasn't very clean. Roberts, who never missed anything, said, 'Personally I always use blotting-paper,' and went on whistling. If I hadn't known him, I shouldn't have known what he was talking about. I said, 'Oh, do you ?' and rang the bell. I gave the maid my card, and asked if Sir William could see me, and at the same time Roberts gave her a wink, and indicated the back door. She nodded to him, and asked me to come in. Roberts went down and waited for her at the basement. I felt safer.

Sir William was a big man, as big as I was. But of course a lot older. He said, 'Well, Sergeant, what can I do for you ?' twiddling my card in his fingers. He seemed quite friendly about it. 'Sit down, won't you ?'

I said, 'I think I'll stand, Sir William. I wanted just to ask you one question if I might.' Yes, I know I was crazy, but somehow I felt kind of inspired.

'By all means,' he said, obviously not much interested.

'When did you first discover that Perkins was blackmailing Lady Hedingham ?'

He was standing in front of his big desk, and I was opposite to him. He stopped fiddling with my card, and became absolutely still ; and there was a silence so complete that I could feel it in every nerve of my body. I kept my eyes on his, you may be sure. We stood there, I don't know how long.

'Is that the only question ?' he asked. The thing that frightened me was that his voice was just the same as before. Ordinary.

'Well, just one more. Have you a Corona typewriter in your house ?' You see, we knew that a Corona had been used, but there was nothing distinctive about it, and it might have been any one in a thousand. Just corroborative evidence again, that's all. But it told him that I knew.

He gave a long sigh, tossed the card into the waste-paper basket, and walked to the window. He stood there with his back to me, looking out but seeing nothing. Thinking. He must have stood there for a couple of minutes. Then he turned round, and to my amazement he had a friendly smile on his face. 'I think we'd both better sit down,' he said. We did.

'There is a Corona in the house which I sometimes use,' he began. 'I dare say you use one too.'

'I do.'

'And so do thousands of other people—including, it may be, the murderer you are looking for.'

'Thousands of people including the murderer,' I agreed.

He noticed the difference, and smiled. 'People' I had said, not 'other people.' And I didn't say I was looking for him. Because I had found him.

'So much for that. There is nothing in the actual wording of the typed message to which you would call my attention ?'

'No. Except that it was exactly right.'

'Oh, my dear fellow, anyone could have got it right. A simple birthday greeting.'

'Anyone in your own class, Sir William, who knew you both. But that's all. It's Inspector Totman's birthday to-morrow'—as he keeps telling us, damn him, I added to myself. 'If I sent him a bottle of whisky, young Roberts—that's the constable who's in on this case, you may have seen him about, he's waiting for me now down below'—I thought this was rather a neat way of getting that in—'Roberts could make a guess at what I'd say, and so could anybody at the Yard who knows us both, and they wouldn't be far wrong. But *you* couldn't, Sir William.'

He looked at me. He couldn't take his eyes off me. I wondered what he was thinking. At last he said : 'A long life and all the best, with the admiring good wishes of—how's that ?'

It was devilish. First that he had really been thinking it out, when he had so much else to think about, and then that he'd got it so right. That 'admiring' ; which meant that he'd studied Totman just as he was studying me, and knew how I'd play up to him.

'You see,' he smiled, 'it isn't really difficult. And the fact that my card was used is in itself convincing evidence of my innocence, don't you think ?'

'To a jury perhaps,' I said, 'but not to me.'

'I wish I could convince *you*,' he murmured to himself. 'Well, what are you doing about it ?'

'I shall, of course, put my reconstruction of the case in front of Inspector Totman to-morrow.'

'Ah ! A nice birthday surprise for him. And, knowing your Totman, what do you think he will do ?'

He had me there, and he knew it.

'I think you know him too, Sir,' I said.

'I do,' he smiled.

'And me, I dare say, and anybody else you meet. Quick as lightning. But even ordinary men like me have a sort of sudden understanding of people sometimes. As I've got of you, Sir. And I've a sort of feeling that, if ever we get you into a witness-box, and you've taken the oath, you won't find perjury so much to your liking as murder. Or what the Law calls murder.'

'But *you* don't ?' he said quickly.

'I think,' I said, 'that there are a lot of people who *ought* to be killed. But I'm a policeman, and what I think isn't evidence. You killed Perkins, didn't you ?'

He nodded ; and then said, almost with a grin at me, 'A nervous affection of the head, if you put it in evidence. I could get a specialist to swear to it.' My God, he was a good sort of man. I was really sorry when they found him next day on the

Underground. Or what was left of him. And yet what else could he do ? He knew I should get him.

I was furious with Fred Mortimer. That was no way to end a story. Suddenly, like that, as if he were tired of it. I told him so.

'My dear little Cyril,' he said, 'it isn't the end. We're just coming to the exciting part. This will make your hair curl.'

'Oh !' I said sarcastically. 'Then I suppose all that you've told me so far is just introduction ?'

'That's right. Now listen. On the Friday morning, before we heard of Sir William's death, I went in to report to Inspector Totman. He wasn't there. Nobody knew where he was. They rang up his block of flats. Now hold tight to the leg of the table or something. When the porter got into his flat, he found Totman's body. Poisoned.'

'Good heavens !' I ejaculated.

'You may say so. There he was, and on the table was a newly opened bottle of whisky, and by the side of it a visiting-card. And whose card do you think it was ? *Mine !* And what do you think it said ? "A long life and all the best with the admiring good wishes of"—*me !* Lucky for me I had had young Roberts with me. Lucky for me he had this genius for noticing and remembering. Lucky for me he could swear to the exact shape of the smudge of ink on that card. And I might add, lucky for me that they believed me when I told them word for word what had been said at my interview with Sir William, as I have just told you. I was reprimanded, of course, for exceeding my duty, as I most certainly had, but that was only official. Unofficially they were very pleased with me. We couldn't prove anything, naturally, and Sir William's death had looked as accidental as anything could, so we just had to leave it. But a month later I was promoted to Inspector.'

He filled his glass and drank, while I revolved his extraordinary story in my mind.

'The theory,' I said, polishing my pince-nez thoughtfully, 'was, I suppose, this. Sir William sent the poisoned whisky, not so much to get rid of Totman, from whom he had little to fear, as to discredit you by bringing you under suspicion, and entirely to discredit your own theory of the other murder.'

'Exactly.'

'And then, at the last moment he realized that he couldn't go on with it, or the weight of his crimes became suddenly too much for him, or——'

'Something of the sort.   Nobody ever knew, of course.'

I looked across the table with sudden excitement ; almost with awe.

'Do you remember what he said to you ?' I asked, giving the words their full meaning as I slowly quoted them. ' "The fact that my card was used is convincing evidence of my innocence." And you said, "Not to me."   And he said, "I wish I could convince *you*."   *And that was how he did it !*   The fact that your card was used *was* convincing evidence of your innocence !'

'With the other things.   The proof that he was in possession of the particular card of mine which was used, and the certainty that he had committed the other murder.   Once a poisoner, always a poisoner.'

'True . . . yes . . . .   Well, thanks very much for the story, Fred.   All the same, you know,' I said, shaking my head at him, 'it doesn't altogether prove what you set out to prove.'

'What was that ?'

'That the simple explanation is generally the true one.   In the case of Perkins, yes.   But not in the case of Totman.'

'Sorry, I don't follow.'

'My dear fellow,' I said, putting up a finger to emphasize my point, for he seemed a little hazy with the wine suddenly ; 'the *simple* explanation of Totman's death—surely ?—would have been that *you* had sent him the poisoned whisky.'

Superintendent Mortimer looked a little surprised.

'But I did,' he said.

So now you see my terrible predicament.   I could hardly listen as he went on dreamily : 'I never liked Totman, and he stood in my way ; but I hadn't seriously thought of getting rid of him, until I got that card into my hands again.   As I told you, he dropped it into the basket, and turned to the window, and I thought, Damn it, *you* can afford to chuck about visiting-cards, but I can't, and it's the only one I've got left, and if you don't want it, I do.   So I bent down very naturally to do up my boot-lace, and felt in the basket behind me, because of course it was rather an undignified thing to do, and I didn't want to be seen ; and it was just as I was putting it into my pocket that I saw that ink-smudge again, and I remembered that Roberts had seen it. And in a flash the whole plan came to me ; simple ; fool-proof. And from that moment everything I said to him was in preparation of it.   Course we were quite alone, but you never know who might be listening, and besides'—he twiddled the stem of his empty wine-glass—'p'raps I'm like Sir William, rather tell the truth than not, and it *was* true, all of it as I told the Super, how Sir William came to know about Totman's birthday, and knew that those were the very words I should have used.   Made it very convincing, me just repeating to the Super what had really been said. Don't think I wanted to put anything on to Sir William that wasn't his.   I liked him.   But he as good as told me he wasn't going to wait for what was coming to him, and he'd done one murder, anyway.   That was why I slipped down with the bottle that evening, and left it outside Totman's flat.   Didn't dare wait till the morning, in case Sir William closed his account that night.'   He stood up and stretched himself.   'Ah, well, it was a long time ago.   Good-bye, old man, I must be off.   Thanks for a grand dinner.   Don't forget, you're dining with *me* next month. I've got a new cocktail for you.   You'll like it.'—He swaggered out, leaving me to my thoughts.

'Once a murderer, always a murderer. . . .'   And to-morrow he will wake up and remember what he has told me !   And I shall be the only person in the world who knows his secret ! . . .

Perhaps he won't remember.   Perhaps he was drunk . . .

In vino veritas.   Wasn't it the younger Pliny who said that ? A profound observation.   Truth in the bottle. . . .

'Once a poisoner, always a poisoner.' . . .

I feel I ought to do something. . . .   *What ?* . . .

'I've got a new cocktail for you.   You'll like it.'

Yes, but—shall I ?

'Mr Bearstowe Says . . .'

By Anthony Berkeley

For the first few months of the war Bloomsbury was able to carry on much as usual. Besides, to give a beer-and-sausage party, or even to attend a beer-and-sausage party, seemed a subtle defiance of Hitler and all his wars. That, at any rate, was the impression that Roger Sheringham was receiving at a party which he found himself unaccountably attending in the month of November, 1939.

Roger did not care much for parties, even beer-parties; nor did he care much for Bloomsbury. For that matter Bloomsbury cared even less for Roger Sheringham. Either it knew him not or, if it did know, despised his best-selling capacities—and was inclined to go a few steps out of its way to let him know it. In due course, therefore, Roger, tired of being snubbed, betook himself and his tankard into a corner and surveyed the smoke-wreathed hubbub with a surly frown.

Like gravitates to like. Into Roger's corner there imperceptibly edged a woman, obviously as lonely as himself but wearing in place of a surly frown a fixed and determined smile. Roger surveyed her. She was a somewhat faded lady, of middle middle-age, who had once been prettier than she was now. Her clothes were worn as wrong as even female Bloomsbury can wear clothes, but, unlike theirs, were expensive. She was clearly out of place, and Roger decided that behind the fixed smile she was unhappy.

'Do you want to get away?' he said suddenly. 'I do. Let's go.'

The lady started. She seemed unused to being addressed by strangers, even at a Bloomsbury party. 'Go away?' she repeated vaguely. 'Oh, *no* ! I think it's wonderful !'

'Do you?' Roger said glumly. 'What in particular?'

'Oh, well . . . everything. I mean, all these authors and . . . and poets and people. Oh, I do so wish I could write. Perhaps you write. Do you?'

'No,' Roger said firmly.

'It must be wonderful to be able to, don't you think? Well . . . Mr Bearstowe says he believes I could, if I could find a theme. Er . . . you know Mr Bearstowe's work, of course?'

There seemed so much appeal in the question that Roger, rather to his own surprise, succumbed.   'Of course.'

She's in love with him, he thought without enthusiasm, as he noted the pleasure, singularly tinged with relief, or even gratitude, which at once illumined his companion's face.   He wondered who this Bearstowe was, and why he was not looking after his own, as he prepared for the worst.

He received it.   A flood of Mr Bearstowe promptly poured over him.   'Mr Bearstowe says . . .'   Roger wondered how Mr Bearstowe found time to say so much.

But all is salvage that falls into a novelist's dustbin.   Fascinated, Roger began planning a short story.   It would be called 'Mr Bearstowe says . . .', and it would be about . . . well, it would be partly about Mr Bearstowe, of course.

'By the way, is Mr Bearstowe here?' Roger asked.   It is as well to have a working idea of one's characters' appearance.

'Oh, yes,' the lady said eagerly.   'He's over there.'   Her glance appeared to indicate a group of three bearded young men, one tall, one short, and one middling.   There was nothing to show the height of Mr Bearstowe.   Roger could not decide whether he should be the tall, cadaverous young man, the short, bouncing young man, or the middling, might-be-anything young man.

There must be a triangle, of course.   The faded lady's husband . . .

'Of course my husband isn't much interested in that sort of thing,' the lady supplied, rather wistfully.

'Of course not,' Roger said with gratitude.   No, of course the husband mustn't be interested.   The husband must be a self-made man, who married a little above him and now thinks he married below him : a self-opinionated, self-satisfied man, who . . .

'You see, my husband doesn't care for me to go to concerts without him, and as he doesn't care to go himself . . .'

'Exactly !' . . . who rules his wife out of school as well as in, and won't let her go to concerts.   Excellent.   Probably one of those short, pompous little men.

'How tall is your husband?' Roger asked abruptly.

The lady looked taken aback.   'How tall?   Well, I don't really know.'

'Oh, come, you must know whether your husband's tall or

short,' Roger said impatiently. Ridiculous woman ! It was important that the husband should be short, because then Mr Bearstowe could be the tall, cadaverous young man.

'No, I think he's just about . . . average.'

'In a country of dwarfs the average man is a giant,' said Roger, inaccurately as well as inanely ; but he judged that this was the sort of thing that the lady attended Bloomsbury parties to hear, and it seemed a pity that she shouldn't have at least one gem to carry away with her.

He was going on to supply more, out of sheer kindness, when his companion uttered a sudden exclamation and made a rush for the door. Through the doorway Roger just had a glimpse of a blond head throwing an abrupt nod in her direction, and Mr Bearstowe passed—the secret still unsolved. All three young men had been blonds.

'Gentlemen prefer to be blonds,' Roger muttered sourly.

'Was that an epigram, my sweet ?' asked a familiar voice.

'Crystal !' Roger exclaimed with relief. 'Fancy seeing you in this bear-pit. And talking of bears, who is Mr Bearstowe ? You know him, of course. You know everyone.'

'Michael Bearstowe ? Yes. Well, I don't know quite how to describe him. He would be a dilettante, if he had any money. But he hasn't. So he dilettants on other people's.'

'He's a sponger ?' Roger asked delightedly. Oh, admirable, sponging, cadaverous Mr Bearstowe, taking the wives of pompous average self-made men to concerts (wife paying) !

'I should say so. Why look so pleased about it ?'

'Because it fits so nicely. Crystal, tell me more of this Bearstowe. My interest in him is insatiable.'

'I don't know that there's anything more to tell you. He's the type who runs after the wives of rich men, and feeds them Culture and Literature in return for temporary loans. A literary gigolo, you might call him. I hear he's got hold of some groceress now and is toting her everywhere.'

'Groceress, Crystal ?'

'The female of a grocer. At least, I understand that the husband makes big noises in Mincing Lane. Isn't that where they groce ?'

'No, I think it's where they drink tea and spit it out again. But this Bearstowe, Crystal . . . has he published much ?'

s

'Nothing, that I'm aware of. Oh, yes, I believe he did have a short story printed in one of the cheap magazines once,' said Crystal, whose job it was to know everything about everyone, and even a few things that they did not know themselves.

'It's perfect !' Roger said ecstatically. 'I shall write the story this very evening.'

Roger did not write the story that evening, or any evening ; and within a week he had forgotten the very name of Bearstowe.

But Mr Bearstowe's story was being written none the less, if by a different hand—and in a different medium.

'She seems terrible upset, sir,' said the Station Sergeant doubtfully. 'Crying her eyes out already, and she doesn't even know the body's been found. I don't know whether she's fit to interrogate, sir.'

'Well, try to get her to pull herself together,' the Superintendent said impatiently. The bathing is dangerous round Penhampton, and one gets so inured to corpses after twenty years' police service that it is difficult to realise that the relatives are not equally hardened off. In his home the Superintendent was the kindest of men, and loathed killing mice.

'You won't want to wait for this, Mr Sheringham,' the Superintendent added to his visitor. 'A woman come to report her husband missing after bathing. As a matter of fact, we've got the body already, but she doesn't know that. I'm afraid she'll go a bit hysterical when she does. They often do,' added the Superintendent with a sigh.

'No, I'll slide out,' Roger agreed. 'In any case, it looks as if the Colonel isn't coming this afternoon ; so . . .'

He broke off. The Sergeant had returned already, with his charge. Roger, having no wish to intrude on the woman's grief, waited for them to pass before slipping quietly out. Then he caught sight of the woman's face and, after a moment of indecision, returned unobtrusively to his chair.

The woman was given a seat facing the Superintendent's desk. She had pulled herself together bravely, but from the clenched hands on her lap it was clear that she was vibrating with nerves.

The Superintendent made soothing noises. 'Now, Mrs Hutton, let me see . . . you're worried about your husband ?'

The woman nodded, choked, and said : 'Yes. He went out

bathing this morning. I was to join him later. His clothes were on the beach, but . . . oh, I'm sure . . . I'm sure . . .'

'Now, now,' said the Superintendent mechanically, and asked for further particulars.

These took some minutes to obtain, but amounted to very little. Mr Edward Hutton, described as a wholesale provision merchant with an office in the City and a home in Streatham, had been staying with his wife in the little village of Penmouth, some five miles west of Penhampton. He had left the house at about half-past ten that morning, telling his wife that he was going to bathe. Mrs Hutton had arranged to join him about noon, but when she arrived there was no sign of her husband, though his clothes were behind the same rock that he always used for undressing purposes. Mrs Hutton had called and searched, and then returned to her lodging. In the afternoon, being now thoroughly worried, she had decided to take the only 'bus of the day into Penhampton and report to the police.

The Superintendent nodded. 'Very proper, madam. Now as to your husband's description, can you give us some idea of his appearance ?'

Mrs Hutton leaned back in her chair and closed her eyes. 'My husband is five foot seven . . . no, eight inches tall, not very broad, thinnish arms and legs, 34 inches chest measurement, rather long hands and feet, medium brown hair, clean-shaven, grey-green eyes, and rather a pale complexion ; he has an old appendicitis scar, and . . . oh, yes, there is a big mole under his left shoulder-blade.'

The Superintendent could not restrain his admiration. 'Upon my word, Mrs Hutton, you reeled that off a treat. Very different from some of them, I assure you.'

'I . . . I was thinking it out in the 'bus,' the woman said faintly. 'And . . . his passport, you know. I knew you'd want a description.'

'Yes. Well . . .' Surreptitiously the Superintendent studied the description of the body now in the mortuary. It tallied in every particular.

With much sympathetic throat-clearing he proceeded to the distasteful task of warning Mrs Hutton to prepare for a shock. He was very much afraid that in the mortuary now, if Mrs Hutton would come along for just a moment . . .

He sighed again as the woman gave every sign of imminent hysterics.

'He's here already ? Must I see him ? Must I ? Won't . . . won't the description do ?'

It took five minutes to get her into the mortuary to identify the body.

But once there she regained her calm. A curious dead-alive look came into her face as the Superintendent gently withdrew the sheet that covered the dead man's face.

'Yes,' she whispered, tonelessly. 'That's my husband. That's . . . Eddie.'

And then Roger noticed a very curious thing. Like the others' his gaze had been fixed on the sheeted figure on the slab ; but happening, by the merest chance, to glance round at Mrs Hutton, he saw that her eyes were tightly closed. For all she knew, she might have been identifying a piece of cheese as her husband. He nudged the Superintendent.

The Superintendent understood and nodded back. 'I'm afraid, madam,' he said, as gently as he could, 'you must *look* at him, you know.'

Mrs Hutton started violently, opened her eyes, looked at the dead man in front of her, and uttered a horrible, hoarse scream.

For a moment Roger thought she was going into hysterics again. He jumped forward, as did both the Superintendent and the Sergeant, and between them they hurried Mrs Hutton back to the office. The Sergeant produced a glass of water, and within a few minutes the lady was able to stop sobbing and assure them that she was quite all right now, it was just the shock of seeing her own husband, actually lying there . . .

'Shock, yes,' said the Superintendent hastily. 'Nasty thing, shock. I remember . . .'

When at last Mrs Hutton got out her powder-compact, all three men heaved sighs of relief.

Roger, who had at last solved a problem which had been worrying him ever since he first saw Mrs Hutton in the doorway, deemed it a good moment to introduce himself.

'Do you know that we've met before, Mrs Hutton ?' he said, with his best social smile.

She looked at him vaguely. 'No. Have we ? Where ?'

'At a party. I didn't know your name, nor you mine, and I've been wondering why your face seemed known to me. Now I remember. It was at a deadly beer-party about two years ago, soon after the beginning of the war. Do you remember ? In Bloomsbury. By the way, have you seen Michael Bearstowe lately ?'

Mrs Hutton jumped to her feet, her face dead-white. For a moment she gazed wildly at Roger, then she collapsed on the floor in a dead faint.

'That wasn't kind of you, Mr Sheringham,' said the Superintendent reproachfully, when Mrs Hutton had been finally tidied away into the care of the police matron. 'I thought we'd got her round—why, she'd got her powder-puff out and all !—and then you go and do a thing like that.'

'I didn't do anything,' Roger said indignantly. 'I only reminded her of a party we'd both been to and asked after an old friend of hers. Do you faint when people ask after your old friends ?'

'You upset her.'

'Apparently. But that's no reason for you to upset me. I might even try to upset you, in return. I might tell you, for instance, that the last time I saw that lady she was so vague that she couldn't tell me whether her husband was a tall man or a short one. Yet now she not only knows his height to an inch but his chest measurement too.'

'Well, why not ? She remembered it from his passport. She said so.'

'They don't put your chest measurement on your passport.'

The Superintendent frowned. 'What exactly are you suggesting, Mr Sheringham ?'

Roger laughed. 'Now don't get official, Super. I'm not suggesting anything. I merely hand you a queer little discrepancy, and you can do what you like with it. But,' Roger added thoughtfully, 'do you know, I would like to have another look at the body, if you've no objection.'

'Oh, I've no objection. But you won't find anything. The doctor's been over him already, and death's due to drowning all right. Still, have a look at him if you want. I'm afraid I can't stay myself ; I'm late already ; but . . .'

Roger assured the Superintendent that for nothing in the world would he detain him longer.

Roger did not have the mortuary to himself. There were two other men already there. The Sergeant, who had been appointed Roger's conductor, indicated that they were the police surgeon and the Detective Inspector in charge of the C.I.D. of the Penhampton Police Force ; and he left him to them.

The sheet had been withdrawn from the body and both men were standing by the slab, gazing down. Roger joined them.

'Pasty-faced beggar, eh ?' remarked the doctor cheerfully.

'Certainly no advertisement for Penhampton's Bonnie Sunshine,' Roger assented absently. He was remembering more and more.

'Mr Bearstowe Says . . .' Yes, and the husband was to have been a pompous, paunchy little bully, who wouldn't take his wife to concerts and wouldn't let her go by herself. Well, here he was face to face with the husband at last ; and he certainly wasn't paunchy, and could hardly have been pompous. But that wasn't to say that he might not have been a bully, Roger thought, looking at the rather weak face and the indeterminate chin : the kind that bullies out of weakness instead of out of strength. Perhaps he was even that pathetic type, the artist *manqué* (his hands seemed to indicate the possibility), *manqué*, and condemned to an office desk in Mincing Lane, and in consequence soured. Yes, and he had inherited the office-desk too, not achieved it ; for this man had never made money, or anything else, if Roger knew faces. Well, it was a story, which ever way it went.

'Notice anything, Mr Sheringham ?' the Detective Inspector asked eagerly.

'No. Why ?'

'I thought you were looking at him a bit hard.'

Roger laughed. 'Afraid not, this time. Except that Mr Hutton wasn't as spruce as he might have been.'

'How do you make that out, sir ?'

'He hadn't shaved this morning.'

'Sorry, but he had,' the doctor corrected with a smile. 'That cut's fresh, at the side of his mouth.'

'Well, he wanted a new blade,' Roger said feebly.

'Like most of us,' the doctor agreed. 'But if you're really

looking for queer details, what do you make of his back?' He signed to the Inspector, and the two of them turned the corpse over.

Roger saw that the skin on the back was badly lacerated from the shoulders to the small of the back, and the elbows were almost raw. 'Barnacles?' he suggested.

The doctor nodded. 'Rocks covered with them. And it was among the rocks that the body was found. Still . . .'

'I see what you mean. If the body was washing about, why was it lacerated only in that particular area?'

'Yes, it's queer, isn't it? No doubt there's some simple explanation. Probably the man who found him pulled him in by the legs. That's all.'

'No, doctor,' put in the Inspector. 'The body was wedged under a big rock at the side of a pool. Trewin, the farm-hand who happened to find him when he went down for a pail of sea-water, says he picked him up straight from the pool.'

'There's an abrasion on the front of the right thigh, where he was wedged,' supplemented the doctor.

'Yes, but that's natural,' Roger said. 'Those scratches aren't.'

'And here's another thing. I've an idea those lacerations were made during life. There were signs of free bleeding—freer than I should have expected.'

'Very interesting,' Roger commented. 'Very queer.'

'Don't think there's anything wrong, do you, sir?' asked the Inspector hopefully.

Roger's reply was lost in the sudden entrance of the Super-intendent.

'Well, it seems we've caught a tartar,' he announced, not without triumph. 'Just had Scotland Yard on the phone. Caught me in the nick of time; another minute, and I'd have been gone. Seems this fellow was wanted by the Yard for black market stuff. They've got a warrant out against him, and they'd just heard he'd been seen in this vicinity.'

'Well, fancy that,' observed the Inspector.

Roger stared down at the dead man. 'You never know, do you? Still, that weak chin . . .'

'Yes, yes; criminal type, obviously,' pronounced the Super-intendent. 'Well, doctor, this is bound to raise the question of suicide. Any chance, do you think?'

'None that I can say. Of course, he may have swum deliberately too far out, but there's nothing to show it.'

'Are you going to check up on Mrs Hutton's statement, Super ?' Roger asked suddenly.

The Superintendent stared.   'We'll make the usual routine enquiry at her lodging.   Why, Mr Sheringham ?'

'I only wondered,' Roger said mildly.   'It would be interesting, for instance, if she took a bathing-dress out this morning, wouldn't it ?   Or if she left the house soon after her husband, and not at noon ?'

'Why, Mr Sheringham,' said the Detective Inspector, whose job it would be to make these enquiries, 'you don't think . . . ?'

'I only think it might be quite an interesting case,' Roger said.

As he trudged along the coarse sand the next afternoon Roger wondered if he were wasting his time and energy.   That Hutton had been murdered, he felt convinced ; and the method was fairly obvious.   But could the woman have done it ?   Physically, yes.   But psychologically ?   Hardly.   She was too vague, too woolly, too . . . too silly, poor woman.

Or did silliness not debar one from murder ?   Murder itself was usually very silly.   Mrs Hutton might not be the stuff of which strong, silent murderers were made ; but mightn't she be a silly murderess ?   She was a hero-worshipper.   How far would hero-worship carry her ?

Roger's plodding feet seemed to be picking out a shambling refrain.   'Mr Bearstowe says . . . Mr Bearstowe says . . .'

And suppose Mr Bearstowe said, 'Pick up your husband's feet when he's bathing and hold them up in the air for a few minutes, out of sheer girlish *élan*, and then I shall be able to marry your Mincing Millions.'

Oh, Mr Bearstowe was in it all right.   Why else faint at the mere mention of his name ?

Yes, and of course there was the evidence of guilt all the time.   First she wouldn't look at her murdered husband at all ; then, when she was made to, took one peep, turned pea-green, and screamed.   If that wasn't presumptive evidence of guilt, what was ?

And reeling off the description in that silly way !   Roger

could almost hear the voice of tuition : 'If they wonder how you've got it so pat, just say you were thinking it out in the 'bus, or remembered it from his passport or something. They won't bother.' And pat she certainly had got it, like a child repeating a lesson. Mr Bearstowe should have devoted more time to his artistic effects.

But the Superintendent had smelt no rat. Roger thought the Superintendent rather a foolish man. Now that Inspector . . .

Yes, there the Inspector was, already. Then this must be the place.

The Inspector was feeling a little guilty himself. 'You know, I oughtn't rightly to be doing this, Mr Sheringham. The Super would be wild. He says it's a straightforward case of accident if ever he saw one, and you've got a bee in your bonnet about murder.'

'I never so much as mentioned the word,' Roger protested.

'No, but it was obvious what you thought. And I couldn't but agree that there seems something fishy about Mrs Hutton. More I think of it, more it seems to me that she acted queer—very queer indeed.'

"Have you checked up at the lodgings ?'

'Yes, but more of a country house than lodgings. Must have been costing them a tidy packet to stay there. They've got money to burn all right, those Huttons, in spite of the taxes and all. Still, her story's all right so far as it goes. She did leave at the time she said, and she didn't take a bathing-dress.'

'Any signs of . . . worry ?'

'No !' said the Inspector emphatically. 'I asked that specially, and she was just as usual before she went out. Didn't answer her husband back when he laid down the law at breakfast as usual, or anything. But when she came back ! Tears ? Floods of 'em ! And before he'd been missing long enough to make any ordinary wife do anything but curse about him making her wait for lunch, mark you.'

'Umph ! Remorse ? I wonder.' Roger felt a little puzzled. Bearstowe would hardly be the type to spring an unexpected murder on a foolish, possibly unreliable woman. He pushed the point aside. 'Anyhow, where's the rock ?'

The Inspector pointed it out. The tide had gone down far enough for Roger, balanced precariously on slippery seaweed, to be able to inspect the crevice in which the body had been wedged. It told him nothing.

He gazed thoughtfully round on the broken, rocky shore, with little waves slapping whitely here and there and the seaweed waving in the pools.

'Well, sir, if you don't want me any more, I think I'd like another word or two with Trewin. You never know. He might have noticed something.'

'Do,' Roger agreed. 'I shall be poking round here for an hour or so if you like to pick me up on your way back.'

But it did not take Roger an hour to find the thing which he had hardly expected to find. In only the third pool which he explored after the Inspector's disappearance, shining merrily on a bunch of seaweed only a few inches below the surface, was a gold ring, simply asking to be found. Scarcely able to believe in his luck, Roger examined it. It was a man's wedding-ring, and the inside was inscribed, 'E.H.—B.G. 18 November 1932.'

Roger turned it slowly over in his hand. It was a chance in a million. And yet what did it prove? That Edward Hutton had been murdered in that particular pool, and none other. Not very much. No hint as to who had murdered him, for instance.

Roger dried himself on his handkerchief, and sat down to await the return of the Inspector.

He came an hour later, bursting with news. 'The woman's in it all right, Mr Sheringham. By a stroke of luck I found a man who was working in this field yesterday afternoon. He says he saw a woman on the beach about half-past three, and the description of the clothes tallies near enough.'

'Mrs Hutton didn't mention being on the beach then?'

'No, sir ; she did not. But that's not all. There was a man with her.'

'Ah !'

'You expected that, Mr Sheringham?' asked the Inspector, a trifle disappointed.

'In a way. Well, what did they do?'

'By the looks of it they came out of a little cave under the cliff here. I must have a look there later. The farm-hand thought they might be a larky couple, so he watched ; but after a minute or two the man went back into the cave and the woman went off along the beach.'

'Did you get any description of the man ?'

'Nothing particular. Orange pullover, grey flannel trousers. Clean-shaven.'

'Clean-shaven, eh ? Yes, well, he would be, of course.'

'Sir ?'

'He had a beard last time I saw him, but beards are much too distinctive. Look here, Inspector, it's time I told you a few things. Let's sit down.'

They found a rock and made themselves comfortable in its lee. Roger lit his pipe, and then told his tale.

'Mind you,' he concluded, 'there's no evidence that the man's Bearstowe. After all, it was over two years ago and she may have got a new hero by now. But it's worth making a few enquiries.'

'I certainly will, sir. This alters everything. The Super's bound to O.K. me spending a bit of time on the case now. And what are you going to do, sir ?'

'Me ? Do you know,' said Roger, 'I should awfully like to ask Mrs Hutton why she fainted at Bearstowe's name. I do so wonder what she'd say.'

Roger did not put this interesting question, however. (For one thing he was not sure that he had the moral courage.) Instead, he left Mrs Hutton in peace and went up to London.

His objective was Crystal Vane, and he was lucky enough to catch her the first time he rang up her flat. Crystal was writing what she called one of her 'sob-articles' when he arrived, but she put it aside readily enough to answer Roger's questions.

Yes, so far as she knew the affair of Michael Bearstowe and his groceress had survived the war to date ; Michael was on a good thing there, and it wasn't likely he'd let it go ; no, he hadn't been called up—total exemption on some grounds or other ; oh, yes, conscientious objector, naturally.

'Would you say that Bearstowe was utterly unscrupulous in attaining his own ends ?' Roger asked carefully.

'If you mean, would he boggle at a little thing like seducing his groceress if it was going to pay better dividends,' Crystal began.

'No, no. Worse than that. Stick at absolutely nothing, I mean.'

But Crystal's journalistic nose scented news, and Roger had

to promise her the first chance when the story broke. Then they discussed the possibilities. In the end Crystal gave it as her opinion that Mr Bearstowe was probably quite unscrupulous enough for murder if driven to it, but it wouldn't be *like* him.

'I see,' Roger said thoughtfully. 'Then I wonder what did drive him. Something big, presumably. Money-troubles, do you think? They can be big enough, in all conscience. But what drove *her*? She doesn't look to me unscrupulous at all. It must have been something even bigger. Love, I suppose. You know, there's something queer about this case, Crystal. It doesn't seem quite to fit.'

'Why do you assume Mrs Hutton was driven at all?' Crystal asked. 'You say she was perfectly normal that morning. A woman of her type couldn't appear normal with her husband's murder in the offing.'

'No. In fact she may not know it was murder at all, even now. Why shouldn't Mr Bearstowe have said it was an accident, and she must just keep his name out of it for convenience? Yes! That explains her part much better. And yet . . . that excessive grief, for a husband she couldn't have loved? I don't know. No, it doesn't fit, somehow. I think I'll take a walk to Streatham.'

But Streatham, it seemed, had nothing to tell Roger. Nor had Mincing Lane, where the offices of Hutton and Edwards were ominously closed. Enquiries as to Edwards showed only that there was no Edwards.

But at Cartwright Mansions, W.1, where Mr Bearstowe had a flat of surprising opulence for one with no means, the porter told Roger that Mr Bearstowe was away on holiday; nor was it known when he would be back. Nor was it even known where he was; the porter thought, camping.

So that was one point established, at any rate, Roger considered, or perhaps two—or even three. At any rate, he might as well take them back with him to Penhampton the next day, little though they amounted to. What I want, Roger thought, is a couple of nice, juicy coincidences.

He got one at Paddington the following morning, when he ran into Mrs Hutton by the bookstall.

Mrs Hutton appeared confused, and dissembled her joy at the meeting; but Roger was officiously helpful, and gladly paid the excess fare over his third-class ticket for the privilege of travelling first with Mrs Hutton. Mrs Hutton could not escape without rudeness and she lacked the capabilities for that useful gift, which in this country is the prerogative of the very Upper or the Pretty Well Lower classes.

But Roger learned little. The carriage was too full of people (with third-class tickets) to allow of intimate conversation, and Mrs Hutton was obviously far too scared of her companion to respond to intimacy even had they been alone in the middle of the Sahara. In fact all Roger could learn was that Mrs Hutton was very, very much on her guard. And why should she be that, if innocent ?

As the train got into its rhythm, Roger listened to the refrain of the wheels.

'Mis-ter BEAR-stowe-says, Mis-ter BEAR-stowe-says . . .'

'You don't need to look at him when you identify him. Just keep your eyes closed and say it's your husband. They won't notice.'

Had Mr Bearstowe said that ?

But why not look at a dear husband, so sadly and accidentally drowned ? Is one frightened of a dead husband, that one cannot look at him ? No, it didn't fit. Mrs Hutton must have some guilty knowledge, even if she wasn't privy before the fact.

Roger looked at the faded, once-pretty face. Mrs Hutton caught him at it, started violently, blushed unnecessarily, and looked away.

Dash it, Roger thought ; the woman's as nervous as a kitten. Why ?

By the time the train reached Penhampton he still had not found the answer.

But if Roger felt that he had little to show for two days' work, that was certainly not the case with Detective-Inspector Brice. Almost before Roger had had time to ask for a cup of police-station tea, the Detective-Inspector had burst into his story.

"You were right, Mr Sheringham. We've found Bearstowe. Got on his track, that is. He was camping on the cliffs, not a mile from the scene of the crime.'

'Ah !' said Roger, and noted that it now was officially a crime.

'And about half-past one—that's a couple of good hours

after the murder, by our reckoning—at half-past one he was seen by the farmer on whose land he was camping, he was seen taking his tent down.   And he bolted for it, Mr Sheringham.   Packed his tent and things, all lightweight stuff, into the holder on his bicycle, and rode straight off.   Didn't even wait to pay the farmer what he owed him for milk and such.'

'I don't think I should pay too much attention to that,' Roger murmured.   'I should say that was fairly typical.'

'Anyhow, he did.   Now here's another point.   When the farmer saw him, about half-past one, he hadn't shaved off his beard (yes, he still wore a beard ; I found that out).   When he was seen round about three o'clock, on the shore, he had.'

'Ah !' Roger said again.   'Yes, that's interesting.   Sure of it ?'

'Absolutely.   The farmer was doing a bit of hedging, not fifty yards away.   He says he could see Bearstowe quite plainly.'

'How was he dressed ?'

'The same.   Pullover and grey trousers.'

'Any trace of the tent or bicycle ?'

'None.   He must have hidden 'em before he doubled back to meet Mrs Hutton, and afterwards he picked 'em up and he's made off with them.   We've put out an all-stations request for any solitary camper to be interrogated, anywhere.'

'Quick work.   Now here's another point.   I take it that your times are correct ?   What time does the doctor say that death occurred ?'

'Round about eleven o'clock, he thinks.   Anyhow, not before ten or after one.   He was dead when Bearstowe took down his tent, if that's what you mean, sir.'

'Yes, partly.   And when he was taking down his tent, at one-thirty, Bearstowe had his beard.   Less than two hours after he hadn't.   Well, here's my point.   How did Bearstowe get hold of a razor ?   Men with beards don't carry them.'

The Inspector beamed.   'That question occurred to me, sir.'

'I'm sure it did.   I just meant, if he had a razor with him, wouldn't that show that the murder was premeditated ?   If he hadn't it was probably done on the spur of the moment.'

'Well, he hadn't,' the Inspector said with pride.   'He got hold of one, and I can tell you where he got it from.   Look at this schedule, please, Mr Sheringham.'

Roger looked. The paper contained a minute inventory of the belongings of the late Mr Hutton, as left in his rooms ; it was complete down to spare collar-studs. Roger ran his eye quickly down the column. A shaving-brush and soap were listed ; there was no razor.

'I say, that's good work,' Roger said warmly. 'You mean Mrs Hutton took it to him at three o'clock ?'

'That's what she met him for, the second time,' said the Inspector, flushed with pleasure.

'The second time ? Oh, I see. You mean, she met him first at twelve, and took instructions. Yes, of course.' Roger drank his tea. 'Well, that certainly seems to put the case in the bag, Inspector. So all you've got to do now is to find Bearstowe.'

'Yes, and Mrs Hutton,' said the Inspector, not without resentment. 'Gave us the slip yesterday she did, and got away to London. Went up to meet Bearstowe, for a tenner. We'll pick her up again all right, but she may have tipped him off that—oh, there you are, sir "

'Ah ! Mr Sheringham !' said the Superintendent genially. 'Well, you were right, sir. I don't mind admitting it. And now we've got you and Mrs Hutton together again. Yes, our chap picked her up at the station and brought her along. Didn't want to come, not a bit. What do you say, Brice ? It's your case, but I think it's time we asked Mrs Hutton a few questions. Eh ?

'I quite agree. Well, we'll see her in here. No, don't go, Mr Sheringham. You were in at the beginning, so you may as well see the end.' He leaned over the Inspector's desk and pressed a bell.

In less than two minutes Mrs Hutton was once again sitting on a police-chair confronting the Superintendent ; but this time it was a frankly terrified woman, and a police official who no longer spoke kindly. Roger looked at her, waiting like a cornered mouse for the spring of the cat, and felt rather sick. She was such a silly woman. Who but a woman of almost sublime silliness would bring her lover a razor with which to shave off his beard, but omit to bring shaving-brush and soap ?

Suddenly something in his brain went 'click !' and he saw the whole thing.

He glanced quickly from the Superintendent to the Inspector, calculating his chances. No, there was not a second to lose. In another moment the Superintendent might ruin the whole thing. He must charge in, and brave the wrath that would certainly come.

'Superintendent, may I ask Mrs Hutton just one question first ?'

The Superintendent looked surprised but gave permission, not very graciously.

Roger moved his chair so that he could look at the woman more directly. 'Mrs Hutton, do you mind telling me this : are you sure you really know what happened on Penmouth beach that morning ?'

Mrs Hutton's jaw dropped. Obviously she had not expected the question ; equally obviously, she did not know how to answer it.

Roger followed it quickly with another. 'Do you know, for instance, that *murder* had been committed ?'

Mrs Hutton started to her feet, prepared to scream, thought better of it, and fainted.

'Mr Sheringham !' exclaimed the Superintendent, in real anger.

Once more Mrs Hutton was borne unconscious into the back regions.

'Listen, Super !' Roger pleaded. 'The whole point was that Mrs Hutton never knew that murder had been committed. If you'd broken it gently, you'd have given her time to adjust herself to the idea ; and she might have decided to help cover it up. Now she's had a bad shock—and she'll talk !'

'Humph !' The Superintendent chewed his moustache, by no means mollified.

'We've been making a mistake from the beginning,' Roger continued urgently. 'A fundamental mistake. I've only just realised it. You see, this murder *was* planned. A long time ago, I fancy. A pit was carefully dug for us, and we fell into it. At first sight, I must say, it looks a terrific gamble, and yet . . . police procedure is so rigid. Yes, that's the clue. Police procedure is so rigid. Your own procedure protected the murderer, Super. He'd banked on it.'

The Superintendent raised heavy eyebrows. He did not look convinced.

'It was clever,' Roger continued musingly. 'He killed two birds with one stone, you see. That warrant for Hutton's arrest . . . he must have got wind of it somehow. By the way, was Hutton insured ? I think you'll find he was. Yes, of course he must have been. Heavily. That's another thing Mrs Hutton was intended to do : collect the insurance money. That was to be a tidy windfall for him to cash in on, you see, even if everything else went up the spout. Of course the bathing appointment was carefully arranged. Right time, right place, deserted beach and all the rest. And then . . . up with his heels in some convenient pool, and what does it matter if his back gets scratched on the barnacles so long as his head stays under water ? Nothing simpler ! Then wedge the body where with any luck it won't drift loose for a few tides ; and even if it does, what's the odds ?

'Mrs Hutton of course knew nothing in advance. That puzzled me from the first. How could such a foolish woman, however amiable, be trusted with murder-plans ? Obviously not. And naturally, when she met him on the beach, he told her it was an accident. But what a convenient accident ! It could be made to fit right in with their own plans. So he told her the tale, and about the warrant and everything, and how the authorities would probably confiscate everything by way of a post-mortem fine except the insurance money, and why he must be kept out of it all, and what she must do. I expect he had some difficulty in rehearsing her, owing to floods of tears ; that's why he didn't emphasise the importance of details as he should have done. And so, of course, she managed to give things away. She would. That was the one flaw in his plan, having to rely on poor Mrs Hutton. But of course he had no choice. Lucky for us that he hadn't.

'So that was that. And if things went right, there was his future all nicely secured, and—his hated rival out of the way ! Yes, I think he was really jealous. He must have been fond of Mrs Hutton in his own way. After all, she suited him very well. Anyhow, he couldn't stand having a rival in her regard, so . . . exit rival ! Hence those tears. She was fond of the rival, you see. Much too fond, in his conceited opinion.

'Now shall I tell you what suddenly gave it away to me ? It was that shaving-brush and soap. How like Mrs Hutton, I

T

thought, to take her lover a razor to shave off his beard with and not take the shaving-brush and soap ; and I wondered if even Mrs Hutton could have been so silly. Well, of course she wasn't. The shaving-soap wasn't taken because soap doesn't lather in sea-water, so it would be no use. Ridiculous little point for such a case to hang on, isn't it ? But the case does hang on it. Because Mrs Hutton wouldn't know a thing like that. Therefore it wasn't she who left the shaving-soap behind, therefore it wasn't she who took the razor, therefore——'

'Then who did take the razor ?' interrupted the Superintendent.

'Of course, the murderer ! Just as he brought that false beard to Penmouth with him, bought probably months ago. By the way, how delighted he must have been with that orange pullover. You see, any bearded face surmounting an orange pullover is just the same at fifty yards as any other bearded face surmounting——'

'Here, what's all this ?' The Superintendent looked his bewilderment. 'False beards ? Orange pullovers ? What do you mean, Mr Sheringham ?'

'I mean,' said Roger gently, 'that you shouldn't have relied on Mrs Hutton's sole identification of her husband's body. You see, the body you've got in that mortuary isn't Hutton's. It's Bearstowe's.'

The Squire of England
By Bernard Darwin

'I hope the light and shade of my Sporting Portrait will be found correct ; and the likeness most clearly show to the sporting world that the appellation of a NONPARIEL (*sic*)—a PHENOMENON—and an OUT-AND-OUTER apply, in every point of view, to the character of George Osbaldeston, Esq., and the motto to be placed under it

'What man dare, I dare !'

Thus Pierce Egan with a final burst of eloquence in the dedication of his Book of Sports. To his vocabulary I make no pretensions, but in a lower key I will try to do my best for the Squire.

There is one sentence of his own which gives an obvious clue to his character and career : 'I freely confess that chaffing challenges and the love of fame have always egged me on.' There at least he saw himself with clear eyes, and if he loved fame he has had his heart's desire. It is now more than seventy-six years since he died at the age of eighty, and he is still, as one of his contemporaries called him, the Squire of England. No one has usurped his title. The modern heroes of the Quorn or the Pytchley are mere local celebrities in their narrow world, but those who know nothing of hunting have heard of George Osbaldeston.

It is true that, save for one most fortunate circumstance, he would be known but dimly, except to those who burrow in the sporting literature of the past. There he constantly crops up ; in the stately praises of Nimrod in his *Quarterly* article ; in Dick Christian's lectures so admirably recorded by the Druid ; in the annals of old cricket with Lambert and Lord Frederick Beauclerk ;

267

in pigeon shooting matches at the Red House ; in the Ring as referee in the fight between Caunt and Bendigo ; on the Turf and particularly in the unattractive story of Margrave's St. Leger and the mystery of Ludlow. In the *Sporting Magazine* and its rival the *New Sporting Magazine* we may constantly meet with references to him. 'Every schoolboy,' allowing a certain latitude to that expression, knows two facts about him, that he fought a duel with Lord George Bentinck and that he won a great match by riding 200 miles in something under nine hours on Newmarket Heath. There is at least ample opportunity for learning what he did, and he did more than any other man has ever done in his own line of country. As to what manner of man he was, however, we might have gleaned comparatively little but for the fact that as an old man he set down his autobiography to please his wife (it is in some respects a strange document for the purpose), and he then discovered yet one more, and this time an unsuspected, talent ; he could write.

This invaluable manuscript was in the possession of Mr Williams, grandson of Mrs Williams whom the Squire married as her second husband. It was rescued only just in time, for the rats had made a meal on it and some parts were lost, but the bulk luckily remained. It was published in the *Field* some eighteen years ago and subsequently in book form, together with an excellent commentary by Mr E. D. Cuming. Mr Cuming must have spent treasures of care in verifying and correcting the Squire's facts, none of which the Squire had looked up, and in supplying the dates which he never professed to know. Here we have a portrait of a man and, within narrow limits, the portrait of an age. The Squire had had as little education as need be ; he had only been at Eton for five halves and was then in all probability removed by his mother lest a worse thing should befall him ; there is no reason to believe that at Brasenose he ever opened a book ; he certainly had no time to do so afterwards, being, as he says naïvely, 'absorbed in hunting, racing, shooting, tennis, rowing, ladies, etc.' He had, however, something better than reading—a natural gift. He possessed in a high degree that which George Borrow admired in the compilers of the Newgate Calendar, the art of telling a plain story. Not only that, but he had a knack of picturesque phrase. Words torn from their context rarely do the writer justice, but I will take the risk of quoting two instances.

Of the jumping of a favourite hunter, Elmhirst, he wrote : 'I could only compare the sensation of riding her over fences to being carried in a chair by a sling.' Of the pursuit of a deserter who had hidden in the Sussex woods and terrorised the neighbourhood he thus described the final scene : 'The militia-men did not try to take him alive, but shot him like a dog where he lay crouched.' I hope I am not wrong in thinking that there is a plain tale supremely well told ; it is so vivid and so perfectly economical of words.

So now, with the Squire to help us, we gain an infinitely clearer conception of him than we could ever have had by poring over files. He springs up before us no mere legendary hero of a hundred feats, but a very human man intensely alive and made up of the strangest and most contradictory qualities. We see him, and this must come first, as a man of the most dauntless physical courage, whether in a personal encounter with no matter whom— and he was only a little fellow of 5 ft. 6 in.—or in any breakneck attempt. Yet at the same time he was singularly lacking in moral courage, unable to face his own affairs when they badly needed looking into ; ready to trust anyone rather than enquire if he were honest ; utterly without the resolution to say no, and once even allowing himself to be blackmailed on a palpably unfounded charge of foul play at cards in order to avoid public unpleasantness. We find him an inveterate chatterbox, who never stopped talking even at the covertside, 'always so chaffy' as Dick Christian said, and yet with a strong, underlying element of reserve. He was in the main a very good-natured man, ready either to give praise or to make allowances, and at the same time he seems in his book to suffer from a constant sense of irritation, sometimes against his best friends, and a feeling, too often well-founded, that he has been 'done.' He was a gentleman by birth and breeding and yet oddly uneasy lest the fact be not recognised. He was quick to snuff an offence, but too soft-hearted to nurse even the most just resentment. At one moment, if things went well, he was in hilarious spirits, and at the next, if they went ill, he was despondent and miserable. He was so vain that he could be flattered or dared to almost anything ; and yet so shrewd a judge of what he and other men could or could not do that he was an ill man to bet against. No one had a greater power of taking delighted pains over the things that interested him, and no one was ever more careless and dilatory over those that ought to have interested him and did not. Finally, if there is one of his stories which seems better than another to give a comprehensive picture of the man, his pluck, his vanity, his certainty that only fraud could have beaten him, it is that of a certain race in which both girth and surcingle flew so that his saddle turned round and he was sent sprawling. He is lying with his head on the knees of Peter Crawley, famous as the Young Rump Steak, and, says he, 'I could only articulate that if I had not fallen I must have won and then became insensible.'

I have tried to set forth the strange mixture of anomalies that was the Squire. Now let me tell something of what he did, and it must take a little while because, admittedly in the days when there were fewer specialists, he was the great all-rounder. Some of the traits in his character which have been suggested may appear as I go along. But first of all let us have a very little history and a very few dates. George Osbaldeston (his name should be pronounced as if there were an acute accent on the e) was born in London in 1786. He was the son of George Osbaldeston and Jane, daughter of Sir Thomas Head of Langley. He was descended from Mary Osbaldeston, of an old Yorkshire family, who married Robert Mitford of Mitford Castle. Her daughter Philadelphia married the Rev. John Wickens, D.D., and their son George (the Squire's father) inherited a share of the Hutton Bushell estate from a relation, Fountayne Osbaldeston, and took his name. George was the youngest of five children, a much-desired son coming after four disappointing daughters. His father died when he was six, and he was brought up—and spoilt—by his mother, a clever but injudicious and extravagant woman. When he came of age, after his brief career at Eton and Oxford, with much festivity, the roasting of oxen and the striking of medals, he was unfettered master of a fine estate, and in the course of the next sixty years—'a life of plunder' as he called it—he ran through about £300,000.

He soon built kennels at Hutton Bushell and bought his first pack of hounds. Hunting must come first among his many activities, and save perhaps for Tom Smith, 'the best man that ever came into Leicestershire,' according to Dick Christian, there has never been a more celebrated Master of Hounds. He hunted, as he himself recorded, the Spilsby and the Burton in Lincoln-shire ; Mr Musters's in Notts ; Lord Vernon's in Derbyshire ; the Atherstone ; the Holderness (he appears not to have been officially Master) ; the Thurlow in Suffolk ; the Quorn twice ; the Pytchley, and the Hambledon in Hampshire. I have not the knowledge even if I had the wish to appraise him as Master, nor surely is it necessary. He is said to have learnt much, as is likely enough, from his famous huntsman, Tom Sebright, who afterwards went to Lord Fitzwilliam ; he was sometimes criticised by the Meltonians who, as he himself complained, were almost impossible to please ; but his place has long since been established. His keenness was never in doubt ; he found a fox even by moon-light and was called 'The Moonlight Hunter.' Neither was there any doubt of his knowledge of hounds. Even the *New Sporting Magazine*, which apparently disliked him, declared 'as a breeder of hounds Mr Osbaldeston has raised himself to the very pinnacle of fame.' That fame was spread abroad by Furrier, a noted sire, Vaulter, Vanquisher, and the rest of his beloved 'children' as he called them.

He was a splendid horseman, beyond all question. After a terrible accident in which he was ridden over and his leg was broken so that he was kept out of the field for two years, he developed a natural distaste for anyone close behind him, but this in no way affected his dash as a rider of steeplechases. He rode six in all and won them all, the best known of them being that in which on Clasher he beat the great Dick Christian himself on Clinker. On this occasion he dropped into poetry, but kept his verses secret till he was too old to be challenged to a duel by the fire-eating Captain Ross, Clinker's owner. He made many more such matches, but for one reason or another they did not come off. It is likely enough that the other party thought better of it, for when any hypothetical question was put to Dick Christian the old roughrider's opinion was always the same, 'I think the Squire would have outrode him.' He was anxious to ride a match against Tom Smith, but his challenge was declined, and the Squire, who could be desperately jealous, accused him of cowardice. However, he made amends by a fine compliment : 'I shall always respect his memory, he was one of the most honourable men that ever lived.'

Something must clearly be said of the Squire's match against time at Newmarket in November, 1831. There was a report that Bob Ridsdale, a well-known sporting character and a 'confederate' of John Gully's in St Giles's Derby, was going to ride from London to York in ten hours. Of course the Squire said he could do that easily enough. Of course General Charritie, who never seemed to learn wisdom and was always making matches against the Squire, betted him a thousand guineas that he could not ride 200 miles, with unlimited horses, in ten hours. Of course the Squire won, for he did it, finishing 'as gay as a lark,' in 8 hrs. 42 mins. He had his own hunters and galloping hacks, and Gully lent him some racehorses. One adventure he had when an ill-behaved horse called Iky Solomon tried to bolt with him into a plantation ; but Iky was soon caught, the Squire remounted, not much time was lost, and he was winning all the time. There was a great crowd of spectators at the finish and the victor's way was shouldered for him through the press by John Gully and Tom Oliver. Somebody said he ought to have a dose of salts, to which the Squire answered, 'Damn your salts ! I'm so hungry I could eat an old woman.' He galloped into Newmarket with a guard of honour, was rubbed down with oil, got between blankets for an hour and a half, and then kept it up with a cheerful party at the Rutland Arms till two o'clock in the morning.

What a man ! And yet, alas ! no human triumph is complete. It began to be said that after all he had not done so very much and that there was an unnamed seven-stone jockey who could easily beat his record. Instantly challenges flew like hail. He would ride that jockey 200 to 500 miles for £20,000 ; he would ride any man for anything and was always to be heard of at Pitsford near Northampton. Nobody took up the gauntlet. Perhaps people knew better ; perhaps they said it was only the Old Squire. That scoundrel Bland had done him over his bets ; he was left with little but the glory, and that had been traduced and marred by envious tongues.

The Squire was a fine driver whether of a coach or the two invincible trotters Rattler and Tom Thumb. He won a bet by driving a certain team supposed only to be amenable to the coachman Hell Fire Dick, and he did it though the other party to the bet loaded the coach with gigantic guardsmen, a possibility that he had overlooked. The trick was forgiven in victory and the loser gave a magnificent dinner, when nearly everybody got drunk. Not everybody, for the Squire, who said he could never drink much, escaped notice in not filling his glass. 'Much' deserves a liberal interpretation, and no doubt he could carry his wine like a gentleman, but he must have been an essentially temperate man or he could never have accomplished a tithe of what he did. He was no Jack Mytton, and though casual in his morals, never sought his women in squalid places.

Turn to shooting, and the Squire was equally pre-eminent with his gun 'made by the celebrated Joe Manton.' The conditions of shooting have so changed that comparisons would to-day be futile. Enough that Captain Ross, than whom there was no sterner judge, said that he had seen as good a game shot but had never seen a better. As a pigeon shot he was second only to Ross (he would himself hardly admit even that superior) and incidentally is described as having been a rather fussy, fidgety shot, which hardly accords with his reputation in any other branch of sport.

Now let us leave sport and go to games, and first to cricket. The Squire was, as I should judge, an eminently 'useful' rather than an accomplished batsman, but he was a truly formidable fast bowler, and I always regret that he did not stay his full time at Eton ; if he had he might have played in the first Eton and Harrow match and sent my Lord Byron's wicket flying like a catherine wheel. He and Brown of Brighton were by all accounts the fastest of all the underhand bowlers ; he was said to put all wicket-keeping to the rout. His terrific pace made him particularly deadly in single-wicket matches, and as an old man he declared, not with perfect accuracy, that he had never lost one. Oddly enough, the most famous of all his matches was one in which he played an almost entirely passive part and all the glory went to his partner, the greatest player of his day, William Lambert. It was played at Lord's on July 6 and 7, 1810, Lambert and the Squire against Lord Frederick Beauclerk and Howard, a well-known fast bowler. The Squire had been very ill and could scarcely stand. He both wrote to Lord Frederick and sent an emissary to him in Mr Budd to ask for a postponement. Lord Frederick was inexorable and answered laconically, 'Play or Pay.'

'Never mind,' said the Squire, 'I won't forfeit. Lambert may beat them both,' and Lambert agreed with the comment, 'Why, they are anything but safe.'   The Squire claimed a fieldsman in his place ; this was refused.   He then tottered to the wicket and by his own account made a big hit and walked one run before retiring (the official score credits him with three) ; again he claimed a fieldsman and again this was refused.   And the heroic Lambert did beat them both.   'He did make desperate exertions,' said Beldham, who had watched the match, to Mr Pycroft : 'Once he rushed up after his ball, and Lord Frederick was caught so near the bat that he lost his temper and said it was not fair play.   Of course all hearts were with Lambert.   Osbaldeston's mother sat in her carriage, and enjoyed the match.   Lambert was called to the carriage and bore away a paper parcel ; some said it was a gold watch—some bank notes.   Trust Lambert to keep his own secrets.   We were all curious, but no one ever knew.'   If there is a trifle of malice in the Squire's triumph he was entitled to it.   As Lord Frederick retired, bowled by Lambert in his second innings, with one shoulder humped in disgust, the Squire thought he looked like 'Crook-backed Richard.'

That match may have left a coolness, but some years afterwards Lord Frederick had good reason to be grateful to the Squire.   There was another big match, this time with Lord Frederick and Osbaldeston as allies and Lambert on the other side.   The Squire was in agonies of pain, having broken a small bone in his shoulder, but Lord Frederick made him half drunk with sherry and insisted on his bowling ; he got Lambert out for a duck with a shooter and won the match.   The service was ill-requited.   A few years later the Squire, on being chaffed over losing a match at Lord's, lost his temper and scratched his name out of the list of members.   Afterwards he repented and wanted to come back.   Others were willing but Lord Frederick was adamant, saying the insult had been too great.   That is a very black mark against the name of that reverend nobleman who made £700 a year out of his cricket.   Among all the great game-players his seems to me one of the most unlovely characters, unredeemed by a single generous impulse.

Exactly how good at tennis the Squire was I do not know, but he invented a bastard form of it which no one else has attempted.   The incomparable French player Edmond Barre was in England and a match was made of five sets ; the Squire received the odds of fifteen and was allowed to catch the ball and return it by hand while Barre played with a racket in the normal way. The Squire had a special glove made of leather and he was so ingenious and pertinacious in his returns that he made Barre lose his temper. His hand was knocked to pieces and was useless for a fortnight— *but* he won his match.

Again, it is hard to rate him precisely at billiards, but he was undoubtedly a very good player and specialised in what would to-day be called 'marathon' matches. He once played for 24 consecutive hours at the Portland Club, but that was nothing to a feat at Newmarket. For three days and nights in succession he went to the races all day and played billiards all night, merely washing and changing his clothes at intervals. On the first two nights he won his matches. On the third his opponent was a professional in disguise, and he lost. The poor Squire was always being 'done,' but he comforted himself with the thought that the professional was exhausted at the end, whereas he himself could have gone on for many more hours.

There was one thing the Squire never did. 'I am not,' he said, 'a piscator.' However, he distinguished himself on the water. A crew of Guards officers did a good time, esteemed a record, over a long distance and were lionised accordingly. The Squire was not going to stand that, and though he was over forty, and had not sat in a boat since he was at Eton, he was after those Guardsmen's blood. By his own account he attacked them at once, but this is clearly a mistake, and according to Mr Cuming there was an interval of several years, during which the challenge must have lain festering in his breast. Then he collected a four, himself and three other amateurs, possibly rather dubious ones who were, as he shrewdly discovered, just as good as the professional watermen. He won the race ; he had shown those soldiers what was what. Nor did he stop there, for he took to his new pastime enthusiastically, became a 'patron of the aquatiques' and rowed in various 'ran-dan' races against professionals with rather modest success.

Well now, if I may address myself to the reader, 'Have you had enough ?' 'For heaven's sake,' he may reply, 'spare us any more.' Yet I have only touched the fringe of the Squire's achievements. As he said after that billiards match at Newmarket, I could go on for many more hours. I will be merciful and let the poor exhausted reader off any further details if he will admit that there never was and never can be again such a wonderful little man as George Osbaldeston.

Pierce Egan hoped that the light and shade of his portrait would be found correct, and there must, I fear, be a little shade.   There were at least two episodes in the Squire's career which to our nice, modern notions approach the shady, and they cannot be passed over.   As to one of them he largely disarms criticism by his perfectly candid account of it.   He thought apparently that he had done nothing unbefitting a man of honour, and the reader must judge for himself, always bearing in mind the different standard of sporting morals in those days, when the rule was 'Play or Pay,' when everything was a 'match,' and anything within the four corners of its terms was permissible.   The other incident is now wrapped in a mystery which it is impossible to disentangle. The Squire may have been wholly innocent.   It may be that the worst that can be said of him is that he was not sufficiently particular as to his company ; but I confess that the affair leaves a nasty taste in the mouth, and I wish it had not happened.

. The first of these two stories concerns the duel with Lord George Bentinck, and the Squire admits so much that I think we may in the main accept his account.   There was an annual meeting at Lord Wilton's, Heaton Park near Manchester, for which he had a large party at his house, and I cannot help feeling that the beginning of the trouble was a grievance of the Squire's that he was not asked to stay with 'the aristocratic party at the Hall.'   The professed *casus belli* was that this party was unduly favoured by both handicapper and judge.   There was an indignation meeting among the aggrieved owners, and the Squire hit on a plan of agreeable simplicity, namely, 'to purchase horses with whose merits they were unacquainted.'   He bought an Irish horse called The Rush, tried him over the St Leger course against another horse, and seeing some people on the look-out for what they could see stopped The Rush and let the other win. In the first race at Heaton he adopted much the same tactics, and 'Rush was such a beautiful horse to ride that they could not detect any roping.'   Then for the race on the following day he told his friend George Payne, who was staying at the Hall, to get on all the money he could ; he openly told the Judge he should win in a canter ; on his way to the starting point he took 200 to

100 from Lord George Bentinck and he won the race, among some hissing from the 'aristocrats,' with perfect ease. 'Squire,' said William Scott, 'you've done us this time.' 'Yes, Will,' answered the Squire, 'you know I am twelve miles further north than you are.'

For some while afterwards nothing happened, for the Squire could not go to the next Newmarket meeting. He asked George Payne to get the £200 from Lord George, and received the answer, 'I think you had better ask him for the money yourself when you see him in the spring.' The Squire was a little puzzled, but let it pass and waited till the spring of 1831. Then he demanded his money and Lord George answered that he wondered at his impudence in asking for it, that a greater robbery had never been committed and that he had a good mind not to pay. 'You must pay me,' retorted the Squire, adding that the affair would not end there and that he considered himself as much of a gentleman as Lord George or any member of the Jockey Club, though he had no title to his name. 'Can you count?' asked Lord George. 'Yes, I could at Eton,' said the Squire. The money was handed him and, bristling with indignation, 'his hackles set,' the Squire went to seek a friend.

The Squire's account of the duel at Wormwood Scrubs is briefly this, that he suspects the pistols were not loaded with ball; that he is sure Colonel Anson deliberately gave the word 'Fire' when he was not looking at his adversary; that Lord George fired first and missed and that in these circumstances he himself shot wide. All this may be true, but I am afraid the Squire is disingenuous as to his motives for firing at random. He was a very fine pistol shot; he could have killed his man, and until the night before he meant to kill him. On that night, however, he met George Payne at the Portland Club and Payne later told Lord Chaplin what passed between them. 'Osbaldeston,' he said, 'you and I are very old friends; you know Bentinck was right; it was a damned robbery; and if you kill Lord George to-morrow morning there will not be a single gentleman in England who will ever speak to you again.' The Squire turned and left without a word. He was puzzled; he thought it all very unfair, but can we doubt that he took George Payne's words to heart and resolved accordingly? The story rings true. Whether he ever thought that perhaps he had gone too far will never be certain. At any rate, after some years the quarrel was partially healed. The Squire, who did not bear malice, refrained from blackballing Lord George for the Bibury Club ; Lord George sent his compliments and offered to show the Squire his horses. The two men were utterly unsympathetic and could never have liked one another, but they exchanged dignified courtesies.

The other story is vaguer, more complex and less pleasant. A horse called Ludlow, belonging to a not very reputable Mr Beardsworth, was favourite for the St Leger of 1832. A day or two before the race Doncaster was full of rumours that he had been sold to some person unknown, who had betted against him and proposed to make him safe. Among others named was the Squire, who was said to 'stand a very heavy shot against Ludlow.' Mr Beardsworth denied the sale for a while and then there appeared a certain Mr Bond, a bejewelled Oriental personage, generally known as 'Death on the pale horse,' and the owner of the Athenæum, not the resort of Bishops but a gaming house in St James's. Mr Bond had hitherto had nothing to do with racing. By his own account he suddenly thought he should like a horse, and hearing that Ludlow was the best, bought him for 5,000 guineas and backed him for a further 10,000. It would be unmeaning flattery to say that anyone believed him. In his various explanations he referred to a third or sometimes fourth party in the deal whom he could not name, and this was generally supposed to be the Squire. John Gully certainly thought so. 'There was a bit of a breeze,' says a writer in the *New Sporting Magazine*, 'between the Squire and Mr Gully, in which I heard something of buying horses to sell the public,' and this accusation was 'met by the defendant with plenty of noise and bluster.' In another account it is said that Gully clenched his fists and the Squire picked up the poker. There were several stormy meetings and, again in the words of the *New Sporting Magazine*, 'after three hours of speechifying it was found impossible to unkennel the mysterious fox—mind I don't say *hunter*.'

That writer certainly allowed his malice to sparkle out of him too grossly. 'Who are these excessively vulgar, ill-looking fellows, with whom the Squire of Pytchley appears so intimate ? Why, there are Messrs R——n and W——f.' Now R——n was Frank Richardson, generally credited with the nobbling of Bessy Bedlam ; W——f was another notorious rascal, Wagstaff in the words of Silvanus 'an audacious fellow, whose teeth literally fitted into each other, like two cross-cut saws set together, or a shark's.' They were no fit company for any gentleman. As to the race, the favourite was nowhere ; after a mile he was out of it ; 'poor Ludlow was quite worn out by his exertion, and doubtless *had a good night's sleep* after it !' That is the end of the story save that Gully and the Squire were reported to have fought a duel. It is certain that they did not, but Mr Pedley, Gully's son-in-law, told one of his sons, who told me, that he had once prevented a duel. No names were given, but I think there can be little doubt as to the identity of the prospective duellists.

There is no direct evidence, and in any case most of the Doncaster witnesses would be wholly unworthy of credit, but that which makes me uneasy is that the Squire says nothing of all this hubbub in his autobiography. He was admittedly at Doncaster ; he mentions another race there in which he declares his horse was got at, but of the St Leger not one word, though he could not conceivably have forgotten it. There is no such unfair argument as that of 'no smoke without fire,' but it is hard to resist the inference that here for once was something of which he was not proud. I can only console myself with the words of Mr Budd, the cricketer : 'A noble fellow, always straight,' but—well, I am not wholly reassured.

It would never do to take leave of the Squire on so sad a note. Let me, as indeed I must, skip many years and look at him as an old man. Gradually all his estate was sold, and he must have become penniless had he not been fortunate enough to marry Mrs Williams in 1851. She was a well-to-do widow, and a kind-hearted, sensible woman. The Squire had a prodigious respect for her and she kept him in good order, so that for the last fifteen years of his life he had a happy if comparatively restricted life. Mrs Osbaldeston firmly took charge of the money remaining to him, bought him an annuity, and doled it out to him on regular principles.

So we see him at the last in a comfortable house in St John's Wood. In the morning he sits in a flowered dressing-gown, composing his autobiography, taking an occasional sip of brandy and calling ever and anon to 'Mrs O.' to come and help him over those elusive dates. Sometimes he falls into a doze and awakes murmuring, 'People say nothing is perfect ; but my Vaulter is perfect and never told a lie in his life.' In the afternoon he is given a single sovereign and goes off to his club in a cab, and when he returns the sovereign is gone. The old fire is still alive in him—the old challenges are still irresistible. Once when he is near to eighty some brute at his club bets him that he will not sit still in a chair for twenty-four hours. He has only his one sovereign but that he ventures and he wins his last match.

Say what you will, I am devoted to the Squire. He was chock full of weaknesses but he was also chock full of courage, and that is something that no one dare despise. When the gentlemen of the Pytchley gave him a cup they inscribed on it these words, 'To the best sportsman of any age or country'; and, after all, were they so very far wrong? I like to think that his restless spirit has found some little paradise of its own, where there are no dishonest judges, no defaulting 'legs,' no censorious Lord George or ungenerous Lord Frederick, nobody but Furrier and Vaulter, Elmhirst and Assheton, who love him and with whom he can be perfectly happy.